PENGUIN BOOKS

TRUE WEALTH

Juliet B. Schor's research has focused on the economics of work, spending, environment, and the consumer culture. She is the author of *Born to Buy*, *The Overworked American*, and *The Overspent American*. Schor is a professor of sociology at Boston College, a former member of the Harvard economics department, and a Guggenheim Fellowship recipient. She is also a cofounder of the Center for a New American Dream, an organization devoted to ecologically and socially sustainable lifestyles.

TRUE WEALTH

How and Why Millions of Americans Are Creating

a Time-Rich, Ecologically Light, Small-Scale,

High-Satisfaction Economy

JULIET B. SCHOR

PENGUIN BOOKS

Previously published as *Plenitude*

PENGUIN BOOKS

Published by the Penguin Group

Penguin Group (USA) Inc., 375 Hudson Street, New York, New York 10014, U.S.A. •
Penguin Group (Canada), 90 Eglinton Avenue East, Suite 700, Toronto, Ontario,
Canada M4P 2Y3 (a division of Pearson Penguin Canada Inc.) • Penguin Books Ltd, 80 Strand,
London WC2R 0RL, England • Penguin Ireland, 25 St. Stephen's Green, Dublin 2, Ireland
(a division of Penguin Books Ltd) • Penguin Books Australia Ltd, 250 Camberwell Road,
Camberwell, Victoria 3124, Australia (a division of Pearson Australia Group Pty Ltd) •
Penguin Books India Pvt Ltd, 11 Community Centre, Panchsheel Park,
New Delhi – 110 017, India • Penguin Group (NZ), 67 Apollo Drive, Rosedale,
Auckland 0632, New Zealand (a division of Pearson New Zealand Ltd) • Penguin Books
(South Africa) (Pty) Ltd, 24 Sturdee Avenue, Rosebank, Johannesburg 2196, South Africa

Penguin Books Ltd, Registered Offices: 80 Strand, London WC2R 0RL, England

First published in the United States of America as *Plenitude* by The Penguin Press,
a member of Penguin Group (USA) Inc. 2010
Published with a new preface in Penguin Books 2011

5 7 9 10 8 6 4

Charts and graphs by the author

THE LIBRARY OF CONGRESS HAS CATALOGED THE HARDCOVER EDITION AS FOLLOWS:

Schor, Juliet.
Plenitude : the new economics of true wealth / Juliet B. Schor.
p. cm.
Includes bibliographical references and index.
ISBN 978-1-59420-254-4 (hc.)
ISBN 978-0-14-311942-5 (pbk.)
1. Wealth.   2. Sustainable development.   I. Title.
HC79.W4S35 2010
338.9'27–dc22   2009046474

Printed in the United States of America

DESIGNED BY AMANDA DEWEY

To Prasannan

CONTENTS

Preface

In the year and a half since I completed the final revisions for the hardcover version of *True Wealth*, a great deal has happened. 2010 has officially been recorded as one of the two hottest years on record. The once-in-a-hundred-year drought the Brazilian Amazon experienced in 2005 was repeated just five years later. There has been a Russian heat wave, severe flooding in Australia and Pakistan, and, in early 2011, news that China's major wheat-producing area is facing its worst drought in sixty years. Agricultural yields for corn and wheat are in jeopardy, and food prices are again rising sharply, leading to hunger and political unrest. Energy prices are also rising, as evidence mounts that we are reaching a peak in oil production. A growing body of research suggests that the massive BP oil spill created far more destruction to ocean ecosystems than the official story allows. All around the world, there are signs of accelerated climate disruption and ecological distress.

And yet I feel hopeful. The grassroots movement I described in the book is thriving. The push for urban food production has been particularly successful and is moving beyond farmers' markets and gardening to the building of sizable enterprises. These include Will Allen's Growing Power in Milwaukee and the remarkable transformation of Detroit, where participants report they are "turning Motown into Growtown." A large-scale effort is well under way in Cleveland, where the Evergreen Cooperatives launched four sustainable businesses—a laundry, a newspaper, a solar power producer, and an organic farm— all of which are owned by low-income workers from the community. There has been tremendous interest from around the country in replicating the "Cleveland model" as urban locales, facing high unemployment, declining investment dollars, and ambitious targets for carbon reduction, look for new ways to move forward. One of the most exciting aspects of these initiatives is that they are laying the groundwork for moving to an economy that is made up of many types of companies with varied ownership structures, motives for action, and ways of operating in the world. We're leaving behind the twentieth-century idea that there's one best model. That means transcending the domination of corporate megaliths to a much more pluralistic, hybridized collection of smaller, varied enterprises.

On the consumption side, the new consumer practices I identified in the book appear to be expanding rapidly, although there are not yet hard numbers to quantify participants or practices. But car sharing, couch-surfing, sharing of unused residential space (Airbnb), freecycling, tool libraries, and the like are proliferating. There are more and more swapping groups and organizations that allow people to exchange used toys, clothing, books, and household items. There are sites to help people share work space, land for gardening, or storage space. Local collectives are sharing cooking, from just soup to whole meals. There has been a growth of groups that share "time"—that is, trade services among each other ("I'll give you a ride if you watch my child.") People are saving money, lightening their eco-footprint, and building community as they engage in this new world of shared, or connected consumption.

On the economic policy front, however, there is less to be upbeat about. My book situated our environmental challenges within the collapse of the global economy in 2008. The central argument was that our economic system is broken, that standard solutions wouldn't be sufficient—especially to solve the unemployment crisis—and that we needed to move forward with deep transformations that address our ecological footprint and unemployment simultaneously. Developments over the last year and a half support that point of view. I argued that the downturn was far more severe than many economists allowed, that recovery would fail to produce jobs at anything like the rate needed to put people back to work, and that for most Americans, the future held more economic uncertainty and lower real returns for their labor and skills. So far, those predictions are being borne out.

Through nearly two years of "recovery," job growth has been minimal. More than 25 million Americans remain either fully unemployed, underemployed, or have been discouraged from seeking work. Economic Policy Institute economist Robert Scott estimates that in 2010, U.S. corporations created more jobs abroad than domestically (1.4 million versus 1 million). Substantial productivity growth of 3.5 percent in 2009 and 2010 further reduced demand for labor. Strong outsourcing and productivity growth are two reasons why the standard "trickle-down" approach to job creation—try and rev up the economy as much as possible—will fail.

But it's not only on job creation that standard macroeconomics is failing. Its whole approach is vacuous because it's indiscriminate. How fast can we grow? How big can we get? We remain trapped in this myopic debate when what we need is a conversation not about *how much* but about *what*. What kind of energy system? What kind of transport? Where should investment dollars go? What should people be spending money on? The country has real needs. We've got to reduce carbon emissions; improve education; transform health care; restore degraded ecosystems; shift to safe, organic, localized agriculture; and expand public transportation. The standard approach says the market will sagaciously meet these needs and that decisions about how to deploy our resources should be private. But when income and wealth are so dramatically skewed toward the top as they currently are, and political power is also beholden to wealth, the private market approach produces what those with purchasing power want, rather than what the country or its people need. Standard theory ignores the distribution of purchasing power and comes to incorrect conclusions as a result.

Instead of trickle-down, I argued for reductions in hours of work to make it easier to create jobs and to allocate the jobs we do have more equitably. The latest data on international differences in work time show that the average American now works 350 more hours than his or her counterpart in Germany, a country that weathered the global downturn with almost no unemployment as a result of adjusting hours of work. Recent research from the Organization for Economic Co-operation and Development found that in contrast, U.S. employers deployed few work time adjustments and chose instead to lay off workers at a rate out of proportion to the downturn in GDP. We are living today with that legacy.

How might we shift to shorter hours? We need to build a political consensus on the virtues of using productivity growth to reduce work time rather than to produce more goods. But while that happens, there are policies that may be feasible now. We could start by having the public sector hire new employees at 80 percent time and 80 percent salary. That will expand the number of people who can be hired by anywhere from 10 to 20 percent. As four-day work weeks become more common in the public sector, there will be some spillover to the private sector. This is an approach that was successfully used in the Netherlands when they faced high unemployment in the

1980s. Eventually the 80 percent schedule spread to the entire financial sector as well as other parts of the economy.

A second possibility is already being adopted by a number of states. They are amending their Unemployment Systems to allow companies to put workers on short hours and use unemployment insurance to make up their earnings loss. There has also been a nascent congressional effort to pass a federal law to give this possibility to all states. It's not a panacea, but it's a start, and its cost is neutral so employers have no objections.

Over the longer run, it'll be necessary to change the culture of time use and the incentives facing employers to get the country back to its historical role as a global leader in reducing work hours. If we can manage that, we'll be able to simultaneously cut our carbon and eco-footprints, put people back to work, and enhance the quality of life for nearly everyone. It's a triple-dividend solution.

In the year since the hardcover was published, I have spoken around the country and in Europe to spread its messages. (When I can I'm using teleconferencing to avoid high-emissions air travel). I have found enormously receptive audiences everywhere. In Europe, the mainstream political discourse in a number of countries has moved into figuring out to manage the post-growth transition, create alternatives to GDP, and achieve the shift to sustainable living. In the United States, where the dominant discourse remains trapped in old paradigms; the action is at the grassroots level. I find widespread understanding that our system is failing and eagerness for new solutions. To bring them to scale, we'll need to work less and grow and share more.

But that's not enough. I am frequently asked about the politics of making this transition. It's complicated and difficult, but there *is* a path that will get us from here to there. It involves making alliances between people who have lost their jobs and those who care about planetary degradation. It requires cross-generational linkages, as well as cross-race and cross-class alliances. And to get a critical mass of active citizens, it requires engaging people around their everyday concerns and supporting them as they discover that to get real change we've got to come together at the local, state, and national levels for collective solutions. I see it beginning in the alternative food movement, in the activism around climate change, and in the exciting initiatives that are happening in cities around the country. I hope that reading this book inspires you to become a part of these efforts to build a secure, fair, and workable future for the planet and all its inhabitants.

Chapter One

INTRODUCTION

Global capitalism shattered in 2008. The financial system came frighteningly close to a total collapse and was saved only by government guarantees and massive injections of cash. An astounding $50 trillion of wealth was erased globally. Economic pain drove people into the streets around the world, from Iceland to Greece, Egypt to China.

Since then, the global economy has been rescued, but it hasn't been fixed. That will require fundamental changes. Climate destabilization, economic meltdown, and the escalation of food and energy prices are warning signs from a highly stressed planet. Ecologists have defined a number of safe operating zones for the earth's complex systems and are finding that human activities have already led us outside a number of them. But the mainstream conversation has been stalled by fatalism. We're better at identifying what can't be done than what we need to accomplish.

There *is* a way forward, and I call it plenitude. The word calls attention to the inherent bounty of nature that we need to recover. It directs us to the chance to be rich in the things that matter to us most, and the wealth that is available in our relations with one another. Plenitude involves very different ways of living than those encouraged by the maxims that have dominated the discourse for the last twenty-five years. It puts ecological and social functioning at its core, but it is not a paradigm of sacrifice. To the contrary, it involves a way of life that will yield more well-being than sticking to business as usual, which has led both the natural and economic environments into decline.

Like most of the sustainability visions that have been offered in recent years, plenitude requires that we adopt cutting-edge green technologies. Without them we cannot ensure the survival of what humans have constructed, and we risk plunging into a hellish future. But it's not a techno-fix. Solving our problems in the time we have available is not possible if all we do is change our technology. We will not arrest ecological decline or regain financial health without also introducing a different rhythm of work, consumption, and daily life, as well as alterations in a number of system-wide structures. We need an alternative economy, not just an alternative energy system.

A body of research, writing, and practice on economic alternatives has been developing. It is part of the larger movement for sustainability that began in earnest in the 1980s. At first, these perspectives had a hard time piercing the bubble surrounding the growth economy. Today, there's newfound receptivity as people recognize that a true recovery will require more than lifelines and bailouts.

The logic driving plenitude is largely economic, focusing on efficiency and well-being. I'm betting that the intelligent way to act, for both individuals and society, is the one that will make humans, non-human species, and the planet better off. Plenitude promises smarter economic arrangements, not just technological improvements. It's a way forward that emphasizes innovation, macroeconomic balance, and careful attention to multiple sources of wealth. In this way, it departs from messages of voluntary simplicity and critiques of consumer culture that contend that less is more, that income and consumption are overrated. Research has shown that outside of poverty they are, but that realization doesn't take us far enough. The bigger prize, true affluence, comes through changes that yield new efficiencies: getting more from less.

The version of plenitude that I describe here is addressed in large part to inhabitants of wealthy countries and wealthy inhabitants of poor ones. But most, although not all, of the principles of plenitude and the economics underlying it are also relevant for lower-income households in poor countries. In its general outlines, if not specifics, it's a widely applicable vision of economic life.

Plenitude is also about transition. Change doesn't happen overnight. Creating a sustainable economy will take decades, and this is a strategy for prospering during that shift. The beauty of the approach is that it is available right now. It does not require waiting for the clean-tech paradigm to triumph. It doesn't require getting government on board immediately. Anyone can get started, and many are. It was the right way to go before the economic collapse, in part because it predicted a worsening landscape. It makes even more sense in a period of slow growth or stagnation. As individuals take up the principles of plenitude, they are not merely adopting a private response to what is perforce a collective problem. Rather, they are pioneers of the micro (individual-level) activity that is necessary to create the macro (system-wide) equilibrium, to correct an economy that is badly out of balance.

That balance won't develop automatically. All large-scale transformation requires collective arrangements to succeed. We need environmental accounting, a mechanism to reduce carbon emissions, and an end to fossil fuel subsidies. We need new labor-market policies. We need to reform our health care, education, and retirement security systems. But while we work for those changes, here's a vision for a way to live that respects the awesome place we call earth and all who live upon it.

The Fundamentals of Plenitude

From the perspective of the individual, there are four principles of plenitude. The first is a new allocation of time. For decades, Americans have devoted an increasing fraction of their time and money to the market—working longer hours, filling leisure time with activities that require more income per unit of time, and buying, rather than making, more of what they consume. It's time to reverse this trend and diversify out of the market. This doesn't just mean the stock market, although its recent volatility suggests that's one market to which this point applies in spades. Today's smart strategy for many, if not most, households will be to begin a shift away from the formal and centralized sets of institutions and arrangements that are called the market. By "the market" I mean business-as-usual (BAU) economic activity. BAU is a term that came out of the climate discourse to indicate what would happen if we didn't address rising emissions. Here I use it to indicate the continuation of the current economic rules, practices, growth trajectory, and ecological consequences of production and consumption. It especially refers to the large corporate entities that dominate the market and are heavily invested in it. For individuals, relying less on the market spreads risk and creates multiple sources of income and support, as well as new ways of procuring consumption goods.

Concretely, what this means is a moderation in hours of work. For time-stressed households with adequate incomes, it likely means making trade-offs of income for time. Reclaiming time frees up resources to invest in ecologically restorative activities and creates the opportunity to replenish the human connections that were depleted in the boom years. Of course, millions have had an altered equation of time and money painfully thrust upon them through unemployment or other losses of income. For that group, which already has a surfeit of time and not enough money, the advice involves moving forward with plans that are less centered on full-time employment in the BAU economy and more oriented to the emergent sustainability sector, which includes both businesses and the parallel economy developing amid the wreckage of the collapse. This encompasses areas such as household food cultivation, home construction and renovation, and community initiatives such as barter and bulk buying.

This brings us to the second principle of plenitude, which is to diversify from the BAU market and "self-provision," or make, grow, or do things for oneself. Indeed, the rationale for working fewer hours in the market is not only, or even primarily, about reducing stress in daily life (although that is certainly important). Recovering one's time also makes self-provisioning possible and reveals a liberating truth: The less one has to buy, the less one is required to earn. The downturn has accelerated what was already a robust rediscovery of doing for oneself among sustainability pioneers. Plenitude aspires to transform self-provisioning from a marginal craft movement into something economically significant. That requires raising the productivity of the hours spent in these activities. As I argue later in the book, new agricultural knowledge and the invention of small-scale smart machines make it possible to turn household provisioning into a high-productivity—and economically viable—use of time.

These ideas reverse the direction most households have taken in recent decades and contradict what modern economics preaches, which is that specialization, in one skill or one job, is efficient. Specialization may have made sense when the market was offering better returns. Even as wages stagnated, ultra-cheap consumer goods were hard to turn down. Today, in a world of ecological and economic uncertainty and distress, putting all one's eggs in the basket of the capitalist market looks like a more dubious proposition.

The third principle of plenitude is "true materialism," an environmentally aware approach to consumption. In the United States, the speed of acquiring and discarding products accelerated dramatically before the crash. Consumers knew relatively little about where purchases came from and the ecological impacts of their production, use, and disposal. But many people do care, and want to lighten the footprint of their spending.

Perhaps surprisingly, the route to lower impact does not require putting on a hair shirt. Nor does it entail making consumption less important. Indeed, the plenitude consumer is likely passionate about consuming, and deliberate in the creation of a rich, materially bountiful life. We don't need to be less materialist, as the standard formulation would have it, but more so. For it is only when we take the materiality of the world seriously that we can appreciate and preserve the resources on which spending depends. Living sustainably does mean we can't reproduce a lifestyle of gas-guzzlers, expansive square footage per person, bottled water, and outsize paper consumption. But it doesn't mean we can't have fabulous clothes, low-impact electronic gadgetry, great local food, and a more leisurely mode of travel. Plenitude means that you will actually have time to take the slow boat to China if that appeals.

The final principle is the need to restore investments in one another and our communities. While social bonds are not typically thought of in economic terms, these connections, which scholars call social capital, are a form of wealth that is every bit as important as money or material goods. Especially in times of distress, people survive and thrive by doing for one another. Interpersonal flows of money, goods, and labor are a parallel system of exchange and savings. One casualty of an intense market orientation is that community has gotten thinner and human ties weaker. People haven't had enough time to invest in social connection outside their primary families. By recovering hours, individuals are freed up to fortify their social networks.

These, then, are the individual principles of plenitude: work and spend less, create and connect more. In turn they yield ecological benefits—emit and degrade less—and human ones—enjoy and thrive more.

Shifting the Economic Conversation

In the fall of 2008, as panic swept through the financial system and the economy began to implode, there was a widespread sense that changes, even big changes, would be necessary. Business-as-usual was suddenly called into question. Even capitalism itself was up for discussion. Within six months, only 53 percent of adults would agree that "capitalism is a better system" than socialism. (Twenty percent preferred socialism and 27 percent were not sure. Adults under thirty were about evenly divided between the two options.) But gradually, as conditions stabilized, the status quo reasserted itself. The mainstream conversation about how to reorganize the economy was back in neutral, especially when it came to fundamental questions about how our system is affecting the planet.

Some things did change. After three decades of dominance, conservative economics had lost credibility. Everyone agreed that we couldn't go back to the policies of the previous decade. In the United States, the litany of no-longer-permissibles included the mushrooming of household debt and a national savings rate of zero, the massive excess of imports over exports, an annual flow of $453 billion for imported oil, and a financial system run amok. The country needed more savings and investment, and the constituency for getting off fossil fuels had grown. But the backdrop for these views was a return to some version of normal, albeit a slimmed-down model. As a result, what was offered was a series of Band-Aids—bank and insurance company handouts, tax cuts to induce spending, automobile industry bailouts, and extended unemployment benefits. Some hoped that financial regulation and health care reform would be sufficient to ensure long-term stability. It's a long shot.

One reason the conversation reverted to its usual outlines is that macroeconomists, who focus on growth, employment, and the overall economy, have been slow to incorporate ecological data into their worldview. During 2007 and 2008, the same period that the housing and credit markets were collapsing, dramatically bad news was surfacing on the climate front. Developments since the 2007 Intergovernmental Panel on Climate Change (IPCC) report, whose data ended in 2006, have been grim. Arctic sea ice was melting at hitherto unimaginable rates, and oceans were rising at more than double the IPCC report's maximum possibility. Drought conditions were spreading. World emissions were sharply up in 2007, and in June 2008, James Hansen, NASA's leading climate scientist, told Congress that the CO_2 target "we have been aiming for is a disaster." By February 2009, the news was worse, with scientists reporting that the speed of climate change was already beyond anything considered in the last round of models. Hansen and his colleagues warned that carbon dioxide levels beyond 350 parts per million are incompatible with preserving a planet "similar to that on which civilization developed." But we were already at 385 and rising.

Yet it was as if the people charged with tending the economy were unaware of the breaking news on climate. The main conversation was about how to put more money into people's hands and how to get them back to buying cars, any cars; building more houses, whatever their dimensions; and accumulating more stuff. The bailout and recovery efforts cost trillions, yet only 6 percent, or $52 billion, of the stimulus was actually "green." Amazingly, General Motors and Chrysler were handed $30 billion without a requirement for conversion to hybrids, much less any provision for the far more fuel-efficient mass transport that the nation desperately needed. The approach relied on reviving a highly destructive pattern of consumption and growth and the fiction that our economic system is basically sound. Barack Obama tried to do more to address ecological impacts, but has made limited progress. As the world was hurtling toward an ecological precipice of unfathomable dimensions, the macroeconomic conversation was basically about how to get there faster.

What's more, the problem extends beyond climate. Research from the traditional sciences, as well as the thirty-year-old field of sustainability, is finding that ecosystems of all types are under threat. Humans are degrading the planet far faster than we are regenerating it. Dead zones are proliferating rapidly in the oceans; farmland is morphing into desert. Biodiversity is shrinking, and we're into the sixth mass extinction of species. If current trends continue, some scientists have warned that by 2050 the oceans will be devoid of fish, the primary source of animal protein for a billion people.

This is not to say that economists were intellectually stuck. Many were embracing key features of Keynesian economics, despite the fact that much of the profession had roundly, and self-confidently, rejected these ideas in the previous decades. Rediscovered Keynesian ideas included the wisdom of running government deficits, an understanding of the volatility of investors' "animal spirits" (optimism), and, above all, the fact that the market does not necessarily self-correct. However, the point of recent economic policy has been to put the pieces "back together" again, that is, to return to what we had, rather than to transform the system.

By contrast, on the street, people began moving on almost as soon as the economy started sinking. After the crash, the savings rate shot up and discretionary purchases plummeted. Research on how consumers were experiencing the collapse found that they were making major adjustments in their attitudes to spending, debt, and lifestyle. A declining fraction of the population considered appliances such as dishwashers, air conditioners, microwaves, TVs, and cable and satellite dishes to be necessities. Interview research in late 2008 found a five-stage process that began with a "goodbye *homo economicus*" epiphany and continued through to a recalibration of what is important in life. People talked about a shift from an economy of "me" to an economy of "we," from status-oriented spending to reengaging with the difference between needs and wants. The anthropologists who conducted the study were surprised to find this "larger, more existential debate." But the public is aware that the American way of life is not sustainable. Surveys I worked on as early as 2004 found that more than 80 percent of the population agreed that protecting the environment would require "most of us to make major changes in the way we live." The years since then have increased ecological awareness and urgency. There's no consensus on what to do, but there's recognition that business-as-usual is failing.

Brand economics has been tarnished. This comes after a period of unusual prestige. Within universities, the discipline had been riding high. Among the public, there has been tremendous interest in how economists think, with Paul Krugman's hugely popular writing, bestsellers such as *Freakonomics*, and ongoing columns, such as David Leonhardt's for the *New York Times*, devoted to the profession. But, with some notable exceptions, economists failed to see the financial, housing, and economic crises coming. Princeton's Uwe Reinhardt noted that they "slept comfortably" while Wall Street imploded. Yale's Robert Shiller has invoked the concept of "groupthink" to explain why. Whatever the reason, what occurred in 2007 and 2008 was a monumental blunder. We can't afford a repeat when it comes to the health of the planet.

And we don't have to. What's odd about the narrowness of the national economic conversation is that it leaves out theoretical advances in economics and related fields that have begun to change our basic understandings of what motivates and enriches people. The policy conversation hasn't caught up to what's happening at the forefront of the discipline.

One of the hallmarks of the standard economic model, which hails from the nineteenth century, is that people are considered relatively unchanging. Basic preferences, likes and dislikes, are assumed to be stable, and don't adjust as a result of the choices people make or the circumstances in which they find themselves. People alter their behavior in response to changes in prices and incomes, to be sure, and sometimes rapidly. But there are no feedback loops from today's choices to tomorrow's desires. This accords with an old formulation of human nature as fixed, and this view still dominates the policy conversation. However, there's a growing body of research that attests to human adaptability. Newer thinking in behavioral economics, cultural evolution, and social networking that has developed as a result of interdisciplinary work in psychology, biology, and sociology yields a view of humans as far more malleable. It's the economic analogue to recent findings in neuroscience that the brain is more plastic than previously understood, or in biology that human evolution is happening on a time scale more compressed than scientists originally thought. As economic actors, we can change, too. This has profound implications for our ability to shift from one way of living to another, and to be better off in the process. It's an important part of why we can both reduce ecological impact and improve wellbeing. As we transform our lifestyles, we transform ourselves. Patterns of consuming, earning, or interacting that may seem unrealistic or even negative before starting down this road become feasible and appealing.

Moreover, when big changes are on the table, the narrow trade-offs of the past can be superseded. If we can question consumer-ism, we're no longer forced to make a mandatory choice between well-being and environment. If we can admit that full-time jobs need not require so many hours, it'll be possible to slow down ecological degradation, address unemployment, and make time for family and community. If we can think about knowledge differently, we can expand social wealth far more rapidly. Stepping outside the "there is no alternative to business-as-usual" thinking that has been a straitjacket for years puts creative options into play. And it opens the doors to double and triple dividends: changes that yield benefits on more than one front. Some of the most important economic research in recent years shows that a single intervention—a community reclamation of a brownfield or planting on degraded agriculture land—can solve three problems. It regenerates an ecosystem, provides income for the restorers, and empowers people as civic actors. In dire straits on the economic and ecological fronts, we have little choice but to find a way forward that addresses both. That's what plenitude offers.

The Road Ahead: Economic Performance 2010–2020

A core principle of plenitude—diversifying out of the BAU economy—is predicated on a view about what the future holds. After the crash, economists put forth a wide range of predictions about the depth and length of the downturn whose only common denominator was uncertainty. The severity and uniqueness of the event led to un-charted territory, in which large-scale models, never all that accurate, were highly unreliable. Economists reverted to simplified mental schema, instinct, and estimates of probabilities. Even a year later, no one really knew whether the green shoots and early signs of growth would last after the stimulus dollars dissipated. The future may bring recovery, stagnation, or even another downturn. What I am about to say must be understood in that context.

The economy is broken in fundamental ways, as are the local and global ecosystems on which it depends. Quick fixes won't solve its problems. Creating a truly sustainable system will require ecological restoration and technological innovation, over a period of many years. Plenitude is a strategy for thriving during that transition. The basic ideas of the plenitude approach were formulated during a period when the economy was expanding, but many, including me, questioned its ability to continue with business-as-usual. As a result, the plenitude logic is most apparent during rough periods for the conventional market. But even when growth resumes, the approach remains relevant. That's because it's oriented to the medium term, the next decade and beyond.

A key prediction is that the days of sky-high market returns are over. The twin bubbles in finance and housing were a mirage. We now know that many of the gains were illusory, such as, for example, billions in fictitious profits in the financial sector. Rising prices for land, housing, and other assets were propelled by unrealistic valuations. The BAU economy is in for a long slide.

The view that future returns will be lower comes in part from looking at historical data. Figure 1 charts the rate of profit for the U.S. economy from 1948 to 2005. It shows that in addition to short-term ups and downs, profitability has long swings. From 1948 until 1982, the long-term trend was down. The stagflation of the 1970s led to a major restructuring that began in the early 1980s. Then profits began to rise, and were on an upward trajectory until the 2008 downturn. It's likely the peak has been reached and we're in for another decade or two of slide. There will be less income for individuals and households. Debt-fueled growth will be replaced by higher household savings, which means that fewer dollars will be available for consumption. Indeed, as is often the case, factors that led to high profits, such as the erosion of workers' earnings and the breakdown of effective regulation, resulted in vulnerabilities down the road. One doesn't have to believe we're facing a decade of stagnation to think we're headed for a less prosperous period.

FIGURE I Profitability of the U.S. Economy, 1948–2005

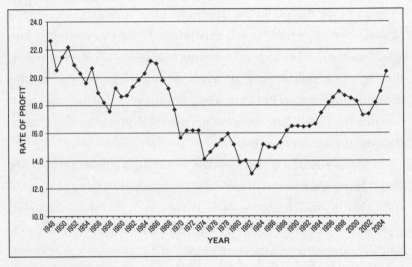

Source: Wolff (2009, Chapter 2)

The dominance of the United States globally is also on the wane, and there's nothing like a worldwide downturn to bring that reality home. For decades, the country has benefited from its special position in many ways. Americans could live beyond their means with a whopping trade deficit because others have been willing to accumulate the dollars that flow outside the nation's borders. But the economic collapse made foreign investors and central bankers nervous about all currencies, including the dollar. American workers have long enjoyed a wage gap relative to those in poorer countries; however, open markets and international competition erode wage differences. Companies have used the downturn to reduce compensation and locate even more jobs offshore.

Even when growth picks up again, there will be large sectors in permanent decline—automobiles, industrial farming, and perhaps even fossil fuels will be smaller and less profitable industries, if they're profitable at all. With a downturn this severe, there will be a protracted and difficult process of weeding out low-performing industries, companies, and products, or what the Austrian economist Joseph Schumpeter called creative destruction. It will take time to re-create the classic conditions for prosperity, such as confidence, financial regulation, monetary stability, consumer demand, and a steady policy hand. Due to the complexity of the global economy, the challenges are far greater than we've ever faced.

As we move forward, the fatal flaw of the current growth regime—climate change and other ecological limits—will rear its ugly head. These problems have already started to affect the bottom line, reducing profits and incomes. Examples include the soaring food and energy prices of 2006 and 2007; the proliferation of extreme weather events, like droughts and floods in the southeastern United States; and agricultural losses due to disrupted ecosystems and species die-offs. Most economic calculations on climate change deal with future costs, but in 2009, a research group released one of the first reports to detail the human and economic costs already being paid. Three hundred and fifteen thousand people are currently dying from climate-change-induced weather and other impacts each year; 325 million others are seriously affected; and the annual price tag is $125 billion, with the vast majority of financial damage occurring in wealthy countries. (The majority of deaths are in poor nations.) Hurricane Katrina alone is estimated to have cost $100 billion. These numbers are expected to rise dramatically in coming years.

Ecological devastation will not only lower the average returns available; the market will also become more volatile. The instability of climate and the running down of ecosystems are not smooth processes. Expect a rockier road.

Does it have to be this way? What about the much-vaunted ability of the market to generate productivity growth, technical change, and wealth? Technological optimists see green innovation as the platform for a new round of growth and stability.

To see how this will likely play out, we need to unpack the idea of growth. This overused term lumps together two very different dynamics, only one of which is really expansion. *Intensive growth* means using a fixed set of resources with greater efficiency. This productivity growth is rightly understood as the cornerstone of economic progress. As we begin to produce more sustainably, it'll be because we make technological and other changes that yield efficiencies in the use of natural capital. A shift to organic and local agriculture, passive solar homes, wind power, and other forms of renewable energy will result in genuine productivity increases. Other true efficiencies can be had through information technology and enhanced human capital. To the extent that this kind of growth occurs, it will indeed provide opportunity and real wealth.

But most of the time when people (and economists) use the word *growth,* they are also referring to the process of pulling in new factors of production, or what's called *extensive growth.* It is so named because it extends the scope of the market, or capitalist, sector, as it replaces public, household, or other types of production. Gross national product and other measures of output and income conflate intensive and extensive growth. But the extensive type is not really growth. It's a shift of resources from one economy to another, or the use of a nonrenewable asset. Drawdowns of capital from the natural world to the market economy (e.g., felling timber, mining, overfishing, and using fossil fuels) are one example. If enough extensive growth occurs, the economies from which those resources are drawn become depleted or, if the process goes far enough, devastated. Eventually, extensive growth starts to become less profitable because the assets being used up get scarcer. It can eventually lead to blowback, which is now happening with the climate system, oceans, and forests.

While the standard account of economic development stresses factors such as human ingenuity, education, and physical capital, that view is beginning to be challenged by environmental historians and social ecologists. Some historians now argue that much of the growth of the industrial period has been of this extensive type, made possible by tapping into fossil fuel sources. We've long been aware that the industrial revolution depended on coal. What we haven't done is work through the implications of that for the post-carbon era. Bill McKibben has put the point powerfully: "Fossil fuels were a one-time gift that underwrote a one-time binge of growth."

The point is also true for other natural resources. Beginning in the sixteenth century, Europe and Asia deforested in order to grow, and resource depletion has been ongoing since then. Over the last few decades, a significant fraction of market expansion has occurred through running down ecosystems. The first national study to assess the extent of the overstatement of growth was done for the 1970s and '80s for Indonesia, and found that half its measured gross domestic product growth disappeared once timber, oil, and soil depletion was factored in. The situation is even starker in China, where torrid growth has created environmental and social havoc. Studies of environmental degradation have found that Chinese GDP was overstated by 8 to 13 percent in the 1990s, and suggest the figure may have grown to as much as 25 percent now. U.S. consumption, fueled by Chinese exports, has become reliant on these drawdowns from nature. A recent estimate of the value lost on a worldwide basis to deforestation alone puts it at $2 trillion to $5 trillion a year.

For the United States, we do not yet know how large the overstatement of market growth has been in recent years. In the early 1990s, the Bureau of Economic Analysis began work on a series of environmental accounts that would allow us to answer that question. But their efforts shortly ran afoul of the coal industry and Republican opposition, and Congress forbade the bureau to continue. The restriction has only been lifted recently, so no comprehensive measures exist. One study of the U.S. electric power industry quantified "off the books" (i.e., currently unaccounted for) liabilities associated with three types of emissions (carbon dioxide, sulfur oxides, and nitrogen oxides). When these are added to official net operating after-tax profits for 2004, the industry total of $22.2 billion in earnings is converted into a net loss of $28.2 billion. Only four of the thirty-three companies included in the study remained profitable after accounting for pollutants they are releasing. Of course, electricity production has a much higher environmental impact than most activities, but reliance on artificially cheap imported fuel, chemical-intensive agriculture, and underpriced manufactured goods creates a similar gap in other sectors. As sustainability asserts itself as an imperative, we can expect to get the necessary environmental accounting.

When the faulty measurement ends, there will be another giant write-down, on top of the financial balance sheet adjustments of 2008 and 2009. There are trillions in fictitious incomes and real costs that haven't been reckoned with yet. If we commit to sustainability, measured annual returns will tend to be lower, at least for the medium term. One consequence is that the business-as-usual market will be relatively disadvantaged, because it is highly resource-intensive. Many large global corporations are especially vulnerable, because they are most dependent on unsustainable practices. If we don't commit to sustainability, the costs of collapsing ecosystems will accelerate, perhaps very rapidly.

Fair enough, but what about the emerging green sector? Won't it be expanding quickly in this scenario, and doesn't it provide an alternative to the diversification strategy? There's no question it's the direction we must go. It will provide real, not fictitious, opportunity. We'll be designing a whole new way to produce and consume based on ingenuity rather than on using up materials. In large part, plenitude is a way to allow individuals to participate in building this new economy. But we're in the early stages of the transition. The experience so far is that companies have been surprisingly slow to embrace sustainable production methods. And no single sector can compensate for the much larger trends from the whole economy. Green businesses will provide only a limited number of jobs, especially right now.

If you're lucky enough to land a good-paying job with a thriving green company, you may want to dive in headfirst. However, as we learned in the 1990s tech boom, there can be an ephemeral quality to a rapidly emerging sector, even for some of the highest-flying companies. In 2008 the surging renewable-energy sector ground to a halt, stymied by the credit crunch. And much of what's passing as green today is sustainable in one, rather than all, of its dimensions. Hybrid vehicles emit less carbon, but their batteries are toxic. They're better than BAU vehicles, but cannot yet be produced in large quantities without negative eco-impacts. So while they're essential, today's green products and technologies are not a magic bullet.

And if the broader economy does recover soon, and global expansion gets back on track? Then we'll be back up against some of the factors that triggered global problems in 2007 and 2008. The prices of food and energy, which were soaring, will likely start rising again. Food (which is eaten by workers) and energy are inputs into virtually everything that is produced. The index of primary commodities, which includes wood, metals, minerals, fuels, and other inputs, rose 23 percent per year from 2003 to 2007, with most explanations crediting strong demand. (Demand from China alone is a major contributor to higher prices.) Food prices rose 9 percent annually. At no time in the last sixty years have commodity prices increased at this rate. Exactly how long it will take prices to escalate will depend on growth rates outside the United States as well as the impacts of climate change. However, once they do, selling one's labor to an employer, buying food at a supermarket, taking an airline trip, purchasing services, or investing in stocks will yield less, in the form of either lower earnings and investment income or less consumer value for every dollar spent.

The bottom line is that room to maneuver is narrowing. In the BAU economy, we're faced with a choice between stagnation and low prices, or growth with high costs and mounting damages. The plenitude path transcends this dilemma. It's parsimonious in the use of scarce natural resources and a heavy user of what can be comparatively in surplus—time, knowledge, technology, and, as we reconstruct it, community.

Plan of the Book

In the chapters that follow, I explore these issues in more detail. Chapter 2, "From Consumer Boom to Ecological Bust," is the story of a rapidly expanding consumer economy and its ecological legacies. This chapter describes the emergence of a fast-fashion dynamic across the consumer market, whereby the acquisition and discard of goods accelerated. I chart a tsunami of sofas, toasters, T-shirts, and other items, as well as the mountains of discards that came in the wake of all this purchasing.

Scientists and engineers have argued since the 1970s that economic growth was the core of the ecological problem. However, as Chapter 3 reveals, mainstream economists have long defended BAU, dismissing the idea that there could be ecological limits to growth. But their optimism is misplaced. Relying on the rationality of markets to ensure the fate of the planet is an irrational, indeed desperate, gamble.

The second half of the book looks toward the future, and what might be. Chapter 4 more closely examines the four principles of plenitude—a new allocation of time through reduced hours of market work, the shift to high-productivity self-provisioning, the development of a low-cost, low-impact, but high-satisfaction consumer life, and the revitalization of community and social connection. The chapter focuses on what individuals can do to gain meaning, financial stability, and control over their economic lives. Chapter 5 looks at plenitude from the viewpoint of the system as a whole, and argues that the personal choices of chapter 4 can lead to balance, efficiency, and wealth creation on a large scale. This logic is easiest to see in the labor market, where individuals' decisions to work less become part of a system-wide solution of shorter hours that reduces unemployment and creates wider employment opportunities.

Where chapter 5 differs most from previous treatments of sustainable economies is its argument that the limiting factor for achieving sustainability is not finance, labor, or natural resources, the building blocks of the industrial economy, but knowledge. As designers and engineers have argued, the true green economy will be built on new blueprints, technologies, and ways of doing things. I show how the plenitude principles, when followed by individuals and small businesses, can be central to the diffusion of smart, ecologically restorative ways to support ourselves. Throughout, the emphasis is on achieving efficiencies that create new wealth. Getting this right involves addressing how knowledge is spread, how skills are developed, and questions of scale.

This conversation is key to recognizing why sustainability is about more than higher energy prices, innovative technologies, and changing the mix of products and activities. Of course, we need all that. But if that's all we change, we're more likely to meet the fate that the trade-off position represents: protecting the environment requires sacrifice and making do with less. BAU with a coat of green paint is not enough. It is only by rethinking basic economic structures that we can figure out how to create durable, true wealth as we regenerate the planet. What was efficient for constructing the nineteenth-century industrial economy is not what's most suited for the resource-scarce system of the twenty-first.

On this point, people are ahead of the economic conversation. In pockets around the country and the world, individuals are busy with new ventures that reverse the structures of scarcity and abundance found in the dominant economy. Their lives are low in conventional consumer goods and high in the newly abundant resources of creativity and community. They are constructing urban cultures with low fossil fuel use, clean food produced through organic farming and permaculture, online networks of product recycling and sharing, bartering of services, ecovillages, and even local alternative currencies. These lifestyles are rich in time, as people reject high-pressure, overly demanding jobs. Ecological visionaries are building transition towns and post-carbon cities. They are learning "one planet living" and other twenty-first-century ways to build community. They are committed to open-source principles, sharing their newly found skills and innovations. They recognize the potential of the small scale. Taken together, these trends already represent a shift out of the conventional economy, and a commitment to alternative economic institutions and different kinds of markets. They aren't on the radar screen as a coherent force yet. But they are the likely normative lifestyles of the future, because they represent economically intelligent ways to live in an era of conventional-resource scarcity.

The global crash that began in 2008 has highlighted the paths that lie before us. We can hold on to business-as-usual, but the comfort of the familiar will likely come at a price of stagnation in incomes, continuing high levels of unemployment, and ongoing destruction of the environment. Alternatively, we can scrap a failing system and go for plenitude, a new route to wealth based on respect for people and the planet.

Chapter Two

FROM CONSUMER BOOM
TO ECOLOGICAL BUST

Before the great crash of 2008, the world economy went on a spending spree unlike any in human history. The combination of sheer population (6.7 billion) and the emergence of a global middle class with money to spend resulted in a truly gargantuan scale of consumption. The United States was at the forefront of this trend, a surprising fact given the unprecedented levels of material comfort its population had already achieved.

The shift toward consumption had been occurring for decades. In 1969 the fraction of gross domestic product devoted to personal consumption stood at 61.5 percent. (The major alternatives are investment, government spending, and exports.) Twenty years later, the consumption share was 65.6 percent, and by 2007 it had topped 70 percent. Expenditures per person hit a peak that same year, at $32,144. It's an extraordinary figure, especially when compared with a global average income of only $8,500, or the fact that more than half the people in the world earn less than $1,000 annually.

From the perspective of fifty years earlier, when the nation was already very prosperous, the expansion of consumption is also striking. In 1960 the average person consumed just a third of what he or she did in late 2008. Since 1990, inflation-adjusted per-person expenditures have risen 300 percent for furniture and household goods, 80 percent for apparel, and 15–20 percent for vehicles, housing, and food. Overall, average real per-person spending increased 42 percent.

This doesn't mean well-being was proceeding apace. Average spending gives information about one spot (or "moment") in a distribution. As has been extensively documented, the distribution of purchasing power was getting vastly more unequal. Since 2000, nearly half, or 47 percent, of the nation's entire income has accrued to the top 20 percent of the population. Before the crash, income inequality was worse than at any time since the end of the 1920s boom, and by some measures had even exceeded that historic peak. Even though consumption was increasing, so too were poverty, indebtedness, and lack of health insurance. Broader measures showed erosion in well-being even as spending was accelerating. The United States, which in 1990 ranked number two in the world on the Human Development Index, had plunged to number fifteen by 2006. The nonstop upscaling of lifestyles was arguably contributing to, rather than offsetting, the deterioration in quality of life.

After the financial crisis hit, attention was focused on fiscal imbalances—a gaping trade deficit of $719 billion and, by 2008, nearly $14 trillion in household indebtedness. Those numbers are important. But the failure has not just been monetary. There's a material dimension that has been overlooked. What transpired in the late years of the bubble was an almost manic speedup in the flow of goods through households and the larger economy. It has been most obvious in apparel and consumer electronics, but it is a more general phenomenon. Notably, every one of those products used up or altered some part of the planet and its ecosystems. New data discussed below shows that material impact is increasing, and ominously so.

There's a curious aspect to the material impact of consumption, when considered from a cultural perspective. Among wealthy countries and wealthy consumers, products have become so abundant and lifestyles so comfortable that the use of goods to meet basic needs (food, clothing, shelter, transport) is often overshadowed by their role as symbolic communicators. Brands, styles, and exclusivity are used to convey social status, construct identity, and differentiate from or join with others. These symbolic aspects of consumption have become more valued.

But as the goods themselves become less important, and their social meanings more salient, their physical or material impact on the planet intensifies. That's because symbolic consumption relies heavily on fashion and novelty. People buy more products and turn them over quickly. I call this the materiality paradox. It describes what happened during the boom, and it's part of why consumption is taking an escalating toll on the planet. Transcending the materiality paradox is one of the urgent tasks we face, and plenitude can help us do that.

Elite discourse remains focused on returning us to the status quo. The operating assumption is the desire to stimulate household consumption. But that raises an obvious question. Is what ails the country a shortage of cars, square footage in housing, television sets, sofas, clothing, dishes, laptops, and cell phones? To see the folly in the "spend our way back to normal" route, we need to look at what was happening before the crash and how it has affected ecosystems and natural resources. Clothing is a good place to start, not because it's the most ecologically significant of the things we consume (it is not), but because it was the cutting edge of a set of unsustainable consumer practices.

Fast Fashion: The Case of Apparel

The most revealing fact about the contemporary apparel market is this: clothing can now be purchased by weight, rather than by the piece, and at a price as low as a dollar a pound. That means it's possible to buy gently used, even high-end apparel for less than rice, beans, or other basic foodstuffs. In historical perspective, this is almost unfathomable.

In the West, apparel has been expensive to produce and has therefore been a high-priced and valuable commodity for centuries. Once fashioned, garments had long and varied lives. A dress or jacket might be born as special occasion wear, then segue into an everyday outdoor piece, then become a garment for indoor sociability, and eventually be worn (and worn out) while doing domestic chores. Apparel also traversed social hierarchies, passed down from elites to their servants. In some households, garments were turned into quilting squares, thereby extending a textile's productivity for years. A piece of clothing might end its useful life as a rag, and literally turn to dust.

While economic growth has rendered all consumer goods far less valuable today than they were in the past, apparel is a special case. According to the historian Beverly Lemire, clothing has been worth so much that it served as an alternative currency in the secondhand economies that have existed for centuries alongside markets in new goods. From the seventeenth through the mid-nineteenth century, apparel was a primary medium of exchange, second only to metals and precious stones. Even in the twentieth century, some used clothing continued to have value in exchange.

This history puts the nearly free gently worn garments of the early twenty-first century into sharp relief. The United States has been piling up mountains of clothing that have virtually no value. There's a profound ecological insight here. The production system drives businesses to use natural resources at hyperspeed, and the consumer system makes the resulting products redundant almost as fast. It's a recipe for disaster.

The accumulation of clothing has been made possible by plummeting prices. At the high end, there has been stratospheric escalation (three-thousand-dollar suits, handbags, and the like), but in the broader mass market, cheapening has been the norm. The outsourcing of production has driven prices down. Global surpluses of labor, including vast numbers of former rural peasants in China, combined with the market power of chains such as Wal-Mart, have led to relentless downward pressure on apparel workers' wages. Other contributors to low prices include artificially inexpensive global shipping, technological innovation in inventory control, and fierce competition among suppliers. In the late 1990s, the Asian financial crisis accelerated the downward price trend as exporting economies endured a severe contraction that further eroded wages. The cost of a dress, a pair of pants, or a coat declined sharply. The consumer price index for apparel, which stood at 127 in 1991, fell to a low of 117.9 in 2006.

For twenty years, consumers have ratcheted up their purchases of apparel. Consider the category of outer- and underwear (which excludes socks and hosiery, but includes all other apparel, such as pajamas, swimsuits, and so on). In 1991 Americans bought an average of thirty-four dresses, pairs of pants, sweaters, shirts, underwear, and other items. In 1996 that number had risen to forty-one. By 2007 per-person consumption had soared to sixty-seven items. American consumers were purchasing a new piece of clothing every 5.4 days.

Higher acquisition has been accompanied by more stylistic change. The industry has shortened the time between the design of a garment and its appearance in the store. The annual fashion cycle has been gradually reduced to a few months, and in some stores the

FIGURE 2.1 Purchases of New Apparel by U.S. Consumers

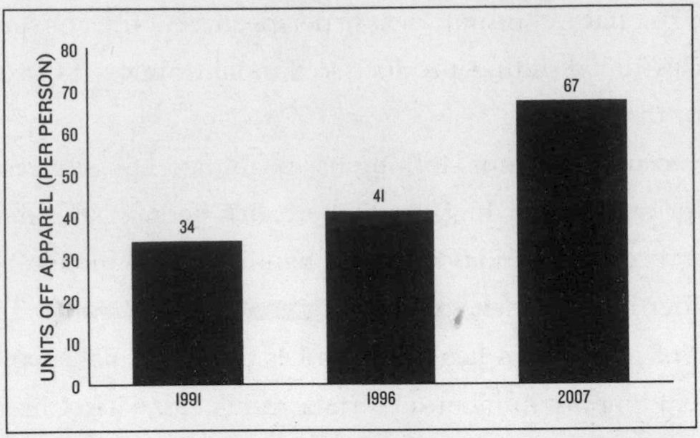

Source: Data on units of apparel from AAFA (2008) and U.S. Census Bureau (2005 and earlier years with missing data made available to author)

floor life of a garment is measured in weeks. As the economics of apparel production have changed, so too have consumers. They have come to expect low prices and frequent design change. Buying is more indiscriminate, and garments are worn fewer times. Shoppers can indulge their taste for novelty, worrying less about whether their wardrobes are versatile and durable. There has been a shift out of what the industry calls basics, which persist over years with relatively slow-moving design, to fashion, which by definition has fast-moving style. People now buy more fashion items, and basics themselves are also more fashionable. It's a fast or McFashion world, in which style is available at mass marketers, such as H&M or Old Navy, at rock-bottom prices.

The concept of fashion is worth considering for a moment. It implies constant movement, even ephemerality. This year's styles must be different from last year's. In *Empire of Fashion,* a history of its rise in the West, the French philosopher Gilles Lipovetsky argues that we embrace fashion because it shows that we can afford to be wasteful, abandoning goods merely because they are no longer stylish. Fashion is to some extent a love of the frivolous, or at least a flight from necessity. By all accounts, fashion is a social, rather than a functional, dynamic. In a fashion-driven world, a piece of apparel, furniture, or electronics can lose its appeal because it is no longer stylish or because it has become too widely available. That's a key distinction between fashion and nonfashion items. Consumers who buy new energy-efficient gas boilers will not be tempted to ditch them because their neighbors adopt them. But once "everyone" has a granite countertop, a pashmina scarf, a pair of UGGs, or a (fill in the blank), fashion-conscious consumers begin to abandon these items. Examples like gas boilers are getting harder to find as more and more of what we buy is sucked out of the realm of the purely functional into the orbit of design and fashion. The British sociologist Mike Featherstone called this trend "the aestheticization of everyday life." By the end of the boom, it was affecting everything from the pencil holder on the desk to the teapot on the stove, never mind the cell phone, its case, and its ringtone.

Fast Fashion Writ Large

Industry has a rather prosaic name for products that move quickly through the market. They're called FMCGs, or fast-moving consumer goods. Traditionally these have been products, such as toothpaste and detergent, that are used up in a flash. During the boom, apparel became an FMCG. So, too, have a number of other products that are considered consumer durables, but whose life cycle is now anything but. Electronics, furniture, and other household items started moving quickly. And as they did, the sheer volume of consumption in the U.S. economy ratcheted sharply up.

Thinking about the volume of consumption is a stark departure from the ordinary practice of economics, which focuses on prices and dollar flows. Dollar data is often very detailed, allowing analyses of buying patterns among groups of consumers or responsiveness to changes in prices. But the number of couches people buy or how much those couches weigh is typically outside the economist's field of vision. Yet those measures are central not only to the consumer experience, but also to the ecological impacts of spending.

The dollar metric can miss the boat in a period like the present, with rapid product innovation and falling prices. Spending data is adjusted for changes in prices, but there is no perfect method to do so, and parsing out changes in quality is complex. One hundred dollars of spending can represent one, two, three, even twenty shirts.

FIGURE 2.2 Prices of Durable Goods

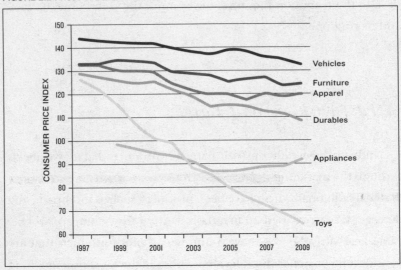

Source: U.S. Bureau of Labor Statistics (2009a)

During the boom, there were bargains galore as goods prices dropped precipitously. In addition to reductions in the prices of

FIGURE 2.3 Department Store Prices

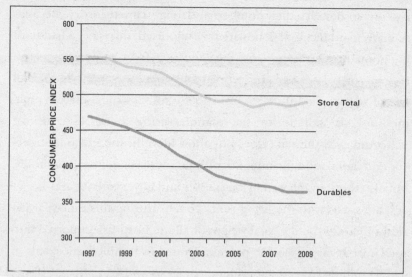

Source: U.S. Bureau of Labor Statistics (2009a)

apparel, the prices of toys fell by nearly half. For other goods, prices rose as the economy expanded in the beginning of the decade, but fell in the later stages of the boom. Furniture, appliance, and vehicle prices declined after 1999. Computer prices (not shown) fell dramatically, to a tenth of their 1991 value. The department store index for durable goods reached a peak of 470 in 1997, then fell a hundred points. Prices for all products at department stores went down as well. As products got cheap, people started buying more.

By how much? To answer that question, we need measures such as the actual number of items or, even better for ecological analysis, the weight of goods. It is hard to find that information because data collection is skewed toward dollar values. The Census of Manufactures periodically publishes reports for some categories, but only a few. Industries do their own research, but it is typically proprietary. (Apparel is unusual, because of its history of international quotas.)

One bright spot in the data landscape is that when products arrive on our borders, their numbers and weights are recorded. Because so many manufactured goods are now imported, this is not a bad starting point. Products come into the country in four main ways—by sea, air, rail, or truck—and the government collects information on all four. I've compiled the data from 1998 until 2007 for selected commodities, as well as for the manufacturing sector as a whole. Unfortunately, the data does not allow identification of purchasers (or end users), and includes not only goods destined for households, but also those purchased by businesses and government.

Let's start with the living room couch. During this nine-year period (1998–2007), the total weight of all the furniture imported into the United States rose 155 percent, from 4,671 million kilograms to 11,894 million. Anecdotal evidence suggests an IKEA effect. IKEA, a low-cost Swedish producer specializing in up-to-date design at bargain prices, opened its first U.S. store in 1985 and subsequently increased its national presence. The large increase in furniture volumes is probably due to the downward price pressure exerted by IKEA and similar retailers, as well as to a growing sensibility of fashion in the furniture market.

FIGURE 2.4 Furniture Acquisition

	1998	2007	Change
Consumer Price Index	133.6	127.1	6.5-point decrease
Weight of imports (in millions of kgs)	4,671	11,894	155% increase
Units of imports (in millions)	327.6	651.3 (2005)	99% increase

Sources: U.S. Bureau of Labor Statistics, U.S. Bureau of Transportation Statistics, WISERTrade

A tally by item, rather than weight, reveals a similar story. Aggregating across fifty-one detailed categories of furniture (mattresses of cotton, mattresses of cellulose, etc.), I found that in 1998,

327.6 million pieces of furniture of all types were imported into the United States. By 2005 imports were twice as numerous, at 651.3 million. The unit data also suggests accelerated buying spurred by the expansion of cheap but fashionable imported furniture.

Do the expanded imports really represent a rise in consumption, or are they just replacing domestic furniture production? I haven't found data on domestic production by volume or in units. However, consumption of domestically produced furniture in dollar terms (defined as domestic production minus imports) rose 25 percent. At the same time, prices fell, so the rise in the number of pieces produced was even larger. Furniture is becoming a faster-moving consumer good.

Consumer electronics are also exhibiting a fashion cycle. The weight of imported electronics, such as computers, cell phones, televi-

FIGURE 2.5 Consumer Electronics

	1998	2005	Change
Consumer price index for information technology	44.3	14.0	30.3-point decrease
Units of imported goods, in millions			
Cell phones	14	177	1,150% increase
Laptops	3	24	620% increase
Vacuum cleaners	67	188	180% increase
Ovens, toasters, coffeemakers	76	227	200% increase
Other small electronics	715	1,400	96% increase

Sources: U.S. Bureau of Labor Statistics, U.S. Bureau of Transportation Statistics, WISERTrade

sions, fax machines, and MP3 players, increased by 75 percent over the period 1998–2007. This is especially notable when we consider that a number of these products, such as laptops, MP3 players, and cellular phones, have been shrinking in size and weight, and laptops have grown in popularity. There has been a shift to thinner flat-panel and plasma televisions. My calculations on imported unit volumes show that these have increased substantially. The number of imported cell phones rose twelvefold, from 14.2 million in 1998 to 177.2 million in 2005. Laptops rose from 3.3 million to 23.8 million, a sevenfold expansion. Furthermore, the increase is not just occurring in newer technologies. Imports of vacuum cleaners more than doubled (67 million to 188 million). Ovens, toasters, and coffeemakers rose from 76 million to 227 million. A subset of ten small electronics categories increased from 715 million units in 1998 to 1.4 billion in 2005, a nearly 100 percent increase. Industry data shows that total purchases of computers rose from 38.9 million in 1998 to an estimated 64.2 million in 2007.

A similar story can be told across manufacturing. The weight of imported ceramics rose by 83 percent, glass and glassware by 61 per-

FIGURE 2.6 The Growing Weight of Imported Goods

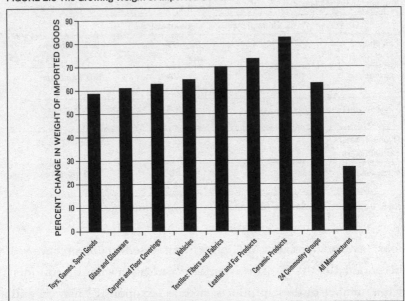

Source: U.S. Bureau of Transportation Statistics, WISERTrade (2009)

cent, leather and fur products by 74 percent, toys and games by 59 percent, textiles by 70 percent, carpets by 63 percent. In a few of these cases, declines in domestic production offset some of the increase, but in others domestic production was an addition to total consumption. The vehicles category is environmentally very significant, because of both emissions and the heavy volume of materials used for manufacture. The material volume of imported vehicles rose 64 percent. Domestically produced consumption in dollar terms increased by 14 percent over the period, and prices of new vehicles fell slightly, indicating that the weight of imports plus domestic production has increased in the range of 80 percent. Other commodity groups with large increases include plastics and rubber, and pearls, stones, metals, and jewelry. Food and pharmaceuticals also increased.

Figure 2.6 also shows the growth in volume of twenty-four commodity groups that constitute most of the consumer economy, as well as data on all commodity imports. Taken together, the twenty-four commodities increased in total weight by 63 percent, or 7 percent a year. For the entire goods sector, which includes more of what business purchases, the total increase over the period was 28 percent, or approximately 3.1 percent annually. The growth in domestic production was in addition to these increases.

Discard Nation

Had the acceleration of consumer purchasing been a one-time spurt or yielded items that would be used and appreciated over many years, its impact could have been manageable. But acquisition has been paired with product abandonment. It's a grand consumer churn, and its speed is unprecedented. Fashions change within months. People grow tired of their purchases more quickly. Products become technologically obsolete or break. Either we're not getting much benefit from what we buy, or we're struggling to keep up with changing styles, or both.

The government doesn't keep comprehensive statistics on used goods, either in the household or as they reenter the market or the waste stream. But there's partial and anecdotal evidence that points to rising household inventories of unused products and discard to various outlets.

When consumers acquire additional goods, they have to find places to put them. The census survey of new housing does not include information on closets or storage space, but new homes have gotten much larger, and anecdotal evidence suggests significant increases in closet and other storage space. In fact, closets have become a mini-industry, with a retail presence (e.g., California Closets and the Container Store). There are numerous books on how to reduce clutter. There is even a profession, represented by the National Association of Professional Organizers, devoted to helping people with their material overload. Another trend is the rise in commercial self-storage. One in ten households now rents storage space, a 65 percent increase since 1995. The industry collects more than $20 billion in annual sales, and has installed 20.8 square feet of capacity per household in the United States.

Consumer electronics are piling up at a rapid rate. The Environmental Protection Agency has estimated that in 2007 alone, 140 million cell phones reached a stage called end of life (EOL). They're ready to be disposed of, having already been stored at home for some time. (The EPA is counting electronics because they contain toxic metals, and there are efforts under way to recycle them, including a few state laws that prevent landfill disposal.) This compares with only 19 million in 1999. Two hundred and five million computers and peripherals transitioned into EOL in 2007 (compared with 124 million in 1999). Since 1980, about 1.2 billion computers and televisions alone have been collected, with another 235 million still sitting in storage in households and offices. For cell phones, computer products, and televisions together, 373 million, or about 1.2 per American, arrived at EOL in 2007. And these are just a few categories—storage and discard are also rising for fax machines and DVD and MP3 players, among others.

Apparel discard has also risen dramatically. The secondhand clothing industry has been estimated to exceed one billion dollars. Much of the supply is exported to low-income countries. In 1991, 316 million pounds of worn clothing were exported from the United States to the rest of the world. By 2004 exports stood at 1.1 billion, an almost fourfold rise. Unpublished regression analyses I have done find that imports of new garments track and predict these exports of used clothes. The more new pieces consumers purchase, the more used ones they give away. Households have also been putting a larger quantity of apparel into the waste stream. In 2007, textiles made up approximately 4.7 percent of the annual municipal waste stream of 254 million tons, which amounted to seventy-eight pounds of textile discards per person.

Another piece of evidence of the exploding supply of used items is the growth of eBay, Craigslist, and other online sites that transfer goods between and among people. The government isn't keeping track of these sites, but they have expanded rapidly. I did manage to find data on exports of used or secondhand merchandise, a grab-bag category that includes items ranging from paintings and drawings to worn clothing, used tires, and postage stamps. Many of the items are industrial, such as backhoes, excavators, and tractors, so it's not a great measure, but it does show that by weight, these exports increased 66 percent from 1998 to 2005.

The Materiality Paradox

The logic of the fashion model is that social and cultural considerations, rather than functionality, drive purchases. Whether for reasons of style, fit, color, design, or even just novelty, in a fashion-driven consumer world, items that still work in the everyday sense of the term are abandoned because they are seen as out-of-date, ugly, ratty, old, or just plain boring. Their social meaning, or what the literature calls symbolic value, is what counts. For decades, theorists of consumer society, most prominently Jean Baudrillard, have written about this symbolic economy.

These postmodern accounts of consumer culture argue that what we now care about as we consume is not products themselves, but the signs and symbols they connect to. Image is paramount. The classic example is the branded athletic shoe, which costs only a few dollars to make, and is not physically distinct from many other shoes. Nevertheless, consumers shell out large sums, which can range from fifty to two hundred dollars, to get these status symbols. Advertising and media have succeeded in cultivating desire for the Apple logo, the Prada triangle, or the Nike swoosh, even more than for the phone, the bag, or the shoe.

Some consumer theorists argue that the emergence of a symbolically driven economy implies that when people crave images and social meaning, the materiality of goods becomes unimportant, which in turn can produce dematerialization. The idea is that we consume images, rather than material products. Virtual possessions in the computer environment Second Life can substitute for offline "stuff." Others predict the material impact of spending will be reduced through technological change. These are comforting thoughts, because material impact is what drives ecological degradation.

The consumer theorists are certainly right about one thing. Symbolic value has become far more important. Expanded expenditures on advertising and marketing, the growth of brand value as a corporate asset, and the emergence of fast fashion are all evidence for that view. But, in opposition to theorists of dematerialization, the materiality paradox suggests that the rising importance of symbolic value increases, rather than reduces, pressure on the planet. That's because sign economies are vulnerable to the dynamics of rapidly changing symbolic value, through the fashion cycle. If what is symbolically valued remains so for only a brief period of time, then replacement goods become necessary. The materiality paradox says that when consumers are most hotly in pursuit of nonmaterial meanings, their use of material resources is greatest. This point brings to mind Raymond Williams's famous quip that our problem isn't that we're too materialistic; it's that we're not materialistic enough. We devalue the material world by excessive acquisition and discard of products. The plenitude principle of true materialism reverses this attitude.

Of course, it's not only the planet that suffers in this stage of consumer culture. The fast-fashion dynamic puts enormous pressure on consumers to keep up with what can at times feel like a dizzying acceleration in norms. It's financially exhausting, and requires time to shop, compare prices, and learn to operate new technologies. Fast fashion fosters an unhealthy dissatisfaction with what one has and anxiety about falling behind. Among the comfortable, it can engender a lack of contentment and gratitude.

The materiality paradox hasn't been recognized, and especially not by scholars of consumption in the wealthy countries. Perhaps the globalization of production partly explains this. It's easier to believe we've left the manufacturing era if sooty factories and mining operations no longer dot the landscape. But examining the data on material flows through the economy and across the globe reveals a far less comforting picture than one gets from the talk about a postmaterial future.

Material Economics

In contrast to predictions of dematerialization, the volume of materials used globally, as well as in each individual region of the world, is rising. The extraction and transformation of resources like fuels, wood, sand, gravel, minerals, and biomass create the pulse of an economy. Until recently, scholars paid relatively little attention to how these materials move through and across economies. But that is changing. One of the most interesting metrics is called material flow analysis. MFA tracks the extraction of resources through production and consumption. The field is still in its infancy, and not well known in the United States, but it is growing, especially in Europe.

FIGURE 2.7 Worldwide Materials Extraction, 1980–2005

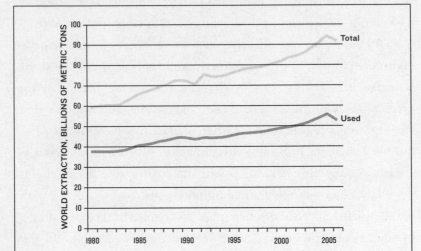

Source: Sustainable Europe Research Institute (2009)

We now have the first comprehensive global estimates of material flows over time. In 1980 humans extracted and used 40 billion metric tons of metals, fossil fuels, biomass, and minerals. (One metric ton equals 2,204.6 pounds.) Twenty-five years later, the annual use of materials had increased 45 percent, to 58 billion. All regions are heavier users, including North America. While 58 billion tons is a very large number, it represents only that portion of extracted resources that actually enter the economy. Another 39 billion or so tons are displaced in the process of production. This unused or wasted extraction is sometimes called overburden. It's the soil that's removed in coal mining, the discarded shells of plants, and so forth. For some commodities, the overburden is enormous. To yield one ounce of gold, a mining company can excavate a hundred or more tons of earth.

On a per-person basis, materials use has been nearly constant over these twenty-five years, as more efficient use of materials has been counterbalanced by expanded production. In 2005, the global average was about 8.8 metric tons, or just under fifty pounds of materials used per day. The U.S. consumer, however, consumed two and a half times the global average, or 23 metric tons. But even this is an understatement, because it doesn't include the flows of imported materials, which are large and have grown rapidly. Unfortunately, the data to track imports and exports by country is not yet complete, but

FIGURE 2.8 Total U.S. Consumption, 2000, in thousands of metric tons

Categories	TMC [1000 m.t.]
Agricultural, grazing, fish, fiber crops	4,122,766
Forestry	657,702
Coal and oil	7,466,204
Natural gas	581,329
Iron ores	372,805
Other metal ores	1,539,492
Industrial minerals	1,767,137
Construction minerals	1,413,704
Total	17,921,137

Sources: Provided to author by Sustainable Europe Research Institute (SERI)

the researchers who are putting it together were able to give me the numbers for 2000. That year, total U.S. material consumption, including imports and overburden, was 17.9 billion metric tons. That works out to 59.8 metric tons, or 132,000 pounds of oil, sand, grain, iron ore, coal, and wood for every person, to produce the United States' GNP. Divide that by 365 and it yields an eye-popping 362 pounds a day. It's not a sustainable number.

The largest category is for coal and oil, and natural gas use is also significant. It is well known that Americans are wasteful consumers of fossil fuels. The housing stock isn't properly insulated, building codes are lax, and easy conservation measures still haven't been put into place. In comparison to citizens of other comparably wealthy nations, Americans have more cars per person, drive more miles, take more airplane flights, and live in larger homes. Most important, the country hasn't moved off coal yet, despite its very high emissions. As a result, in 2006 the average American emitted 19.7 metric tons of CO_2 per year, while the Germans, Japanese, and British were at about 10 tons, the Italians were at 8.3, and the French at 6.7. Given all the discussion about the emissions of China and India, it's worth noting that their per capita rates are low, at 4.6 and 1.3 respectively. But it's also true that in the United States households are responsible for less than half of all emissions—a huge fraction is attributable to industry, whose practices households do not control.

The second-largest category is agriculture. In recent years, there has been a good deal written about how food is produced and consumed in the United States, and the adverse effects of this system on consumers and the earth. Factory farming is chemical-intensive and produces large greenhouse gas emissions. The number of calories produced per person is high, and American patterns of food production are resource-intensive and polluting, especially beef production, which yields excessive carbon dioxide and methane. The average U.S. beef diet emits the equivalent in greenhouse gases of 1,800 miles of driving, and Americans eat more beef (ninety-four pounds in 2005) than people anywhere except Argentina. Research on beef versus vegetable production found that in comparison to asparagus, for example, beef is thirty-six times more greenhouse gas–intensive. And perhaps the most distressing fact of all is that an estimated 40–50 percent of U.S. food is wasted along the chain from farm to table. We're destroying the environment with industrialized food production, a good portion of which just gets driven to landfills, where it rots and releases even more methane.

Housing and construction are also materials-intensive. On the residential side, there has been a trend toward much larger homes. The average single-family dwelling built in 1980 was 1,740 square feet. Twenty years later, it had expanded 45 percent, to 2,521. Ninety-five percent of these homes have two or more bathrooms, 90 percent have air-conditioning, and 19 percent have three-car or larger garages.

The conventional wisdom says that we can continue to grow indefinitely because technological change will allow us to dematerialize. The idea is that GDP can be decoupled from materials use, pollution, and eco-impact, allowing it to rise to the heavens, while its materiality shrinks. While it's true that each dollar of GDP is now responsible for less material flow, over the last twenty-five years, the growth of GDP has canceled out this reduction almost everywhere.

Between 1980 and 2005, the United States and Canada increased their materials use by 54 percent, or about 2 percent a year, even before accounting for imports. Over this period, total materials consumption rose from 6.6 billion to 10.1 billion metric tons. Population rose by 35 percent, less than the materials increase. So not only did total materials use rise, but per-person use also went up. Material flow per dollar of GDP did decline, about 25 percent, but the total growth was more than twice that. Paper is a good example of the failure of technology to reduce material impact. Computers were supposed to yield the paperless society, but in the United States, per-person con-

FIGURE 2.9 Domestic Material Consumption in North America, 1980–2005

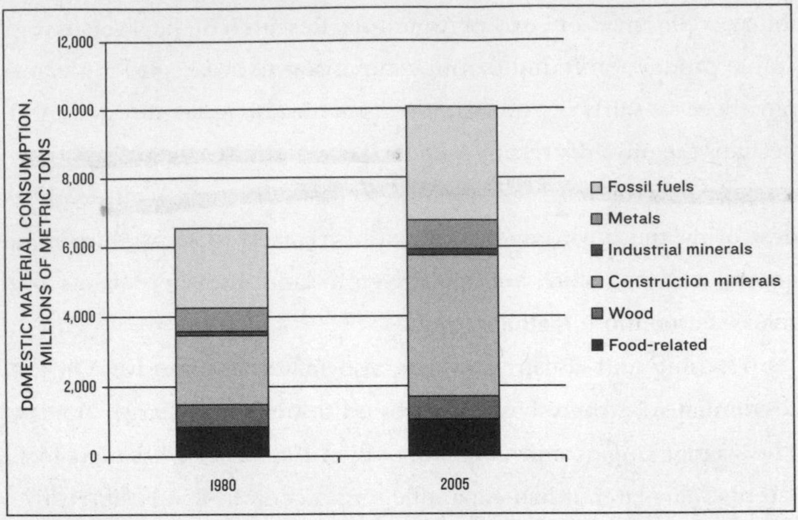

Source: OECD (2008b, p. 40)

sumption of paper has risen since 1980 and stood at 650 pounds a year in 2005, the highest in the world. With 4.5 percent of the world's population, America accounts for a third of paper consumption, almost all of which comes from trees.

Western Europe has done much better than North America, in part because fossil fuel use has fallen, compared with a 43 percent rise in North America. As a whole, Europe increased its materials use only 9 percent, far less than the 54 percent in the United States and Canada. The differences between the two regions' energy consumption also raises the point that not all materials are equally damaging. Fossil fuels, because of their role in climate change, are most problematic. One of the troubling trends of recent years is that wealthy countries have been off-loading a good portion of the burden of their fossil fuel consumption to poorer nations where production is taking place. Chinese factories, for example, are fired by coal, an extremely dirty fuel with an outsize impact on climate. Considering just global warming gases, in 2004 the United States is estimated to have out-sourced 20 percent of its total emissions.

In the 1980s, the bulk of expert opinion settled on lower impact per dollar of GDP, or what is called relative decoupling, as the cure to ecological ills. However, the experience of the last twenty-five years suggests that the market alone will not produce results fast enough to counteract ongoing environmental damage. One reason is the materiality paradox, something neither economists nor other social scientists counted on. Improvements in efficiency and technology have been unable to outstrip the rising material volume of accelerated acquisition. And while weight-reducing innovation is occurring in some products—electronics and camping equipment are obvious cases—not everything is getting lighter. Vehicles, refrigerators, and homes got bigger and heavier. The promise of dematerialization also didn't take into account the enormous expansion of demand for materials from what has come to be known as the Global South, the countries outside the wealthy Western nations that lack the funds to purchase the latest and most resource-efficient technologies.

More generally, dematerialization has been stymied by the failure to incorporate ecological costs, especially for fossil fuels. Western Europe's relative success in containing material flows is due to smart energy policies that raised taxes and reduced consumption. North America, with its subsidies for coal, oil, and gas, has been far more voracious. We shall see in the next chapter that improvements in energy efficiency that are not offset by taxes are effectively price reductions, which spur consumption.

In thinking about solutions, it is important to recognize that consumers have been cut off from the material realities of production. Producers and retailers prefer that consumers not think about the damage their purchases are having on the earth, so information is not typically available, especially at the point of purchase. Does the factory that assembled the cell phone rely on dirty, coal-fired electricity? Are the dyes in the shirt toxic, as is typical in much of the world's apparel? Was that beautiful piece of jewelry made of gold excavated from a mine whose chemical processing is poisoning water supplies and causing cancer in local residents? It's hard and sometimes impossible to even know the answers to these questions, much less be able to stop the destructive practices. This means that fashion cycles can accelerate in products that have extreme impacts, with consumers none the wiser, as the rage for flat-screen televisions reveals. A spate of recent research revealed that some manufacturers had begun using a synthetic gas called nitrogen trifluoride (NF_3), whose climate impacts are thousands of times that of CO_2. So far the quantity of the gas released is tiny, but the example shows that the model of unregulated producers plus uninformed consumers can be disastrous.

The emphasis on dematerialization is one component of a broader approach that says technological improvements, or technology plus ecologically sound pricing, will be sufficient to repair and protect ecosystems. This remains the stubbornly dominant thinking among experts and politicians, even though the numbers don't add up for the short to medium term. Why is there so much resistance to addressing other remedies, such as how fast we grow and patterns of consumer choice? Part of the answer lies in a spirited conversation on the future of the planet that took place decades ago, after which the mainstream discourse declared infinite growth an ecologically viable path.

Are There Limits to Growth?

The 1950s and early 1960s were a heady time at the Massachusetts Institute of Technology. While eventually the institute would be embroiled in controversies over its involvement in the Vietnam War, at this point there was great enthusiasm among the researchers whose inventions lay the groundwork for the computerization and information technology that would reshape the world in the 1990s. Jay Forrester was one such engineer, a young man from Nebraska who arrived at MIT for graduate study in 1939. Forrester started his career working on systems feedback control in military equipment, including submarines. During the Second World War, he was sent to the Pacific theater to repair a radar system aboard the aircraft carrier *Lexington,* and survived a torpedo attack. Forrester returned to MIT in 1947. Under his direction, the institute's first digital computer was created, and Forrester patented the first random-access magnetic computer memory.

In the 1950s, Forrester got involved with business problems and developed a comprehensive theory of management known as systems dynamics. It was a natural outgrowth of computers because it involved taking large quantities of information and analyzing how it moved together as an integrated system. Forrester applied the technique to business organizations, cities, and schools. In 1970 his urban modeling led him to the Club of Rome, a group that had just been founded by Aurelio Peccei, an Italian businessman, to look at "the human predicament" over the long run. In contrast to prevailing enthusiasm about economic growth and future possibilities, the Club saw storm clouds on the horizon. One was population, which was already above 3.5 billion, and at that moment was growing hyperbolically; that is, its growth rate was increasing as population grew. The Stanford ecologist Paul Ehrlich had warned that population was a bomb ready to go off. Would food supplies be adequate to feed the 6 billion expected for 2000? Would there be enough oil, gas, aluminum, and other fuels and metals? Forrester offered to create a systems dynamics model for the entire world and analyze how five key factors—population, food, industrial production, nonrenewable resources (especially fossil fuels), and pollution—might develop over the next 150 years. Within weeks, a delegation from the Club came over to MIT and agreed to finance the project. Forrester turned to the young researcher Donella (Dana) Meadows, a Harvard Ph.D. in biophysics, her husband Dennis Meadows, who was on the MIT management faculty, and others. They helped develop a model that would become the basis of their book sensation, *The Limits to Growth*. When it was published in 1972, it sent shock waves around the globe.

The Limits to Growth was about whether the earth could support continued expansion in people, production, and pollution. The simple story was that all three were expanding exponentially, and at faster rates than counteracting forces, such as cleaner technologies, higher-yielding food grains, or the earth's natural absorptive capacity. If human activity was small relative to the earth, this wouldn't pose a problem, but as humans began to use more and more of the planet's resources, the question of the earth's carrying capacity would inevitably be broached. The sources of degradation (population, production, pollution) would overwhelm the sinks (absorptive and productive capacities). At a 4 percent growth rate (a common range for the global economy), output doubles every eighteen years. As we neared the end of the twentieth century, levels of industrial production dwarfed those of the past. Would this kind of growth continue to be possible?

Systems dynamics research is often structured around scenarios—by setting variables at different rates or changing the core relationships of the model, different outcomes will be generated over various time spans. *The Limits to Growth* asked what would happen over the long run if then-current trends continued, as well as how various kinds of interventions would affect the trajectory. The main finding was that with what we now call a BAU scenario (dubbed the "standard run"), pressures would begin to appear in the early twenty-first century. The most pessimistic of the scenarios foresaw a decline in income starting in 2015. Food production would become inadequate and pollution would begin to overwhelm the capacity of the planet to absorb it. Nonrenewable resources would become more expensive to extract. As the century progressed, environmental imbalances would intensify, eventually leading to collapse.

The book attracted enormous publicity, and eventually sold more than 30 million copies in thirty languages. The 1973 oil embargo and stagflation created a sense that things were going awry. Many in the scientific community signed on to the view that the earth has limited carrying capacity and that humanity needs to be careful not to over-run its resources.

The publication also engendered a vigorous counterattack. Economists led the charge, which is not surprising, given the orientation of the field to a self-correcting market and optimism about technological change. The model didn't incorporate price signals and in its BAU version didn't incorporate pollution reduction. The Oxford economist Wilfred Beckerman lambasted it as "brazen . . . impudent nonsense." The economists' case was most prominently taken up by William (Bill) Nordhaus of Yale, who argued that the *Limits* model failed to incorporate enough technological change, especially of the resource-saving variety. If we are facing limits, he argued, there will be profitable opportunities for avoiding them through innovation. For example, the phenomenal growth in agricultural productivity over the previous century was seen as an indication of future ability to feed even the rapidly growing population of the late twentieth century. Another argument was that known reserves of nonrenewable resources were not good predictors of future supplies, because if scarcities did develop it would pay to devote more effort to exploration and drilling, and reserves would expand. Alternatives for scarce fuels or minerals would be invented. Economists were sanguine about the possibility of surpassing physical realities with human ingenuity.

Another key question was whether unabated exponential growth in population was a reasonable assumption. Europe and North America had already experienced their demographic transitions, with declining birth rates. China and India would not be far behind.

Population fears had surfaced at the moment of maximal growth, without enough credit given to counteracting forces. This is a point that was relevant to the model more generally. The no-adaptation, or standard run, scenario that yielded the worst outcome was unlikely, because its negative effects would call forth responses, a point the systems dynamics researchers understood well.

The debate didn't progress in the way one might have hoped. The two sides published in different journals, and there wasn't much direct conversation. The tone got nasty. It also assumed an unfortunate political hue, with conservatives more likely to dismiss the concerns, and supporters on the other side of the spectrum.

The conventional wisdom was that the economists won the day. One reason is that the shortages the model focused on were food and nonrenewables, such as stocks of oil and bauxite and other minerals. This was partly because of concern about peak oil and a long history of energy modeling. When energy, food, and other commodity prices declined in the 1980s, it was seen as prima facie evidence against the scarcity view and closed the case for some. On this point, there was a well-publicized bet between Ehrlich and an economist named Julian Simon about what would happen to the prices of key minerals, which Ehrlich lost decisively. The economists also correctly foresaw future increases in agricultural productivity, although they missed rising numbers of hungry and malnourished people and the destructive effects of the chemical- and water-intensive farming on which higher yields have been based. They were right that reserves of most materials are limited more by cost than by pure availability, and they made a number of valid criticisms about the structure of the model.

But did the economists win the battle over the model and lose the war about whether we are actually facing limits? It's looking more and more that way.

Evidence on global warming surfaced just as the *Limits* debate was occurring, and the Meadowses and their team wisely warned about this new threat. By contrast, Beckerman dismissed it as a scare story. Nordhaus estimated that warming might be economically beneficial, yielding up to a 5 percent improvement in world output, partly on account of subsequently discredited assumptions about more favorable agricultural conditions in cold countries. We know now that the conventional economic intuition was not only wrong, but spectacularly so.

Soon enough an outpouring of scientific data was reframing the discussion away from the fixed resources highlighted in *Limits* to the renewable systems on which life depends—atmosphere, forests, oceans, wetlands, and soils. By the mid-1980s, ecosystem indicators such as biodiversity were showing sharp declines. Ironically, the new sources of oil and gas that economists correctly anticipated arising were not a solution, as heralded, but contributors to destructive planetary warming. In 1993 a majority of the world's scientific Nobel laureates signed a warning that "human beings and the natural world are on a collision course . . . and that current practices put at serious risk the future that we wish for human society and the plant and animal kingdoms, and may so alter the living world that it will be unable to sustain life in the manner that we know." As the twenty-first century dawned, growth had already triggered dangerous climate change. If current trends continue, middle-range scenarios predict that half the world's population will be facing serious food shortage by century's end, and some analysts find that prediction overly optimistic. Early warnings about BAU growth now look ominously prescient.

Having failed to adapt when the alarm bells were first rung in the 1970s, we are already bumping up against the carrying capacity of the earth. An international collaboration among ecological economists and scientists that attempted to define safe operating zones, or what they term "planetary boundaries," reported in 2009 that of the nine they identified, we'd already exceeded three (climate, biodiversity, the nitrogen cycle), and were approaching limits on four more (freshwater use, land use, ocean acidification, and the phosphorus cycle).

Planetary Ecocide

The debate over limits raised questions of underlying philosophy about how natural and social systems operate. Conventional economic models are more likely to use linear relations, incorporate self-correcting mechanisms that work through market behaviors, and build in a tendency for the system to equilibrate to a fixed point. When scarcities develop, prices rise. The higher price reduces demand and encourages supply, which in turn eases the price pressure.

By contrast, the systems dynamics, climate, and newer combined climate-and-economic models understand that the world is often chaotic and nonlinear, with thresholds, tipping points, and other features that are far less reassuring than the simple market equilibrium story. One factor that leads to instability is feedback loops. These are relationships that intensify effects, either positively (enhancing an effect) or negatively (reducing it). Feedback loops are like superchargers that accelerate a trend in motion. Perhaps the best-known feedbacks are from the climate system. Rising CO_2 concentrations in the atmosphere warm the surface of the earth, causing the melting of permafrost, which in turn releases methane, a powerful greenhouse gas, which causes more warming. Once a system starts to go awry, feedback loops can be especially problematic, because they intensify the bad dynamics that are occurring. But there are also good feedbacks, such as an innovation in clean energy that induces other pollution-reducing technical change.

The biggest news of the last few years is the pace of climate destabilization. Rather than the safer, more predictable straight-line processes that were prominent in earlier thinking and research, scientists are now working through the far more worrisome mechanics of feedback loops. The official word from two thousand scientists who gathered in Copenhagen in March 2009 was that "the climate system is already moving beyond the patterns of natural variability within which our society and economy have developed and thrived. These parameters include global mean surface temperature, sea-level rise, ocean and ice sheet dynamics, ocean acidification, and extreme climatic events. There is a significant risk that many of the trends will accelerate, leading to an increasing risk of abrupt or irreversible climatic shifts." Translation: feedback loops have started, opening the door to the possibility of nonlinear, catastrophic climate change.

The growth of emissions has been rising, with the current annual level of CO_2e, or carbon dioxide equivalent, gases at more than fifty gigatons, or about 7.5 metric tons per capita. In ordinary times, the planet can absorb just under half the carbon that is emitted. But the presence of feedback effects may be reducing this capacity, and what were sinks become sources. Oceans are less absorptive now. On land, heat waves have already begun to reduce photosynthesis. Forest fires are releasing CO_2 and permafrost has begun to thaw. A longer growing season could operate in the opposite direction, but there is increasing fear that the bad feedback mechanisms will predominate. Polar ice caps are shrinking and the Greenland ice sheet is melting twice as fast as anticipated. Sea levels are rising, with some predictions of at least two meters by century's end. Higher sea levels will wipe out small island nations, turn coastal dwellers into migrants, and contaminate the water supplies of many of the world's largest cities.

Many scientists are worried that these apocalyptic scenarios may occur if we don't act promptly, although the power of feedback loops is still being debated. There is growing recognition that the goal the global conversation had been looking toward—a two-degree Celsius (3.6-degree Fahrenheit) rise—will yield disaster, because the planet is warming faster and the feedback loops are happening far more quickly than anticipated.

Forecasts of a BAU growth path predict dramatic increases in CO_2 concentrations. The Stern Review, an influential 2006 report by Nicholas Stern of the U.K. Treasury, suggested that BAU could yield 550 parts per million by 2035 and more than 650 ppm by 2100. Others are predicting as much as 1,000 ppm by 2100, but that pessimistic scenario assumes no policy response, which now seems unlikely. How much warming does the current path create? The latest major business-as-usual scenario, from MIT, predicts a catastrophic rise of five degrees Celsius by century's end. Disaster scenarios are being spun in which few species survive and large swaths of the planet are uninhabitable. Alternatively, nature may take revenge earlier, with climate destabilization causing famines, droughts, and storms that disrupt economic activity and make ordinary growth impossible. At a minimum, a one-degree Celsius warming in the system is inevitable, with more likely. We need to abandon BAU as soon as possible and begin to pull carbon out of the atmosphere. There is a growing international movement to make 350 ppm the target, but to achieve it, we need to start now.

The difficulty is that, as with material flows, the emissions trajectory has been relentlessly upward. Most ominously, between 2000 and 2007 anthropogenic emissions rose four times faster than in the 1990s, more than even the most extreme scenario considered by the IPCC in 2000. The rate of increase in atmospheric CO_2 was 2.2 percent in 2007, far higher than the 1.5 percent of the 1990s, and above even the 2.0 percent prevailing since 2000. In the United States, the latest data shows the necessary turnaround hasn't yet occurred. Although emissions per dollar of GDP have fallen by 30 percent since 1990, and per capita emissions have stabilized, total emissions are expanding, albeit slowly. Early reports are that the economic crash has reduced global emissions, but the numbers are not yet available. It's essential that recovery not restart the fossil fuel juggernaut.

Scientists are gathering evidence about how climate disruption is affecting ecosystems, species, and planetary balance around the world. Changes are greatest at the poles, but they are happening all over. NASA's James Hansen reports that arid subtropical climate zones are expanding poleward and that an average expansion of 250 miles has already occurred. Enterprising biologists at Harvard and Boston University compared present-day New England flora and fauna with what Henry David Thoreau and others documented, and found that more than 60 percent of the species that were around in the 1850s are either gone or will be soon, including some of the most "charismatic," such as orchids and lilies. Mountain glaciers, on which hundreds of millions depend for water, are disappearing. Coral reefs are dying. Drought is intensifying, not only in sub-Saharan Africa, but in Australia, the southeastern United States, and other areas. The southwestern United States is at risk of becoming a permanent dust bowl, as are other parts of the planet. Climate change is already putting ecosystems at risk, and as they decline, they exacerbate climate instability. But planetary distress is also evident outside the realm of climate.

We are in the midst of what biologists refer to as the sixth mass extinction. The last one happened 65 million years ago, with the loss of the dinosaurs. Among birds and mammals, extinction is occurring at a hundred to a thousand times natural rates. A major study by the International Union for the Conservation of Nature found that 38 percent of the 45,000 species they studied are currently threatened with extinction. A quarter of all wild mammals are at risk of disappearing. A U.S. report on birdlife released in 2009 found that a third of all bird species were already endangered, threatened, or in serious decline. In addition to climate change, the main drivers of species decline are habitat loss, overexploitation (as in fishing), pollution, and invasive alien species. The Living Planet Index of the World Wildlife Fund, which follows 1,686 vertebrate species, has declined by 30 percent since 1970. Terrestrial species have declined by 33 percent, freshwater species by 35 percent, and marine species by 14 percent. These are unprecedented developments in human history and represent losses of incalculable value. Anthropocentric valuations stress the role of species in ecosystem functioning, the loss of potential drugs and technological advances, and the benefits humans get from being able to see and interact with plants and animals. Worldviews that do not measure nature solely in terms of its value to humans recognize the collapse of biodiversity as a profound loss on its own terms. Zebras, hippos, polar bears, elephants, lynxes, and many other wondrous creatures are in jeopardy.

A comprehensive assessment of the state of the world's ecosystems was carried out by the United Nations in 2005. It found that 60 percent, or fifteen of the twenty-four major ecosystem services it studied, are being degraded or used unsustainably. It concluded that over the last fifty years humans have changed ecosystems more "rapidly and extensively" than in any comparable period in human history. Most ominously, the study found "established, although incomplete evidence" that this degradation was increasing the likelihood of nonlinear changes and collapses in the ecosystems (analogous to the abrupt climatic responses discussed above). Air quality, erosion regulation, water quality, wood fuel, natural buffers for weather hazards, and pest regulation all declined.

The oceans are a particular source of concern. The combination of overfishing, destructive trawling methods, toxins, and acidification caused in part by climate change are resulting in a collapse of ocean ecosystems. Stocks of large open-ocean fish have plummeted, with estimates of decline ranging from 65 to 90 percent. Coral reefs may be completely gone within a few decades. Surface warming has already begun to inhibit vertical mixing of ocean waters. Together with chemical runoff, this creates a condition of oxygen depletion called hypoxia that kills off multicellular life. In 2008 scientists found 405 oceanic dead zones, in comparison with 49 in the 1960s. Ecologists and oceanographers are watching in horror as once diverse and spectacular ocean habitats turn into the equivalent of algal deserts, great reservoirs of slime.

The Human Footprint

While learning about ecocide can be demoralizing or overwhelming, simplified measures are proving useful for mobilizing a public response. That's the theory behind the ecological footprint, an evocative metric developed in the 1980s by University of British Columbia ecologist William Rees and his then–graduate student Mathis Wackernagel. The footprint measures the amount of land and shallow sea area used to produce the food, fuel, plastics, metals, wood, fibers, and other resources consumed by a household, business, city, area, or nation. For the household, it takes into account how far food travels to reach its table. It looks at the number of trips taken in cars and trains, the size of the house, how warm it is kept in winter, and how much air-conditioning is used in the summer. It includes a measure of how much ecosystem capacity is needed to absorb the carbon the household burns. It is expressed as a land area, which highlights the fact that what people consume ultimately depends on cropland, forests, and fisheries. Eco-footprint analysis is the basis of the widely reported statistic that if everyone on the globe lived as Americans do, we'd need five planets to support the human population.

The five-planets calculation is of course an overly simplified one, and the footprint is a highly aggregated concept that leaves out many things, such as toxic substances. It's not a measure of impacts, on either ecosystems or human health, although it does have strong connections to them, especially through its treatment of carbon. It's undergoing a continual process of refinement and improvement, and is being adopted by governments, companies, and communities around the world.

Footprint research also analyzes the existing biological capacity of the earth in comparison with what humans are using. Biocapacity is not a fixed number because land is brought in and out of cultivation; new technologies improve the productivity of land, enabling more production on less acreage; degradation turns arable land into desert; and fisheries rise and fall. Between 1961 and 1995, measured global biocapacity increased slightly, but it has fallen since then as ecosystems have degraded. When the human footprint is below the world's biocapacity, we're in a viable situation. When it exceeds it, we've begun to eat into natural capital and are undermining the reproduction of future generations.

FIGURE 2.10 Ecological Footprint, Carbon Footprint, and Biocapacity

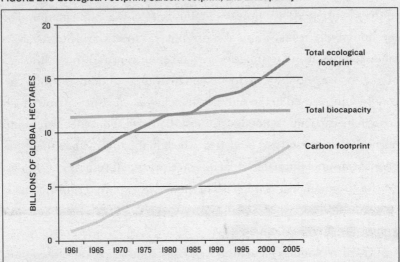

Source: Global Footprint Network (2009)

By these calculations, the world first reached its limits in 1986. Since then resource use has increasingly outstripped biocapacity. According to the latest data available (2006), there are about 1.8 available hectares (or 4.5 acres) for every person globally, but we're using 2.6, for a per capita deficit of 0.8. We've entered the zone of what the Meadowses and others called overshoot, and are living beyond our planetary means. By this measure, we are operating 40 percent above biocapacity.

FIGURE 2.II Ecological Footprint per Capita, Selected Nations, 2006

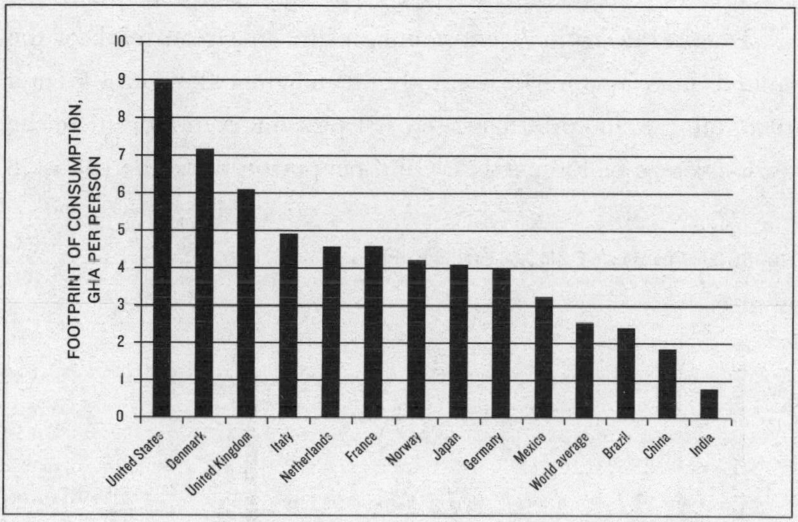

Sources: Global Footprint Network (2009) and Ewing et al (2008), "Table I: Per-Person Ecological Footprint of Production, Imports, Exports, and Consumption, by Country," Appendix F, pp. 4I–45

Global calculations are useful for some things, such as measuring planetary trends. National numbers allow us to see which countries are consuming beyond their means, or beyond fair global allotments. The United States once had the world's largest per capita footprint, but the United Arab Emirates currently exceeds it by a hectare. Americans each consume 9.0 hectares, or five times the global biocapacity of 1.8 hectares. The biggest component of the U.S. footprint is carbon emissions, which account for about 70 percent of the total

(6.4 hectares). The large, wealthy countries of Europe (Germany, France, Italy, Spain) and Japan have per capita footprints that are about half that of the United States (although colder Denmark is higher, at 7.2), and the United Kingdom is at 6.1. Perhaps the most important lesson North Americans can take from the footprinting exercise is that it is possible to have materially rich lives with far less impact on the earth. It's also useful to recognize that in the Global South, including China and India, per capita impact remains low. The Chinese footprint is 1.8 hectares; India's is only 0.8. Brazilians and Mexicans are a bit higher, at 2.4 and 3.2 respectively.

Despite the nation's enormous wealth, the tread mark of the United States is getting heavier rather than lighter. Between 1961 and 2005, the U.S. footprint has risen 181 percent, even more than the world average of 150 percent. On a per-person basis, the rise is 78

FIGURE 2.12 Changes in Ecological Footprint, 1961–2005

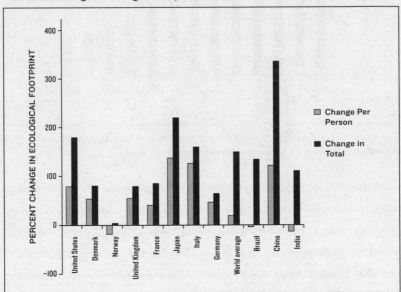

Source: Ewing et al (2008), "Table 7: Percent Change in Population, Ecological Footprint, and Biocapacity, 1961 to 2005", Appendix F, pp. 67–71

percent. Unfortunately, the United States is not unique, although it is extreme. As a group, the rich countries have expanded their footprints considerably more than the middle- and low-income ones, and not just on a per capita basis (where the gap is largest), but even in terms of total impact. In contrast, the average Indian has a lower footprint now than in 1961, despite a dramatic increase in income. So does the average Brazilian. China's growth is substantial in both per capita and aggregate terms (122 and 336 percent respectively), but has started from a very low base.

This data also shows that even very wealthy countries can remain rich and reduce their footprints. The average Norwegian has a 19 percent lower footprint today than he or she did almost half a century ago, even with a per capita income that is about eight thousand dollars higher than the U.S. level. The Finns and Swedes barely raised their footprints over this period. Their incomes are not quite at U.S. levels (they're about nine thousand dollars lower), yet these rank among the richest societies in the world.

The footprint concept has also been used to look at water use (although the word *footprint* is something of a misnomer in this case). Many predict that water will be to the twenty-first century what oil was to the twentieth: an increasingly contested resource. While measuring what is termed water stress is complex, a common estimate is that about a third of the world's population now lives in areas with moderate to heavy stress on water supplies. Water-intensive farming and warming-induced drought and desertification will intensify these pressures. Privatization, which has proceeded far in some countries, threatens equitable solutions. Analyses from the IPCC's Fourth Assessment Report suggest that by 2050 the number of people living in water-stressed areas may increase dramatically, with worst-case estimates reaching 6.9 billion.

The water footprint shows how much water a nation relies on,

FIGURE 2.13 Annual Water Footprint Per Capita, Selected Nations

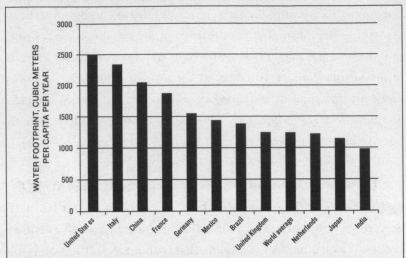

Source: Hoekstra Chapaggin (2007), "Table 3: Composition of the Water-Footprint for Some Selected Countries. Period: 1997–2001," p. 42

including both domestic uses and use of imported products. As with other ecological resources, the United States has outsize habits. Its water footprint is the world's highest, at 2,483 cubic meters per capita. That's twice the global average of 1,243, and twice the level of comparably rich countries. The U.S. figure is so large because of the nation's water-intensive agriculture, meat-heavy diet, suburban lawns, and high consumption of consumer electronics, apparel, and other commodities. It requires 2,000 liters of water to produce one T-shirt, 2,400 for a hamburger, and 8,000 for a pair of leather shoes.

The ecological and water footprints together cover land, atmosphere, shallow sea, and fresh water. What they make clear is that BAU growth in global resource use is not viable. For the United States, they reveal a level of consumption that is ethically indefensible and strategically unwise. But perhaps most important, these metrics also indicate that such profligacy is unnecessary. Comparisons with comparable countries show the United States could halve its ecological and water footprints and retain, by almost any accounting, lifestyles of affluence and abundance. Even more telling is the fact that others are managing to reduce impact without putting on a hair shirt. And, if Americans were willing to make even more far-reaching changes, their footprints could be reduced considerably below half what they are today, even to globally fair, indeed imperative, levels, without undue sacrifice.

Taking Stock

We are living in extraordinary times. The consumer boom of the 1990s and 2000s was a historical anomaly. Goods moved at hyperspeed through the retail and household economies. Material flows, predicted to decline, accelerated. Never have so many bought so much for so little. But like all binges, the consumer extravaganza had to end. Now we've got twin crises—financial and ecological—and today's best thinking understands we'll have to solve them together.

Economists, however, have worked to protect business-as-usual. Bullish on markets, this thinking also extends to their views about the environment. The standard logic says that incorporating full ecological costs will avert planetary disaster. The experience of the last few years should give us pause about this sanguine conclusion. From the financial, commodities, housing, and other volatile markets, there has been enough evidence of herd behavior, irrationality, corruption, and short-termism to question the view that markets will necessarily yield predictable and sustainable outcomes. Entrusting the fate of the planet purely to the rationality of markets is a dangerous leap of faith. To see how and why economists came to their position, let's take a closer look at how they think and at the practice of environmental economics.

Chapter Three

ECONOMICS CONFRONTS
THE EARTH

Both the original *Limits* theorists of the 1970s and the expanding sustainability movement of the 1990s found one group particularly reluctant to address the threat of business-as-usual: mainstream economists. A fateful methodological choice made by the discipline helps to understand why.

The canonical models used by the mainstream are addressed to what happens within markets, rather than to economic dynamics more broadly. Because air, water, and many natural resources are neither owned nor priced, the effects of economic activity on their health and functioning do not fall within the purview of the standard treatments. When environmental impacts have been addressed, it has been as externalities, that is, effects that occur outside markets. Over time, the study of environmental impacts moved out of general economics and into a subfield that sought ways to internalize these effects, that is, bring them inside the market calculus.

Outside the subfield, most economists have practiced their craft as if nature did not exist. They do not incorporate natural resources into basic accounting categories and data collection. In addition, market prices do not include ecological costs, an omission that introduces a systematic bias into the analysis and evaluation of virtually all market outcomes, albeit one that has been largely ignored. Goods or activities that degrade the environment (without paying for that degradation) are priced too low. Those that are particularly dirty are especially underpriced and overproduced. As a result, the market generates too many plastics, toxic chemicals, and fossil fuel–dependent trips and too little music, organic food, and solar power. These distortions matter for almost all economic analyses, not just those under the heading of environmental economics.

The failure to institute full-cost pricing underpins the materiality paradox. It is only because goods have been artificially cheap that consumers were able to, and wanted to, purchase so many of them and discard them so readily. The same point applies to producers, who would have done more to clean up their factories, farms, offices, and products if they had been held responsible. In both cases, if people were paying for the ecological consequences of what they produce and consume, market decisions would be very different.

There's also a resulting macro, or system-wide, failure that is rarely considered. Not accounting for environmental impacts means that the economy is generating too much production and growing too fast overall, relative to what is efficient. This result is not just in the eyes of environmentalists, but according to the ironclad logic of the standard market model. Such an approach may have been justifiable in a world where environmental impacts were small. Today, they're looking more and more like the main event. But economists haven't seen it that way. While it's difficult to be precise about exactly where on the spectrum the median economist now sits, it is generally thought that until quite recently most rejected the need for vigorous collective action on climate, in contrast to scientists' thinking.

Frustrated with the practices of the mainstream, two decades ago an interdisciplinary group called the Society for Ecological Economics was founded. Economists, natural scientists, engineers, systems dynamics researchers, and others came together around the view that ecosystems should be at the core of economic analysis. They were especially interested in what conventional economics wasn't measuring or studying. These dissenters recognized a fundamental point about how our system has been operating. If the market economy gets large, and nature remains external to it, threats to basic ecosystem functioning will arise. The market is driven to exploit free resources, and so to cannibalize its very conditions of existence.

Ecological economics has mostly been ignored by the mainstream. However, now that many more economists have recognized the urgency of climate change, there's a new openness to thinking about our overall dependence on ecosystems, a central insight of ecological economics. But even if economists suddenly get religion regarding the planet and its ecology, incorporating it into the DNA of economic thinking will require sociological changes in the field itself. The methodological choices made long ago to treat nature as an external effect have resulted in a literal externalization. Environmental issues are studied outside of general economics, and many environmental economists are located outside economics departments proper. The economics department at Harvard, with fifty-five members, has only one whose main area is environmental economics. Stanford, a university with a strong institutional commitment to environmental issues, also has just one. In contrast to the natural science disciplines, where the study of climate change and biodiversity has attracted large numbers of researchers and a voluminous body of findings, economics has contributed fewer voices to this discussion. Environmental economics has also been closely intertwined with energy economics, which in turn has ties to energy companies and interests. (The subfield is often called environmental and

energy economics.) And in the last few decades, special interests acting against environmental protection, often from the energy sector,
have enlisted economics to water down regulations and forestall
action. Researchers have also found other biases in the way environmental economics is practiced. Studies have found that economists'
calculations typically underestimate the benefits and overstate the
costs of ecosystem protections.

Getting to a sustainable economy will require a fundamental shift
in outlook. It makes little sense to treat the profound degradation
now occurring in the earth's ecosystems as a glitch in an otherwise
well-functioning system. Merely internalizing the externality of pollution, or slowing degradation by shifting technologies or reducing
overall growth, will be insufficient to achieve true efficiency and future abundance. To get that, we need to realize that core aspects of
economic life are transformed as we focus on preserving nature. We'll
need to value natural capital, a trend that has begun in earnest. But
in addition, the plenitude approach argues that we need to rethink
the scale of production, how knowledge is accessed, skill diffusion,
the ownership of natural assets, and mechanisms for generating
employment. These questions move beyond the prescriptions of conventional economics, to a deeper reconceptualization of how to organize an economy when natural resources are valuable, jobs are
scarce, and equity matters.

Resources, Cornucopias, and the Miracle of the Market

In the 1970s, when the alarm bells about ecological overshoot
were first rung, mainstream economists were dismissive. Wilfred

Beckerman, claiming to speak for the field, expressed what "most of my economist colleagues have always known," that "the problem of environmental pollution is a simple matter of correcting a minor resource misallocation." Beckerman overstated the case, but he was right that the discipline has historically tended to optimism about the environment and is adept at creating narratives about why solutions for environmental problems will naturally emerge.

Economists have seen the very idea of ecological limits as a re-hash of the discredited theories of the early nineteenth-century political economist Thomas Malthus. Malthus believed that population growth would outrun increases in agricultural productivity, so that food production would fail to keep up with mouths to feed. He fore-saw rising poverty and famines. The standard view is that he got it wrong, given the tremendous increases in agricultural productivity and the demographic transition toward lower birth rates. (With a sixth of the world's population, or a billion people, already hungry, 1.4 billion living in one-dollar-per-day poverty, rising food prices, and intensifying competition for land between energy and food uses, one might be forgiven for wondering if the case against Malthus isn't absolutely closed.) Neo-Malthusians, as the *Limits* school was branded, were thought to have repeated Malthus's mistakes. When the oil price increases of the 1970s resulted in exploration and discovery, it was taken by some as evidence of the fatuity of the whole approach. As a discipline, economics lined up to say that rather than facing up to limits to growth, we should be trying to promote more of it.

This approach originally carried through to thinking about climate change. As I noted in chapter 2, when climate change was discovered, influential economists rejected the idea of timely action to reduce emissions. The Yale economist William Nordhaus said climate change might even end up improving well-being through effects such as more productive agriculture and the benefits of a warmer climate in colder countries. He also took the view that for the United States, the greenhouse effect might on balance be economically advantageous. Economists and scientists were on opposite sides of the fence.

The upbeat prognoses of economists were due to a number of factors. Many were not in close conversation with ecologists, who were charting ecosystem degradation. This was partly just disciplinary Balkanization, but was also due to economists' views about the market. A standard assumption is that the market will price resources rationally, given accurate information about future supplies and costs, and incentives to internalize ecological impacts. If a natural resource is becoming scarce, its price will rise because it has become more expensive to obtain or produce. A higher price will reduce demand for the resource and will also induce economic actors to find new sources or develop alternatives. Lower oil prices in the 1980s and falling food and other commodity prices in the 1980s and 1990s led many economists to be skeptical of claims that resources were becoming scarce.

One of the presumptions of the optimists is that there are ready substitutes for nature, so genuine limits are rare and not worth worrying too much about. If we chop down all the forests, we can rely on tree plantations. If we overfish the oceans, we start fish farms. The utilitarian origins of economics loom large here, as well as its secularism and human-centered focus. Rather than being seen as something intrinsically precious, nature is regarded as an ordinary input into production, and it is assumed that we can get along with a lot less of it. This is one legacy of the industrial-era view that producers can easily interchange machinery and human labor. If nature does have intrinsic value, it is as something to consume, rather than as an input into what we produce. We can buy more nature, but have to sacrifice income to do so.

The strongest version of eco-optimism has been espoused by people such as Julian Simon, Herman Kahn, and Milton Friedman, and more recently Bjørn Lomborg. They've been dubbed Cornucopians, because they believe that there are no physical limits to growth. They predict the future holds unlimited riches via the wonders of population growth, which results in more smart people and more human ingenuity. That ingenuity discovers substitutes for nature, which are then diffused through the market. Their view is that more population is a good thing and that limits thinking has been repeatedly disproved. In its most extreme versions, this position effects a peculiar transference. Rather than worshipping the miracle of nature, it's the market that is revered. Cornucopians have tended to be political and polemical, extreme free marketeers who reject the science of climate change and environmental degradation.

Few economists go all the way with the Cornucopians, but a larger number are believers in a more moderate variant of eco-optimism, which argues that growth itself will save the environment. Represented in a concept called the Environmental Kuznets Curve, it is modeled on studies of inequality carried out in the 1950s and '60s by the economist Simon Kuznets. Kuznets saw a humpback data pattern across nations. At a given point in time, some had low levels of both income and inequality, some had more inequality and more income, and some had high incomes with low inequality. From this finding, most economists came to believe that countries must endure a growing concentration of income as they develop, but that once they become wealthy, they can buy themselves more fairness. Of course, in recent decades wealthy countries are getting more unequal again, even as they grow.

Whatever the merits of the Kuznets model, and they have been debated, it was applied to the environment. The argument is that as poor countries begin to develop, they grow fast, pollute wantonly, and worry about the impacts later, after they've gotten rich. Such a view has become conventional wisdom for nations such as China and India. By this reasoning, one gets the counterintuitive result that the solution to environmental problems is to grow faster.

The Environmental Kuznets Curve was originally measured for individual pollutants such as sulfur dioxide and nitrogen oxide, which have been regulated in wealthy nations. The evidence was statistical

FIGURE 3.I Environmental Kuznets Curve (EKC)

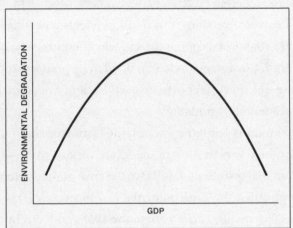

and economy-wide, and the actual mechanisms that drive the finding were not tested. One assumption was that richer economies shift to less polluting services. Another was that as citizens get wealthier, they pressure the government to crack down on polluters and clean up the air, water, and toxic wastes of industry.

As it turns out, the Environmental Kuznets Curve findings haven't held up well, especially beyond the original cases of specific pollutants, and those results have also been questioned on technical grounds. The hypothesis is completely wrong for greenhouse gas emissions, which do not decline at any level of income. (Rich countries have been the biggest emitters.) Ecological footprint also grows with income, and even in wealthy countries, many ecosystems, such as fisheries, water systems, and soil systems, continue to decline. The Environmental Kuznets Curve, a more nuanced form of market-based eco-optimism, turns out to be an unreliable guide to sustainability.

The assumptions of eco-optimism about the behavior of markets are also hard to defend, especially after the experience of the last few years. The miraculous market view says the market will be cool, calm, and collected, correctly forecasting future scarcities. We've witnessed the tech bubble of 2000, the housing and financial bubbles that popped in 2007 and 2008, and the wild gyrations of oil prices in 2008 and 2009. These are clearly examples of irrational pricing, which have had painful consequences. What if we're in a yet-to-be-discovered myopic moment with respect to natural resources? If investors have a bias toward good news, as some economic theory predicts, prices will not reflect true scarcity. If market participants are like most people and have tended toward denial about climate change, today's prices will fail to account for the need to switch out of fossil fuels and into clean energy sources. These effects mean that market outcomes will be unreliable signposts of ecological health.

Massive government subsidies are another reason prices are not accurate reflectors of ecological realities. Each year, the U.S. government underwrites the oil, gas, nuclear, and coal industries to the tune of tens (or, depending on one's definition, hundreds) of billions, allows them to emit carbon without financial liability, and supports a massive automobile infrastructure and chemical-intensive farming. Finally, the assumption of an all-knowing market requires almost superhuman informational and processing demands. Investors have to understand the scientific evidence, combine it with economic, political, social, psychological, and demographic data, and predict market movements. Relying on market prices as indicators of the state of the natural world is risky, if not reckless.

Trade-off Economics: The Unbearable Costliness of Nature

Accounts that emphasize the ability of the market to develop alternatives for nature or to clean up the messes caused by growth tend to be thinking in the medium or long term. In the Environmental Kuznets Curve story, it's only after decades of economic development that people begin to take action to clean up their air, water, and soil. In the short run, the economic thinking has mainly been of the sort that earned the field its moniker as the dismal science. Protecting nature is seen as costly, and we are told we'll have to give up things we value dearly to do it. Environmental economics frequently operates in the realm of trade-offs: a cleaner climate means more expensive energy, saving species costs taxpayer money, and preserving forests eliminates jobs.

The logic behind the trade-off view is that competition and markets ensure the economy is more or less operating at full capacity and resources are efficiently deployed. People and firms have already made the choices that optimize their well-being. They're working as many hours as they want, and purchasing the goods and services that best meet their needs. Firms have already chosen the best technology available, given current prices. Environmental protection is thought of less in terms of making the economy more productive than of leading us to different choices. If we want more forests, we make do with less furniture.

This logic can be represented in a production possibilities curve. An economy can only get as far as the frontier represented by the curve. It is assumed this is where the economy usually is, so that more nature means less production. This is the logic behind many economists' skepticism about the existence of win-wins, or free lunches,

FIGURE 3.2 Production Possibilities Curve

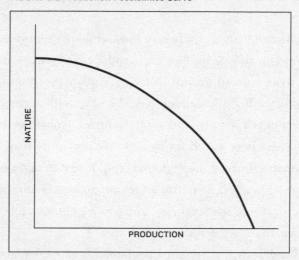

which are represented by positions inside the curve. (From inside, it's possible to increase both income and the protection of nature, by moving rightward and upward, out to the frontier, where the curve lies.) If win-wins do arise, astute actors will notice and gobble them up. The closer one hews to orthodox economic thinking, the less likely one is to believe that economic actors are currently failing to take advantage of profitable opportunities. (An exception is when government policies push an economy inside the curve. The Princeton economist Uwe Reinhardt derided his brethren after the crash for this attitude of *"Est, ergo optimum est, dummodo ne gubernatio civitatis implicatur"*: It exists, therefore it must be optimal, provided that government has not been involved.)

One assumption of the trade-off view is that the additional production or income gained by degrading the environment is highly valued. This is taken for granted even in wealthy nations. Plenitude questions that assumption, and is supported by more than a decade of new findings showing that the link between well-being and income is less straightforward than previously assumed. But environmental economics hasn't incorporated this work into its theories or tool kits. Standard methods still overvalue income and undervalue nature.

On climate change, defenses of inaction have dominated the national economic debate until recently, with pessimistic assessments of even the weak aims of the Kyoto treaty. William Nordhaus, despite having adjusted his calculations over the years, still argues that the 80–90 percent reductions in wealthy countries' emissions that scientists and others have called for by 2050 are too costly relative to expected benefits. Instead, his "optimal" response is to allow emissions to increase 25 percent. Better to let temperatures rise and suffer the ecosystem damage, sea level rise, and loss of life, as well as to risk catastrophe, than to pay for cleanup.

Nordhaus's DICE (Dynamic Integrated Climate-Economy) model represents the best known of a larger class of mainstream economic models built around trade-offs that have been used to counsel policymakers about how to respond to climate change. They're termed IAMs, or integrated assessment models, because they combine assumptions about the physical world with macroeconomic equations. Their prescriptions present a revealing paradox. They take climate change seriously, but a number of them suggest doing almost nothing for at least the next few decades.

The paradox is resolved by looking carefully at the details of these complex and technical models. Economists, including a number within the ecological economics camp who have studied them, find that a few subjective (and hard to defend) choices about damages, benefits, and how to treat future generations are responsible for many of the conclusions. The best known of these controversies concerns the discount rate, or how the model balances money today with money in the future. DICE uses a high number to "discount," or reduce the value of, future income and consumption. Its assumption is that a dollar in the future is worth less than a dollar today because future generations will be richer than people are now. Since *we* (today's generation) value money more than *they* (tomorrow's richer generations) will, it's not "efficient" to have us pay to stop climate change. Let *them* (the people around in 2050) pay, even if *we* caused the climate change. This assumption, presented as scientific, stacks the deck against action, because the costs pushed off to future generations are so heavily discounted (in the ordinary sense of the word). Sometimes the rates used are so high that they drive the results of the model. Furthermore, the assumption of a high discount rate assumes away the possibility that climate change will be sufficiently destabilizing to make future income growth negative, an outcome that is looking increasingly possible. If that's the case, the discount rate should be negative, because future generations will value (and need) money more than people living today do.

But the problems go far beyond discount rates. The economists Frank Ackerman and Ian Finlayson, of the Stockholm Environment Institute and the Massachusetts Executive Office of Energy respectively, discovered that DICE arbitrarily added a large benefit to warming, positing that the preferred average global temperature is that of Houston or Tripoli (twenty degrees Celsius/sixty-eight degrees Fahrenheit). This is a questionable assumption in itself, but particularly egregious given that much of the world's population lives in places that are already too hot and getting hotter and that recent evidence suggests higher temperatures will substantially reduce the incomes of the global poor. DICE also assumes that preventing 2.5 degrees of warming, an increase that, if it occurs, will create hundreds of millions of climate refugees and may trigger catastrophic outcomes, is worth only $5 billion to the American public. But we are already seeing hundreds of billions of dollars in climate-related losses from the warming that has occurred. Other problems with IAMs include attributing lesser value to the residents of poor countries where more damage will occur, arbitrary estimates of how damages will develop, overly simplistic projections of technological change, and the failure to take uncertainty seriously.

Rooted in these highly subjective assumptions, the DICE model and similar IAMs work to justify BAU. They embody a support of the status quo that scientists believe will yield disaster. Nevertheless, a 2009 review by Geoffrey Heal of Columbia, a leading environmental economist, characterized the profession at large as holding a presumption against the need for strong action. Apparently trade-off economics is alive and well. Environmental protection has been pitted against growth, incomes, jobs, and well-being. The thinking has been short-term, and the basic assumption is that interventions do not shift the frontier out but either move us along it or, even worse, push us inside by skewing incentives and undermining the business climate.

Is the assumption that we're on the curve with respect to ecological limits the right one?

Since the downturn began, the answer has obviously been no. In a recession, workers are idle, businesses are running below capacity, and we're operating inside the frontier. That's why there were fewer economists than usual opposing stimulus dollars for green-jobs proposals. The opportunity cost of redeploying labor to home insulation or building wind turbines is low. Moreover, because of ripple effects, government action to put people to work can spur more private-sector growth. It's an opportune time for environmentally positive policies.

The changed discourse also indicates that these conversations do not happen in a political vacuum. Through the Bush years, pessimistic assessments dovetailed with the business backlash against environmental regulations. Numerous industry-funded studies of both U.S. regulations and global climate policy claimed that environmental protection is too costly. The Bush administration was very active in using economic arguments against environmental improvements. It's a different ballgame now, with the Obama administration taking the view that action to address the environment, and climate specifically, will be economically beneficial, in both the short and the long term.

Leaving aside the current collapse, are we generally in a world in which we must rob Peter to pay Paul? At the heart of trade-off thinking is the assumption that nature is a consumption good—forests, seascapes, or preserves must be "purchased" to be enjoyed. However, nature's far more important role is as an input into production. By this logic, using up nature erodes our ability to create future income, an effect not taken into account with a static formulation such as the production-possibility curve, or its more sophisticated formulations in model form. Preserving nature shifts the curve out. Pioneered by ecological economists, a larger body of research is developing methods to value nature as capital and calculate the ongoing services that ecosystems provide. This work has the potential to revolutionize the cost-benefit calculations of environmental economics, and is beginning to make headway. For example, when climate models include ecosystem services, the case for urgent action is much stronger.

By contrast, trade-off economics, particularly standard cost-benefit analysis, has tended to use a partial accounting, and is more tied to the short run. It also appears to have a systematic bias. A series of studies has found that economic calculations done to assess the potential impacts of environmental projects tend to overestimate costs and underestimate benefits. There are many cases of environmental protections that have been far less burdensome than opponents expected. Trade-off thinking has typically left technological change outside its purview, so that policies to protect the environment aren't credited with spurring nature-saving innovation. (When they do, the frontier is pushed out to the right, thereby transcending the trade-off.) Newer thinking recognizes that once we're in a technological transition, for example to clean energy, innovation is more rapid and less costly than initially assumed.

A Breakthrough on Climate?

In 2006 Nicholas Stern, chief economist for the U.K. Treasury, came out with a game-changing report, in which he argued that not stopping global warming would be more costly than vigorous action today. The Stern Review argued that if we don't act, at least 5 percent and maybe more than 20 percent of world GDP might eventually be lost to climate damages. The cost of keeping warming to what was then considered an acceptable level (two degrees Celsius) would be much less, on the order of 1 percent of GDP. (More recently, the bad climate news has led Stern to advocate for a lower CO_2 target, with a 2 percent price tag.) Stern, who also relied on an IAM, squarely repudiated trade-off pessimism, contending that there are many policy interventions for which the benefits outweigh the costs. Action to prevent climate change—rather than being a drag on growth—*is* the growth strategy. Since the publication of the Stern Review, many more economists, including highly influential ones, have come out strongly in favor of concerted action. They're arguing that solving the climate crisis will not be particularly expensive. It's a free, green lunch.

Cost calculations are becoming increasingly optimistic as the climate of opinion among economists has finally begun to shift. Jeff Sachs, director of Columbia's Earth Institute, estimated on the basis of a bottom-up study of the costs of specific interventions that it would cost a mere $1.8 trillion a year globally to keep emissions from growing, a "tiny fraction" compared to the benefits of heading off ecological disaster. A 2007 study by the consulting firm McKinsey found that the first 40 percent of projects, including building insulation, fuel economy, new water heaters, and industrial efficiencies will actually save money over their lifetimes, so they're clearly win-win. Two years later, an update concluded it would be possible to reduce emissions 70 percent below BAU by 2030 with relatively modest costs (less than 1 percent of that year's gross world product).

Economists are also putting forward novel arguments in favor of action, such as the idea that even if the likelihood of extreme climate destabilization is small, humans are risk averse. Cutting emissions is an insurance policy against a low probability but catastrophic event. (In fact, the catastrophe scenario is now looking more probable.) The trade-off mentality is also being abandoned in the search for double dividends. The green stimulus creates jobs and helps the environment with the same money. Double dividend thinking is evident in proposals that use carbon-pricing policies to reduce taxes economists don't like because they are believed to distort choices. Win-win thinking is on the rise.

At the heart of the issue is a simple but powerful point. The very existence of an environmental effect outside the market (an externality) means that the market has not found an efficient outcome. Climate change is the most serious market failure in human history. With an externality this large, the system is *by definition* far from its frontier, and trade-off thinking must be wrong. Efforts to curb emissions will necessarily have benefits that exceed costs, once we properly account for impacts. That means it must be win-win. Even if there are losers, such as coal and auto companies and their workers, there'll be enough benefit from stopping climate deterioration to compensate them for their losses.

But the new thinking on climate has only taken us so far. Climate models and projections assume high rates of output growth, not just for the developing world, but also in countries such as the United States. McKinsey assumes a doubling of gross world product by 2030. Sachs assumes output will expand six times by 2050. Nordhaus assumes a quadrupling in per capita consumption by 2105, plus more than 2 billion additional people. Emissions are factored in, but not the impacts of growth on biodiversity, fisheries, soil quality, water availability, and toxic emissions. Can we possibly tolerate a sixfold increase in production? That massive increase in income will show up as demand for already overburdened resources. It won't do to just assume production without impact. These days more economists working on ecological issues are in serious dialogue with scientists, and keenly aware of the problem of biodiversity. But the circle hasn't been squared.

Can Technology Save the Day?

Most people are counting on technology to pull off that trick. Even non-Cornucopian economists, who tend to see technological change more as a tortoise than a hare, are getting upbeat about clean energy. The new conventional view is that climate change can be solved by innovative technologies and market incentives such as a price for (or tax on) carbon. There's palpable excitement about plug-in hybrids, smart grids and smart homes, renewable energy, and reflective roofs, as well as a significant government role for turning these ideas into realities.

There's reason for optimism, and not just on energy. The last few decades have witnessed enormous progress in the first stage of a sustainability revolution employing ideas such as zero waste, eco-efficiency, and biomimicry (the practice of applying nature's own parsimonious and evolutionary wonders to manufacturing and design). A few of its pioneers include the environmentalist entrepreneur Paul Hawken, architect William McDonough, physicist and activist Vandana Shiva, energy expert and technologist Amory Lovins, writer Janine Benyus, and green chemist Michael Braungart. Many others are now joining them in imagining and inventing natural alternatives to toxic chemicals; lighter, stronger materials; alternative energy systems; comprehensive recycling; and clean nanotechnologies. The most far-reaching of these developments follow the ecological principle that waste equals food: that all by-products from manufacturing or agriculture become inputs into some other production process. Wastewater from bathing irrigates plants, which in turn help to heat and cool structures. It's a closed-loop process. Rainwater recycling is also getting popular. Composted food nourishes soil. There are already transformative examples, such as passive solar buildings that use smart design, good construction, and human body heat to maintain warm temperatures without fossil fuels. We have cars that can travel a hundred miles on a gallon of gas and cars that run on alternative fuels. We are starting to eat high-productivity organic food and clothe ourselves in recycled materials. Across energy, agriculture, manufacturing, design, and transport, there's a clean, green production movement emerging, much of it truly inspiring in its ingenuity.

Some on the technology side assume that change will be costless—that resource savings will at least pay for the cost of the innovation. It's a world of win-wins or even triple wins, with the environment and the corporation and the consumer (or worker) gaining. A classic example is creating an energy-efficient workplace that uses natural light and heat, which not only slashes energy costs and emissions, but also improves labor productivity, lowers manufacturing outlays, and makes employees happier. The initial investment more than pays for itself. Under these conditions, going green raises income and well-being.

Some, such as the journalist Thomas L. Friedman, are looking to clean tech to invigorate the U.S. economy by propelling the next round of growth.

There's no debate about the need to produce differently. And nearly everyone agrees we need to price carbon. But will this be enough?

Not surprisingly, most of the political action on climate has so far been directed at technology. It's what the market does well, and it poses no political threat to business-as-usual. More far-reaching change, in growth aspirations, the basic structures of the economy, or the consumer culture, is barely under discussion. In the McKinsey studies, the reigning assumption was to calculate emissions reductions without behavior change, which is deemed "difficult" to achieve.

But the experience to date with nature-saving technological change should make us wary of the wave of optimism sweeping the conversation. To keep the discussion in perspective, consider that we need to begin pulling carbon out of the atmosphere and regenerating ecosystems now, not just in 2020 or 2050.

Let's start with the question of diffusion. What determines how quickly, or whether, new technologies get adopted and used? It's a hard question to answer and not one that we have a really good answer to yet. But we do know certain things. First, the pure efficiency properties of a technology are not determinative. We must also consider the economics of diffusion. Technologies differ in the way they combine factors of production: labor, machinery, knowledge, finance, managerial inputs, and so on. For companies or households to adopt new techniques, the economic as well as the technological calculus has to be favorable. The 1970s were a period of rapid progress in alternative energy and green technology, and technologists tended to assume that these innovations would spread because they are technologically superior. But the shift to nonpolluting sources stalled out.

One reason is that energy prices, which were high in the 1970s, dropped in the 1980s. Other costs also played a role. In the 1980s, real wages fell, on account of globalization and weak labor demand. And credit was costly. That configuration depresses the rate of technological change. Unfortunately, it's also the set of conditions we currently face. Government policy can alter cost conditions, but its power is not unlimited.

There is also a political economy of innovation. Firms are reluctant to install technologies whose gains they cannot capture. A decentralized system of solar and wind, for example, may have technical superiorities such as avoiding the power loss that accompanies long-distance power generation in centralized facilities. But if the technologies are small-scale and easy to replicate, large firms have difficulty capturing the profits that make investments desirable. Especially in the energy sector, market control, pricing, and the distribution of returns must be added to considerations of technical efficiency to predict what will and will not get adopted.

Rebounds and the Paradox of Technological Change

A shift out of fossil fuels will slash greenhouse gas emissions. But that will take some time, and while we're getting there, the standard view is that we'll be turning to hybrid vehicles, home insulation, enhanced fuel and appliance standards, and other measures that still rely on fossils, but more efficiently. In economic terms, these gains are equivalent to a reduction in the price of energy, because they yield a given level of energy services with less fuel. The rebound effect occurs when that lower price induces consumers to buy more energy, which in turn partly or wholly cancels out the engineering improvements.

There is now a substantial literature on rebound effects. They were first identified by the British economist William Stanley Jevons, who found that improvements in the efficiency of coal use led to increased consumption of that resource. The Jevons paradox was resurrected in 1980, when the economists Daniel Khazzoom and Leonard Brookes used it to analyze the gains in energy efficiency of the 1970s. They argued for a strong version of rebound, in which efficiency improvements actually increase the demand for energy. If true, it's a classic case of blowback.

The rebound effect consists of a number of different dynamics. The first are direct: substitution and income effects. The substitution effect refers to the tendency to buy more of a product when its price is lower. The income effect occurs when people increase their purchases of energy because the cheaper price effectively raises their real income and allows them to buy more. There are also indirect effects. Improvements in efficiency typically increase the scale of production, which in turn raises energy use.

Researchers have not definitively settled on quantification of these effects, and are discussing a range of estimates that vary by sector and country. For home heating and cooling, the direct rebound appears to be in the range of 30 percent, that is, 30 percent of the efficiency gains are wiped out by higher demand, with a bigger response for cooling than heating. In automobiles, the consensus estimate is closer to 10 percent, although a major U.S. study found a 23 percent rebound. The rebound phenomenon is a stark reminder of the point that engineering specifications are only one part of the picture, and that the economics of technological change can be equally important. It also shows how imperative it is to control the price of energy if we are serious about reducing emissions.

The indirect impacts are more complex and potentially larger. Because energy is an input into many goods and services, enhancements in efficiency can lower the prices of other products, and people will then buy more of them. These in turn require energy to produce, transport, and operate. There's also a scale effect. When the productivity of energy rises, it propels the overall economy, which in turn raises energy use. How large is this type of rebound? We don't know because the methodologies for the macro-level studies are not yet good enough to yield firm conclusions. The backfire case, of more than 100 percent rebound, is unlikely. But the effects are considerable. One study from the United Kingdom found a 26 percent rebound; other methods yield higher numbers. Some analysts believe energy is particularly potent in boosting profits and economic growth. This is precisely the argument that some of the most ardent green energy technologists such as Thomas L. Friedman are using to promote vigorous action to combat climate change.

The U.S. experience over the last few decades is an object lesson in the perils of rebounds. Since 1975, the country has made substantial progress in improving energy efficiency. Energy expended per dollar of GDP has been cut in half. But rather than falling, energy demand has increased, by roughly 40 percent. Moreover, demand is rising fastest in those sectors that have had the biggest efficiency gains—transport and residential energy use. Refrigerator efficiency improved by 10 percent, but the number of refrigerators in use rose 20 percent. In aviation, fuel consumption per mile fell by more than 40 percent, but total fuel use grew by 150 percent because passenger miles rose. Vehicles are a similar story. And with soaring demand, we've had soaring emissions. Carbon dioxide from these two sectors has risen 40 percent, twice the rate of the larger economy.

When the goal is emissions reduction, there are ways to circum-

FIGURE 3.3 Rebound Effect

	Improved Efficiency	Rise in Consumption
Energy	Energy consumption per dollar of GDP fell by almost 50% since 1975	Energy demand increased by more than 40% since 1975
Vehicles	Average MPG has improved by 30% since 1980	Fuel consumption per vehicle remained constant since 1980 due to more driving and more (and larger) vehicles
Aviation	Fuel efficiency per mile has risen by 40% since 1975	Overall fuel consumption increased by 150% since 1975
Refrigerators	Energy efficiency improved by 10% since 1990	Overall number of refrigerators increased by 20% since 1990
Air-conditioning	Energy efficiency improved by 17% since 1990	Overall number of units has increased by 30% since 1990

Source: Rubin and Tal (2007)

vent rebound effects. Keeping the price of energy high is key. But even this isn't a panacea. If there's a tax on carbon, and those tax receipts are spent, they too create demand for products and, by extension, for more emissions. Even if we manage to shift out of fossil fuels altogether, so that energy use does not create greenhouse gases, the economic boost from these new technologies will spur demand for natural resources of all sorts. In the first round, it's the metals, glass, soil, water, cement, and other materials necessary to produce wind turbines, solar panels, and geothermal pumps. In the second, it's the resources to make the TVs, cars, furniture, tourist experiences, food, and other products consumers buy with the proceeds from the nifty new green economy. It's hard to avoid the conclusion that we need to control not only the price of energy, the usual prescription, but also the pace of growth, because efficiency gains propel demand, which in turn causes ecological degradation.

Technological Optimism in the United Kingdom

We now have a real-world experience of the technological approach. In the late 1990s, the British government, under the leadership of Tony Blair, began to get serious about climate change. It's a relevant case for North America, because the economies are similar (often referred to collectively as the Anglo-American model), and the climate discourse also contains many parallels, although the British are much further along. The U.K. debate between those advocating a pure technology and pricing approach and those who think growth needs to be curbed is the topic of a recent study by the sociologist Anders Hayden.

Britain has been described as "carbon crazy," with significant government, business, NGO, and media attention paid to reducing the carbon footprint. Supermarket chains now label packages with carbon scores, and chains such as Marks and Spencer have signed on to carbon neutrality. In 2007 Parliament passed a major climate-change bill that mandated a 26 percent reduction below 1990 levels of greenhouse gases by 2020, and a 60 percent cut by 2050.

On the other hand, the Labour government has been adamant about its commitment to growth, arguing that efficiency, clean energy, and a market for carbon will do the trick. They claim that they can decarbonize, or sever the link between emissions and GDP. The environment ministry has enacted programs on food waste and plastics use to encourage behavior change among citizens, and a variety of efforts to reduce the carbon footprint of businesses. In the academic literature, this approach is known as ecological modernization. It holds that the fundamentals of the market economy can remain intact. Green production, with eco-conscious consumers and a price for carbon, will be sufficient to solve environmental problems.

While the United Kingdom was one of the only successful cases under the first round of the Kyoto agreements, virtually all their emissions reductions came from phasing out coal. During the Blair period, from 1997 to 2006, despite government efforts, carbon dioxide emissions actually rose. Refusal to reconsider their stance on growth has doomed efforts to meet even the now scientifically inadequate targets of the 2007 bill. Projected growth in one sector alone, aviation, will likely account for the entire country's carbon budget in 2050.

The British approach is failing, and dramatically so. That has led to increasing pressure to address growth itself, from a variety of quarters, including from the Conservatives, who have talked about a redirection toward quality of life and new definitions of progress. While unlimited expansion is still the reigning ideology, the obvious inability of technology plus voluntary market behavior to do the job has ignited a serious discussion about other ways forward. The optimism of the first phase has given way to a more sobering conversation. What is most striking about the British experience is how quickly the limits of the ecological modernization approach have been reached. A few years into the experiment, it's obvious that neither the newer, more demanding targets being talked about nor even the original cuts will be achieved without more radical measures.

Acknowledging Overshoot

In the 1960s, when cost-benefit analysis was developed, trade-off thinking was in its heyday among economists, who were using it to think about issues such as inflation versus unemployment, and inequality versus growth. That world was a far "emptier" place, to use the pioneering ecological economist Herman Daly's expression. It wasn't yet known that human activities were destabilizing the climate, levels of production were about a tenth of what they are today, and species extinction rates were much lower. Trade-off thinking made more sense.

Living through ecological overshoot is another story altogether. As ecological economists began arguing decades ago, not protecting environmental assets has become more costly than protecting them. We are running down the stock of natural capital, and as it declines, its ability to produce benefits and absorb costs is diminished. Each year that we fail to act, costs mount, and the window for action narrows. In contrast to trade-off thinking, overreliance on natural resources is what will make us poor, not just in the long run, but sooner than most of us realize. Rather than having easy substitutes for nature, as optimistic economics assumes, many believe we're approaching (or are on) the part of the curve where there are no substitutes. That's where nature is truly of infinite value, and therefore infinitely costly to degrade, an observation that is starting to appear in the economics literature. If we continue to compromise atmosphere, climate, water, and other species, we jeopardize life itself.

In 2004 what many had hoped would be a breakthrough paper was published by *The Journal of Economic Perspectives*. A collaboration of some of the world's most distinguished environmental economists and ecologists, such as Kenneth Arrow, Partha Dasgupta, Lawrence Goulder, Paul Ehrlich, Stephen Schneider, and Gretchen Daily, asked a question that had been off the table since the debate about limits: "Are we consuming too much?" This type of collaboration itself was rare (perhaps a first). The paper stayed within the standard economic framework that takes human well-being as the ultimate goal, and

asked if we are consuming too much either to reproduce today's
levels of well-being into the future or to maximize well-being. The
answer was a definite maybe. (One reason for uncertainty was the lack
of data for key environmental resources, such as fish stocks, clean air
and water, quality soil, carbon-sequestering forests, and biodiversity.)
Sustainability economists saw an important opening, but the paper
failed to engage the mainstream in the conversation that was becoming more insistent in other circles: is growth sustainable? Years from
now, it may be recognized as the first step in a great U-turn.

Economic thinking on climate shifted because estimates of what
would happen without action have grown increasingly dire. That
opened up win-win options. A similar shift is bound to occur for other
types of resource degradation. When we finally and fully tally up the
costs of fishery collapse, soil erosion, desertification, wildfires, loss of
tropical forests, toxic releases, and a mass extinction of species, the
price tag will loom large in comparison to the costs of preserving the
planet. As in the climate debate, it will be clear that regeneration will
be cheaper than suffering the consequences of collapse. What we're
currently doing will be seen as another massive market failure, the
correction of which will improve welfare. And as that realization develops, the question of growth will be back in play.

The Path to Sustainability: Population, Affluence, and Technology

Ecological economists often organize their thinking with an accounting framework developed by two scientists: Paul Ehrlich of
Stanford and Harvard's John Holdren, currently President Obama's
chief scientific adviser. It says that environmental impact is a product

of three things: population, affluence, and technology. Affluence is income per capita, and includes not just what individuals earn, but the entire production of a society. Population measures the number of people consuming that level of income. Technology stands for an operator that translates total production into all of its ecological effects. Strictly speaking, this "technology" concept covers more than the word does in its common usage, because it also incorporates the mix of different products and activities. (A shift of purchasing from transport to entertainment, for example, will reduce impact, even without technological change.) Since the early uses of this framework in the 1970s, more complex formulations have been developed, and the variables have been decomposed into their component parts. But the simple version helps us see a basic fact about our current predicament.

The reality of overshoot means that we must reduce adverse ecological impact, and significantly so. There are three broad levers for doing so. The first, population, has been the object of tremendous efforts since the 1960s. Fertility has come down around the world, and the United Nations' medium scenario is that population will peak at 9.1 billion in 2050. The rise until then is mostly through inertia, as the large cohort of today's youth enter their childbearing years. At the moment, world population is growing at just under 1.2 percent per year.

That leaves income and technology. Before the downturn, the world economy was growing between 4 percent and 5 percent per year, which results in a doubling in about sixteen years. So all the work of reducing impact must be done by technology, and in sixteen years it'll need to do twice as much as today. Reductions in carbon emitted per dollar of income under BAU will be 1.2 percent per year. That just about offsets the population increase, with no contribution to reducing emissions or to counteracting higher income.

Estimates are that we'll need 5–7 percent annual improvements in decarbonization alone, or a quadrupling of carbon productivity, to stay within the now-inadequate two degrees Celsius target. This is already far outside the range of experience. To achieve the safe 350 ppm level, improvements in technology have to be even larger. This simple arithmetic makes clear that we've got to address the growth of production.

But greenhouse gas emissions are not all we need to fix. We've also got to stop destroying habitat, polluting water and land, and releasing toxic chemicals, thereby raising the burden on technology even more. Considering the material flow measures from chapter 2, the prospects for a purely technological solution appear remote. From 1980 to 2005, the weight of the materials used to produce a dollar of GDP fell about 30 percent on a worldwide basis, or 1.2 percent a year. Because output grew more, there was a 45 percent increase in materials use overall. Western Europe has made impressive progress, but measured decoupling in North America has only been about 25 percent, or 1 percent annually, and the real rates for both regions are considerably lower due to unattributed imports. Dematerialization, or delinking income and impact, is possible, but it is proceeding far more slowly than the pace of ecological decline.

The bottom line is that expecting technology to bear the entire burden of ecological adjustment is foolhardy. Even technology plus a carbon price but no other measures to affect energy and nonenergy demand will not suffice. Macro-level rebound research, as well as common sense, points to the need to address the expansion of production. Either we have to grow less or we have to grow very differently. In the United States, per capita annual income is already a historically unprecedented $47,200. It's time to get serious about finding some alternative sources of wealth that will allow us to thrive without destroying the planet.

In rich countries, and the United States in particular, that may become easier than the BAU forecasts imply. The market economy of the future is unlikely to offer the outsize returns of recent years. The smart choices may be those that use exciting new technologies but don't necessarily raise income in conventional ways, or as conventionally measured. That's the basic idea behind plenitude.

Chapter Four

LIVING RICH ON A
TROUBLED PLANET

The limits of the current growth regime are becoming apparent
year by year. As we travel along the planet's shutdown path, food,
energy, transport, and consumer goods will become more expensive. Jobs and incomes will be less available, and the usual way out—a
debt-financed consumer boom—is unaffordable for households and
the planet. With familiar opportunities deteriorating, we'll be ham-
strung if we limit ourselves to past practice. It's time to leapfrog over
the unpalatable trade-offs currently on offer and embrace a new
economy. Diversifying out of the BAU market makes it possible to tap
into neglected assets. True wealth can be attained by mobilizing and
transforming the economies of time, creativity, community, and
consumption.

A Caveat: One Life Living

One innovative effort within the sustainability movement is called one planet living. It's based on the ecological footprint, and attempts to shift individuals and communities to lifestyles that use only as many resources as are currently available if biocapacity were equally allocated across the globe. There's an ecovillage of a hundred homes in South London called Beddington Zero, operating since 2002, where many residents have managed to attain that goal. They're aspiring to zero carbon, zero waste, and local sourcing of food, fibers, and products.

The strategy of diversification outlined below can be a route to a similarly light footprint. But its ability to yield a life of true happiness and well-being is ultimately dependent on a prior principle—one life living. It comes from the idea that most people believe they have only a single chance on earth. To live richly, or with plenitude, one must use that chance in a way that is personally meaningful.

Those in the vanguard of sustainability have found their purpose in helping to save the planet. But for the vast majority of us, ecological living is not the object of our passion. We will understand that it's necessary, and may enjoy it. But deep meaning is found elsewhere, in family, friends, personal creativity, religion, music and art, social justice, science, business, or helping others. Plenitude as an economic strategy cannot supply that meaning: it can only help achieve it. So as you read the pages that follow, keep this in mind. If your work and primary activities give you that satisfaction already, the approach should help you to find more, or protect what you have. If you are still searching for work that is truly meaningful, it will expand your options by reducing what you need to earn. There's just one planet, and for each of us, one life.

Adjusting to Ecological Reality: The Principle of Extra-Market Diversification

In chapter 1, I argued that the business-as-usual economy is in for a rocky period. Profits and incomes will be lower. Prices will be higher. Conventional economic activity will offer less to the average person. If I am right, then for many people, the intelligent response is to begin a shift out of that market, cutting losses by diversifying. BAU is becoming a losing proposition, especially over the longer run. There are going to be new ways of producing and consuming, either because we smarten up or because nature forces us to change. Those who figure this out earlier will be ahead of the game. For some, the best option will be a partial shift, which combines what they've been doing with new activities. For others, who are beginning or switching careers, completely opting into alternatives will make sense. Some will adjust as a household, reconfiguring the work schedules of two earners.

The logic behind the strategy comes out of the theory of time allocation. Formalized in the 1960s by the Chicago economist Gary Becker and others, time allocation is the application of economic reasoning to the question of how an individual (or household) should optimally allocate his or her time across different opportunities, all of which produce value. While economists had long studied this question in reference to labor supply—whether or not to work for pay, and for how many hours—Becker is credited with thinking about the question more generally.

One of the insights of the time-allocation approach is that all activities, whether they are monetized or not, have the potential to yield returns. We recognize wages and salaries as the returns to employment. But activities that do not earn dollars create returns as well. Doing work in one's own household, without a wage, is production. The cooked meal, the completed tax return, and the cared-for child all have economic value. (Economists call these returns to non-market activity shadow wages, an unfortunate term that reinforces the invisibility of this work.)

The reasoning applies even to activities not normally considered to be production. The returns of leisure include pleasure and building skills: for example, by practicing a sport or an instrument or pursuing a hobby. Volunteering creates benefits for the community, and good feelings for the person engaging in it. Even spending time with a friend, something one might consider purely uneconomic, strengthens social networks of support and reciprocity, which in turn creates access to resources. Friendship also yields a return simply because it is enjoyable.

I make this point in some detail, because over the past three decades, Americans have been transferring an increasing fraction of their time into market activity. Households have put more hours into paid labor and reduced time spent in home production. They're compensating in part by purchasing more goods and services, and buying them at later stages of processing (e.g., more prepared foods). With the exception of senior citizens, people are devoting less unpaid labor time to community work. Leisure is also more commodified, meaning that for any given hour of free time, there are more dollars spent. There's less participatory leisure and more spectatorship—a Disneyland vacation (expensive) rather than camping (low on monetary outlays, high on do-it-yourself).

As the future of the BAU economy becomes uncertain, it makes sense to shift time and effort out of the market into the other valuable things we do. These include activities that are not monetized at all, such as building social capital, and those that are pseudomonetary, such as barter; activities that meet needs without a market (growing food) and those that have the potential to create new sources of cash (a small business, especially in the rising green economy). The point is to diversify uses of time and ways of meeting needs.

The advice to pursue extra-market diversification does not apply to everyone. If you are a high earner, market specialization will still make sense. This is also true if you have a valuable niche skill. If you love your job, are not working more hours than you would like, and have absolutely secure employment, your best bet may be your current lifestyle. But for most people at least some of these conditions do not hold.

The BAU economy won't be around forever. As we reinvent production and consumption systems to make them ecologically sustainable, new markets and businesses will emerge and become stable providers of income. But in the transition, the bottom line is: expect a lower bottom line, as conventionally measured. The savvy response is to invest in those sectors and activities that have been neglected. It's time to reclaim hours, build skills, invest in people, save more, and perfect the art of self-provisioning.

Time Wealth

For most people, diversification begins with their dominant asset, labor hours. The first principle of plenitude is therefore reclaiming time. Millions of Americans have lost control over the basic rhythm of their daily lives. They work too much, eat too quickly, socialize too little, drive and sit in traffic for too many hours, don't get enough sleep, and feel harried too much of the time. The details of time scarcity are different across socioeconomic groups, but as a culture we have a shared experience of temporal impoverishment.

The national speedup was largely unexpected. Fifty years ago, the conventional wisdom was that technology would deliver us from toil. But as the country has grown richer in monetary and material terms, we've seen the opposite, a phenomenon I wrote about twenty years ago and called "the overworked American." Core demands of work, commuting, and family life have been joined by escalating expectations in the realms of consumption, technology, and education. Analysts have also used other terms to describe what's happening. The neuropsychiatrist Peter Whybrow called it "American mania." The filmmaker John de Graaf diagnosed "affluenza." It's a way of life that undermines basic sources of wealth and well-being, such as strong family and community ties, a deep sense of meaning, and physical health. That's why reclaiming time is the common denominator of lifestyles at the cutting edge of the sustainability frontier. Not only is adaptation to the new ecological and economic conditions far easier with less time stress, but newfound hours lead to novel financial opportunities.

In the 1980s, when I first became interested in working hours and time use, there was relatively little research on trends in hours. Since then, there have been many new studies. My original findings highlighted the growth of annual hours among those with jobs, particularly after correcting for then-rising structural unemployment and underemployment. There has been controversy among researchers about trends in hours, both because there are competing sources of data collected at different points in the business cycle and because experiences by education have diverged. Employees with low educational attainment have suffered more under- and unemployment, and those with high education are more overworked. And of course hours fell sharply during the recession that began in 2008, as they always do in a downturn. (They will rise as the economy revives.) But *all* sources show that from the mid-1970s until the present, hours of market work have risen.

According to government survey data, the average working person was putting in 180 more hours of work in 2006 than he or she was in 1979. (The increase was from 1,703 annual hours to 1,883.) The trends are more pronounced on a household basis. Married couples aged twenty-five to fifty-four with children were on the job 413 more hours in 2006 than in 1979. Many more men are working schedules

FIGURE 4.I Annual Hours Worked, U.S., 1967–2006

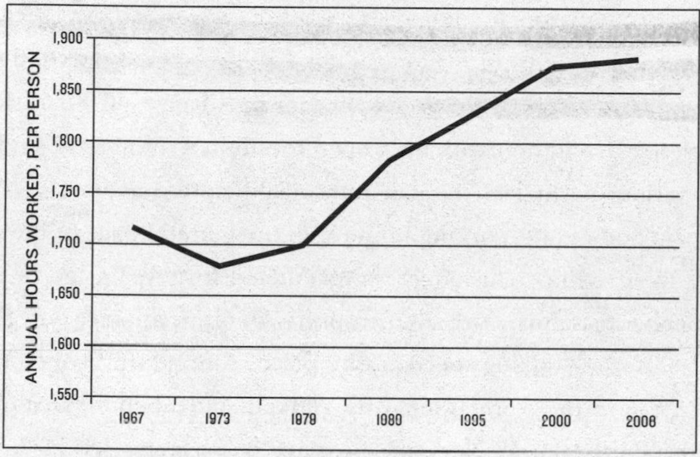

Source: Mishel, Bernstein, & Shierholz (2009), Table 3.2

in excess of fifty hours a week. (Thirty percent of male college graduates and 20 percent of all full-time male workers are on schedules that usually exceed fifty hours.) Another indicator of the extent of market work, the fraction of the population employed, rose from 60 percent in 1985 to 63 percent in 2007.

American schedules are striking when compared with those in similarly wealthy nations, such as Germany, France, Italy, and the Netherlands. Annual work hours in the United States exceed those countries' levels by an average of 270, or more than six and a half weeks (assuming a forty-hour workweek). Even the British, who are significantly poorer than Americans, put in 164 fewer hours a year than their U.S. counterparts. North American schedules (Canadian hours are similar to those of the United States) are considerably above all countries at a similar income level, with the exception of Japan.

Not surprisingly, over the last twenty years, a large number of U.S. employees report being overworked. A 2004 study found that 44 percent of respondents were often or very often overworked, overwhelmed at their job, or unable to step back and process what's going on. A third reported being chronically overworked. These overworked employees had much higher stress levels, worse physical health, higher rates of depression, and reduced ability to take care of themselves than their less-pressured colleagues. Adverse effects of long hours, stress, and overwork have been found in a number of studies, for a variety of physical, mental, and social health outcomes.

As incomes and working hours rise, the general pace of life also tends to speed up. This effect was predicted forty years ago by economic theorists, but it is rarely measured. An international study from the 1990s used walking speed as one proxy. Among thirty-one major cities around the world, New York ranked sixth, behind first-place Dublin. Furthermore, New Yorkers' pace had accelerated in the fifteen years since the measurements were originally taken.

A fast-paced, long-hours, and, for some, high-income lifestyle made a certain amount of sense in an era of expanding profitability and cheap goods. It was especially appealing for professionals whose skills were yielding enhanced earning power. This type of work-centered time allocation is not new. The industrial revolution of the late eighteenth and nineteenth centuries was also a period when expanding business opportunities led to rising hours. Work time grew dramatically as owners of textile factories, railroads, and chemical plants attempted to squeeze every possible ounce of profit from their expensive machinery.

In coming years, I'm betting that for many, the process will run in reverse. The wages and other returns that can be expected from an hour of labor in the business-as-usual economy are going to be lower. For the individual, a sensible response is to work fewer hours. On the other hand, if shorter hours aren't affordable, people may choose to work more. Austerity-minded, trade-off economics says that if the economy worsens and natural resources get scarce, we'll either be living poorer or working longer.

Plenitude suggests a third option: work less in the declining market, but use those freed-up hours productively, to invest in new skills and activities. Some of the time will be deployed to replace higher-priced food, energy, and consumer goods with homemade or community-produced alternatives. Some will be used to invest in social relationships, another form of wealth. And some hours will be spent in high-return leisure activities requiring relatively little monetary outlay. These substitute for the expensive commodities of the faster-paced, higher-income lifestyle.

This vision of a world in which jobs take up much less of our time may seem utopian, especially now, when a scarcity mentality dominates the economic conversation. But there are already signs that a culture shift toward shorter hours and lower-impact living has begun. In 1996, when I first surveyed on this issue, 19 percent of the adult population reported having made a voluntary lifestyle change during the previous five years that entailed earning less money. In 2004, 48 percent did. The higher number likely reflects the aging of the baby-boom generation and a reaction to the excessive work demands of the booming economy of the 1990s and early 2000s. Even New Yorkers' famously fast pace of life stopped accelerating, and held steady over the decade that began in 1996.

Of course, not all these lifestyle changes are permanent. But the survey data suggests that these choices are becoming more common, and they are widespread across the population. In the 2004 group, three quarters reduced their work time either by quitting employment altogether, cutting back on hours within their current job, or reducing the number of jobs they held. The most common motivation was to reduce stress, which was cited by 47 percent of the respondents. Wanting a balanced life or wanting more time were reasons given by about a third, and 30 percent said their change was prompted by the desire to have more meaningful or satisfying work. Twenty-seven percent cited wanting to take care of children.

When I published *The Overworked American* in 1992, the economy offered far fewer opportunities for well-paying part-time work, and employees who wanted to reduce their hours were more likely to have to leave their jobs. Since then, more occupations and companies have offered short-hours options. At the end of 2007, before the downturn, 17 percent of the labor force was working part-time, and for four-fifths of them, this was by choice. According to the most recent figures, 31 percent of the labor force was working in nonstandard employment, which is a combination of part-time, consultant, temporary, and other casual arrangements.

In the surveys I have done, one feature of voluntary shifts to shorter hours stands out. People who make these changes report being very satisfied. In the 2004 survey, 23 percent said they are not only happier, but they don't miss the money. Sixty percent reported being happier, but miss the money to varying degrees. Only 10 percent regretted the change.

The current downturn, difficult as it is, represents an opportunity for expanding the norm of part-time work. In the first year of the recession, many businesses avoided layoffs by reducing hours through furloughs, unpaid vacations, four-day workweeks, and flex time. The Great Depression had a similar effect on hours. By mid-2009, one study of large firms found that 20 percent had reduced hours to forestall job cuts. Past experience suggests that many will love the extra time, particularly those who get a full day off. Some will try to retain their shorter schedules even when their employer can offer more work. In my research, I found downshifters who began with a job loss or an involuntary reduction in pay or hours, but came to prefer their time wealth.

There isn't a one-size-fits-all way to expand time wealth. Those lucky enough to have flexible hours in their current jobs will have the easiest time. Others will quit their jobs, or adjust hours among members of the household. Some young people are starting their working lives with this model, avoiding the high costs associated with a long-hours lifestyle. Of course, for many, earning less money is simply impossible, because their wages are too low. (However, many low-income individuals are already practicing other dimensions of the plenitude model.) Finally, many who have suffered unemployment in the current downturn may choose to return to positions that are not as all-consuming as their previous jobs. If they do, they may find that they are not only improving their own lives, but they have become part of the solution to large, systemic imbalances. Sharing the market work that is available will be essential to reestablishing a fair and well-functioning labor market.

Making Shorter Hours Affordable: Security for All

A characteristic of recent years is that households worked longer hours and bought more stuff, but found themselves unable to afford some of life's basic needs. The costs of medical care, education, and child care escalated while the prices of consumer goods fell. Pensions got unreliable, while low prices for manufactures became a fixture. The prohibitive cost of meeting basic needs created stress and pain, and also introduced market distortions. People remained in jobs they preferred to leave, or worked longer hours than they wanted to, in order to get access to insurance. Inflated prices for higher education left many graduates deeply in debt, opting for second- or third-choice careers that were more lucrative than the fields they were passionate about. Down the line, this inability to choose one's lifework freely can undermine emotional and physical well-being.

To date, none of these problems have been solved. The United States remains famous as the world's only industrialized country without universal health care. Even lower-income nations such as Malaysia, Peru, and Thailand manage what Canada, Western Europe, Australia, and Scandinavia have done for decades. Elsewhere, higher education and child care are made affordable through public support, and pensions are more generous and more reliable. In the United States, financial-sector shenanigans and corporate restructuring have led private companies to default on pension obligations, and 401(k) plans plummeted in tandem with the stock market. As scholars have shown for years, the United States lags behind comparable nations in social spending and provision of these basic services.

Some have found it possible to follow the plenitude lifestyle in the absence of solutions to these collective shortcomings. They use strategies such as buying only catastrophic health insurance, going without insurance, or having one member of a couple work to get insurance while the other opts into informal activity. A few voluntary simplifiers barter for medical services from alternative health practitioners. But these are gambles only the most intrepid are willing to take. Downshifters often move to low-cost areas where everything is cheaper and they can find others pursuing similar lifestyles. Of course, it's much easier to cope with the absence of public provision for basic needs without children to support. And it's more feasible for households that have accumulated nest eggs or have family safety nets.

However, it is inevitable that the adoption of the plenitude lifestyle will be slowed until basic provisions for security are developed. People are more likely to remain in jobs working longer hours than they prefer if cutting back means losing access to benefits. We must make progress toward our common future. This means coming up with systems that provide basic security to all individuals and families—from childhood through old age.

After thirty years of conservative economic policy, the pendulum is swinging back. Reform of health care is on the agenda. There are conversations about improving K–12 education, increasing access to higher education, and reforming the pension system. A few principles should guide these efforts. First, universality is central. The Social Security system, which has been a marvel of low bureaucratic costs and high popularity, succeeds in part because its coverage is so wide. When access to programs is restricted, the costs of maintaining the boundaries and ferreting out free riders can be high, and perverse incentives are introduced. In universal systems, these problems disappear. Single-payer health care systems, which include everyone, are much more cost-effective than private insurance. In the United States, the fraction of health care costs attributed to administration, rather than care, has been estimated to be as high as 31 percent. Second, costs can be kept low by avoiding private profit from essential services. The health care system, which went heavily in the direction of for-profit provision, is in shambles. Higher education, which has few for-profits, is one of the nation's most successful "industries." Wall Street's lobbying for privatizing Social Security should be resisted, in part because it will funnel billions from workers' earnings into fees for bankers and financiers. Third, access to basic needs such as education and health care must be widely affordable. If landing a decent job requires a college degree or training in other skills, then it is incumbent upon society to ensure access for all its members.

While waiting for effective federal programs, there are other options to consider. Some states began health care reform on their own, such as Massachusetts, with its model of universal coverage. In the nineteenth century, trade unions and mutual-aid societies took on the task of self-insuring among their members. Smaller public or nonprofit entities can manage the flows of contributions and bene-fits that are the backbone of health care, pension, and other social security systems. What's essential is that some collective body—be it a government agency, a community, a union, or a nonprofit—take on the task of managing savings, dispersing benefits, and providing insurance. Once individuals know that they will be taken care of if they get ill, that their children can be well educated at reasonable cost, and that they will have a pension at the end of their working lives, they are free to pursue a lower-impact and more satisfying style of life.

Why Working Less Is the Green Solution

Rebalancing between market and nonmarket activity is not only a strategy to improve individual well-being; it is also a centerpiece of ecological sustainability, through the triad of reductions in paid work, income, and marketed consumption. Earn less, spend less, emit and degrade less.

The psychologists Kirk Brown and Tim Kasser measured the ecological footprints of four hundred people, half of whom self-identified as voluntary simplifiers, people who consciously chose to reduce consumption and shift away from material goods. The simpli-fiers' footprint was almost a quarter (23 percent) lower than among a random matched sample. (The simple livers also reported signifi-cantly higher well-being than the random sample.) Analyses of data across nations yield similar findings. A simple graph shows that coun-

FIGURE 4.2 Ecological Footprint and Hours Worked Across Countries, 2005

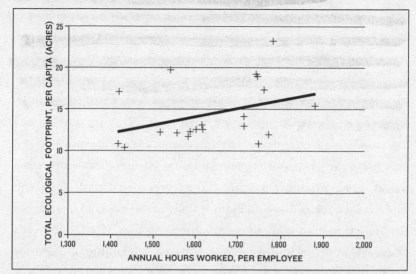

Sources: Ecological Footprint data from "Ecological Footprint and Biocapacity 2005" (Global Footprint Network 2008); Annual hours worked data from The Conference Board and Groningen Growth and Development Centre (2008).

tries with longer annual hours of work tend to have higher ecological footprints. A fuller model, by the sociologists Anders Hayden and John Shandra, found that, controlling for a variety of other influences including income, hours of work remain an important and statistically significant predictor of ecological footprints. A study by David Rosnick and Mark Weisbrot of the Center for Economic and Policy Research estimated that if the United States were to shift to the working patterns of Western European countries, energy consumption would decline about 20 percent.

Why do shorter hours lead to lower resource use? The most obvious effect is through scale. Market work generates income, which is used to buy food, products, energy, and mobility. Purchasing falls when shorter hours are combined with lower income, an effect analogous to reduced spending during a recession. But there are two other channels, both of which are compositional; that is, they affect the mix of products purchased.

The first is income-induced changes in the mix of goods and services, which occur when households cut back disproportionately on resource-heavy vacation travel and home renovation, or the purchase of consumer electronics and other discretionary items. The second is time-induced changes in the mix of products and activities. Households with more time wealth can engage in slower, less resource-intensive activities. They can hang their clothing on the line, rather than using an electric dryer. More important, they can switch to less energy-intensive but more time-consuming modes of transport (mass transit versus private auto, car or train versus airplane). They can garden and cook at home. A Finnish study of the material intensity of time found that an hour of restaurant eating uses 11 kilowatt-hours of energy, while an hour of eating at home (including all travel for food purchasing, gas for cooking, and so forth) uses only 7.4. A French study found that, after controlling for income, households with longer working hours increased their spending on housing (buying larger homes with more appliances), transport (longer hours reduced the use of public transportation), and hotels and restaurants. These have been identified as three of the most environmentally damaging expenditure categories on a number of metrics, such as carbon emissions and ecological footprint.

One big question, which hasn't yet been studied, is whether intentional simplifiers travel more, especially over long distances, because they have more free time. Anecdotal evidence suggests those with high incomes may. If they do, it's a compositional change that may raise eco-impact. However, there's a new trend afoot called Slow Travel, which harks back to leisurely forms of long-distance movement, such as trains, ocean liners, and freighters, that were popular before air travel became so inexpensive. As with the Slow Food movement, its aim is to enhance the quality of the experience as well as to lighten ecological impact.

Provisioning in the Twenty-first Century

Plenitude requires substituting into new, high-benefit uses of time, ideally those that can serve double or even triple purposes. These include producing for oneself, making items that may be sold or bartered for other things, and engaging in activities that are meaningful, skill-building, and contribute to one's standard of living.

The trend toward self-provisioning has already taken hold among small-scale entrepreneurs, voluntary simplifiers, and a group of bioneers, the biological pioneers and ecological inventors who are living low-impact lifestyles with sustainable technologies. Of course, self-provisioning also has a more mainstream history. Some of the activities under this rubric, such as home repair and knitting, have had enthusiasts all along. In other cases, people are returning to lost arts practiced by earlier generations. Popular activities include woodworking, quilting, brewing beer, and canning and preserving. Gardening, hunting, and fishing are other examples, as are sewing clothing, home repair and renovation, and building a computer from components.

People engage in these activities because they enjoy them, they yield better-quality products or products that are not easily available, and they can be less expensive ways of getting access to highly desired goods. Producing artisanal jams, sauces, and smoked meats, or handmade sweaters, quilts, and clothing, makes these pricey items affordable. Social attitudes toward practices such as vegetable gardening and handmade clothing and consumer goods have also changed, so that these are becoming more mainstream choices, rather than the inferior lifestyles of forced circumstances.

Self-provisioning is now thriving. Estimates of the size of this sector are not available, and much of the evidence is anecdotal. We do know that vegetable gardening has exploded. In April 2009, a national survey found that one in five Americans said they were making plans to plant a garden that year. Brewing beer and winemaking have become popular. There's a renaissance in canning and preserving food. After the recession hit, service-oriented businesses such as salons, pet groomers, and nannies experienced a decline in business as people began doing these things for themselves. An annual expo called Maker Faire that started in California has been attracting growing numbers of do-it-yourselfers, or DIYers, and inventors, who use both traditional and high-tech methods. It's spreading to new locations around the country, and attendance has reportedly quadrupled since 2006. Expect these numbers, and all forms of self-provisioning, to be rising dramatically, both because of a culture shift and because in hard times people have more time and less money.

The long-term economic benefit to self-provisioning is that it expands a household's options with respect to employment choices, time use, and consumption. The more self-provisioning one can do, the less income one has to earn to reproduce a standard of living. In recent years, the technical feasibility of home production for basic needs such as food, energy, clothing, and housing has grown. Self-provisioning has become one leg of the stool for living smart and sustainably.

Sound far-fetched, especially for urban households? The merger of sustainability and self-sufficiency has created an explosion of activity and creativity inside and outside cities. The best known of the trends is food cultivation, through organic gardening, urban homesteading, gleaning, and even a movement to grow fresh food "in small places," such as crowded city apartments. Urbanites are moving far beyond herbs and vegetables, by planting fruit trees, putting chickens in their backyards, and keeping bees. People are also going off the grid, with solar panels and passive solar design, geothermal pumps, windmills, and wood pellet and corncob stoves. The alternative energy movement is expanding beyond heat and electricity into appliances. Individuals are building solar ovens and fridges, and even biodigesters, machines that turn household waste into energy to fuel an eco-kitchen. These trends have new names, too: microfarming and microgeneration for self-produced energy. Fourteen percent of additions to solar capacity in 2008 were in off-the-grid installations.

Self-provisioning is also getting popular in housing. As an alternative to high-priced, high-impact, and often shoddy homes produced by commercial contractors, people are building their dream houses with smart design principles, natural materials, efficient energy systems, and often the "free" labor of their families and friends. The movement toward straw-bale homes that has taken off in the Southwest is perhaps the best known of these trends. Straw-bale construction has become prevalent enough that some localities have introduced code for it, and there are even banks that lend for these structures. There are other examples. In West Texas, followers of the visionary Egyptian architect Hassan Fathy established the Adobe Alliance to build homes for the region's many low-income and unemployed inhabitants. These beautiful structures require almost no monetary outlay and are marvels of design and ingenuity. Their crown jewel is the architect and Alliance founder Simone Swan's spectacular domed home. People are experimenting with the use of compressed earth bricks, poured earth, "papercrete" (which uses recycled paper and a small amount of concrete), and a variety of other materials. New Englanders have revived the colonial-era tradition of community barn-raisings, only now they're coming together to build yurts. Yurt construction is also going on elsewhere in the United States, as well as in the Canadian Maritimes, and in the United Kingdom. In Montana, a frugal, outside-the-box couple named Tom and Renee Elpel built a solar slipform house (slipform is a simple stone building method) that looks like it could be in a design magazine, on a ten-dollar-per-square-foot budget and, perhaps more remarkably, a twelve-thousand-dollar-per-year income. Now they've made a career out of their experience, sharing their expertise by writing books, giving workshops, and posting content and communicating on the Internet. As failed housing markets around the country stagnate, expect more real estate refugees to be constructing their own debt-free shelter with recycled, low-cost, or no-cost materials.

The strategy of combining less time on the job with self-provisioning has been most fully elaborated by a visionary philosopher named Frithjof Bergmann, in an economic arrangement he termed New Work. Bergmann conceived of New Work thirty years ago, while teaching at the University of Michigan. Conditions resembled the present, with a deep economic downturn that started in 1980. Industries such as steel and autos were decimated, and Bergmann was living in the heart of auto country. He developed a response to the widespread layoffs and devastation that gripped the state, and particularly Flint, the city where he set up shop.

Bergmann's system had three components. First, radically cut hours in factories, to about twenty per week, in a bid to preserve jobs. Second, help under- and unemployed workers figure out their life's calling, that is, the type of work they most wanted to be doing, and support them to get going with it, irrespective of whether it would yield income. And third, promote a series of advanced or smart-technology methods for producing the basics of life without arduous labor. His term was high-tech self-providing.

Bergmann had begun his academic career in the philosophy department at Princeton in the 1960s. He was interested in human freedom, and intrigued by Henry David Thoreau's well-known experiment in a cabin at Walden Pond. Bergmann resigned his post at Princeton and headed to southern New Hampshire to emulate what Thoreau had done. It was a bold move for a young scholar with a promising academic career.

There was much that Bergmann loved about his time in the woods, but he came to believe that one part of Thoreau's vision was hopelessly romantic: the low-tech approach to labor. Through two brutal winters and with only a handsaw, Bergmann found the endless round of chopping wood, boiling water, and other daily tasks to be arduous, indeed mind-numbing. He ended his experiment with an insight that would guide his subsequent thinking: self-providing is great, but it needs advanced technology to be liberating. This was a crucial departure from one strand of the self-reliance and sustainability movements, which had promoted the return of historical, low-tech methods. Over the decades, Bergmann has collaborated on a series of innovative products that bring self-provisioning principles to individuals, but in ways that require minimal or low levels of human labor.

Bergmann focused his efforts on technologies that address basic consumption needs—food, transport, energy, apparel, furniture, and household goods—so that people can free themselves from the alienation of factory and other bureaucratized work. He collaborated with designers and manufacturers to develop and promote advanced, affordable, and eco-friendly alternatives to the expensive mass-produced components of the mainstream lifestyle. When possible, he aimed for choices that also generated income. In the 1990s, he was active in promoting living wall gardens, which are vertical planting beds that grow vegetables without pesticides, weeding, or much labor. (Small versions are now sold in cooking supply stores, from companies such as AeroGarden.) Bergmann worked with community organizations in the most blighted areas of Detroit and Manhattan to bring these "miracle grow" boxes to unemployed youth and low-income mothers who used them to raise tomatoes and other vegetables, both for their own consumption and to sell at farmers' markets.

Living wall gardens are an example of the innovative technologies now being developed under the rubric of urban agriculture. They take advantage of the fact that plants actually grow from water, sunlight, and minerals, rather than from soil, so that with smart design, it's possible to create lush, verdant plantings on vertical spaces. Living wall systems, which can be used for vegetables, herbs, or just decoration, are available commercially at surprisingly low prices. They're a model of ecological principles and are also being used in green building design. When installed at scale on buildings, they reduce energy consumption by absorbing heat in the summer and insulating in the winter. They also purify the air as the plants take in and process toxins. They can be strikingly beautiful and bring natural systems to dense, urban spaces. The French landscaper Patrick Blanc, who invented the Vertical Garden, has installed arresting plantscapes throughout Paris, and increasingly around the world. In comparison with conventional farming, they are highly efficient in their design and require less labor to sustain, thereby satisfying the principle of high-value activity.

Urban farming is part of a larger movement called permaculture, which aims to revolutionize agriculture by mimicking nature's inherent parsimony. Permaculture's founders recognized that modern agriculture wastes enormous amounts of energy, because single-crop systems are unable to take advantage of synergies among species. They developed high-value ecosystems reliant on the natural labor of plants and animals, rather than polluting fossil fuels or arduous human labor, the two major inputs of recent agrarian systems. Chickens heat greenhouses and peck fields clean. Animals eat pests. Forest canopies fertilize tubers and fruit trees. Roof gardens, some of which include up to 160 species of edible and medicinal plants, are marvels of biological engineering. They heat, cool, and purify air, provide sustenance, can be a source of income, and help cure disease. The labor involved in building and tending one of these wonders is a high-skill, high-productivity diversification out of the traditional market.

Another example of high-tech self-providing involves a dramatically different kind of private transport. More than a decade ago, Bergmann began working with auto engineers in Michigan, some of whom had designed the EV1 electric car, the subject of the documentary *Who Killed the Electric Car?* Bergmann focused on the car because households spend so much money on transport and because the auto is the archetypal industrial product. An innovative car would enhance the credibility of the self-making economy. The goal was a vehicle that was cheap, fuel efficient, versatile, and, in its main departure from current practice, would have its final assembly done by the buyer. It would be available at about a fifth of the cost of an ordinary new automobile. One source of inspiration was the small-airplane industry. Nearly all the small-airplane construction in the country was being done by amateurs assembling planes from kits in their garages. While the designs are there, Bergmann hasn't yet succeeded in mounting the automotive project at significant scale, which is hardly surprising given that auto start-ups require enormous capital. But with hybrid, electric, hydrogen, and Smart cars as the first wave, and the Hypercar and other superefficient options ready to be produced, it's likely there will be some low-cost, high-efficiency vehicles in the near future.

The principle of high-tech DIY finds its most general application in the case of the digital fabricator. Fabricators, or fabbers, are advanced machines that follow sets of digital commands to manipulate and form raw materials to produce actual objects. One type is rapid prototyping machines, which engage in a kind of three-dimensional copying process. The machine is programmed to produce a certain object, the required materials are added, and it begins to create. Humans add the steps the machine can't handle. Scrap plastic is a common input for a fabber, but they also handle metal, wood, and other materials.

Originally the fabricating technology was used almost exclusively by industry, to create prototypes for small-batch production, but that is changing. Led by the physicist Neil Gershenfeld, MIT opened a fabrication laboratory, or fab lab, about ten years ago. It's a collection of some core intelligent machines that together can make a vast array of objects and machinery. In addition to the rapid prototyping machines, a fab lab will include various types of cutting machines, such as laser cutters or water-jet cutters that use intense streams of water, as well as milling machines that are used to make circuit boards, and routing machines. Some of these are relatively miniaturized, such as the desktop milling machines, and others are the size of paper copiers or even larger.

Fab lab machines have been used to make a wide variety of things; indeed, their proponents suggest they can produce almost anything. This includes simple items such as alarm clocks and toasters as well as furniture and clothing. One MIT student produced a bicycle frame from polycarbonate plastic, then began teaching others how to do it. Fab labs can make computers, wireless devices, cell phones, and other electronics. They have also been put to work on really ambitious projects such as wind turbines, solar energy systems, and even ultra-inexpensive prefab houses using cheap materials, churned out to precise specifications. Recently, the MIT group has been spawning fab labs around the world—from inner-city locations such as Boston to global sites from Ghana to India to Norway to Barcelona—and teaching people how to use the equipment. They've opened a fab lab in Jalalabad, Afghanistan, where they're making customized prosthetics, among other things.

The fab lab is the canonical example of high-tech self-providing. Eventually, personal fabbers will be available at affordable prices, and may be as ubiquitous as ovens or refrigerators, but for now, they're being installed at a community level by NGOs. Groups around the world are using the technology for energy-saving devices such as automatic light sensors, bicycles that power appliances, and improvements to clean transportation options. Years ago, Frithjof Bergmann recognized the potential for these machines. If a community purchases a fab lab (the initial setup with machines and supplies was only about twenty thousand dollars) and makes the equipment available, its members can make their own furniture, shoes, clothing, appliances, and other household goods. When labor is "free," the monetary cost of making an item is just the price of materials, which can be very small. In the mid-1990s, as his New Work concept took off in Germany, where unemployment was high, Bergmann began working with cities and towns to establish halls, or New Work centers, to house these and similar machines.

The New Economics of Household Production

The application of advanced technology to household production may seem like an unlikely pairing. After all, high tech has emerged from a complex, modern industrial economy. Producing for oneself is an economic form that was largely abandoned by the early twentieth century as cheap commercial and eventually mass production made it obsolete. But history is not linear, contrary to the economic narratives of modernization theory. We are not moving in one direction toward a more efficient, more specialized, and more marketized world. New technological developments, the growth of literacy and numeracy, and ecological realities are among the factors that make a new direction possible and desirable. It's time to think about smaller-scale enterprises, more diverse skill sets, and the proliferation of invention and creativity.

It is true that the principle of diversification is characteristic of an earlier, preindustrial era. As much scholarship has shown, households have historically engaged in a wide range of productive activities, even when they reside in highly commercial, marketized economies. Across all five continents, agrarian households have produced food to eat and food to sell. They have kept animals and made many of the items they use in everyday life. The females of a household have often been spinners, selling their thread to merchants. Household members have woven cloth, or participated in the putting-out systems of manufacture, where merchants advance materials and buy finished or assembled products. Urban households have followed a similar path, using whatever productive assets they can muster to create multiple sources of income. Women took in boarders, served as bankers in informal currency systems, and sold foodstuffs out of their homes. And these are by no means purely historical curiosities. Many of these practices are still widespread today.

While these arrangements may seem hopelessly premodern, they reflected a sophisticated economic calculus in their environments. Climatic conditions were uncertain, markets were volatile, and collective security was incomplete. Not by accident, these are the characteristics we can expect more of in coming years. A diversified income stream makes sense when the labor market is going through ups and downs, or long-term decline. Facing such a situation, investing all one's time in a single skill set or occupation is riskier than cultivating a number of sources of earnings. Diversified households also use a multiplicity of activities to fill in the slack periods. Historically, agrarian households turned to spinning, soldiering, and even mining during the winter when there were few farming tasks. Contemporary households can apply some of these same principles to take advantage of market volatility, seasonal demand for labor and skills, and, more important, to optimize their participation in an emerging but not yet predictable sustainable economy. The specifics of what and how we produce will be different, but the economic principles behind the strategy remain compelling.

What makes these arrangements worth returning to are the advances of a postindustrial era, which have dramatically increased the potential productivity of the individual, the household, and even the local community. There is now a much wider array of technologies to choose from, some of which are quite productive. Computers and the Internet are obviously in this category, but they're not alone. Innovations such as fabbers radically alter the cost calculus. Making shoes or clothing or even toasters in centralized factories is no longer necessary and may even lose its financial advantage, particularly once environmental costs are incorporated. Small-scale production in households or communities avoids transport costs, which will be rising. It's a produce-on-demand method, so it minimizes waste by avoiding overproduction (a chronic problem in mass production). It incorporates desirable consumer features such as the ability to customize. Small-scale and sufficiency production also match the emergent skill set of the population. In the old mass production system, advanced numeracy and literacy were concentrated in managers and designers, and blue- and pink-collar work was deskilled. By contrast, high levels of numeracy and literacy are required more broadly in a technologically advanced economy, and equally so for the high-productivity, low-impact systems of agriculture and manufacture I have been discussing. As these skills are diffused through the population, the efficient scale of production falls.

I will return to these issues in the final chapter, where I situate them within the macro context. My point here is that a variety of factors have been leading the optimal scale of production to shrink. Some of them are familiar, including the impact of an open-source system, not just in software, but more generally. The economics of information leads to networks and sharing, which in turn reduces the desirable scale. For those versed in the world of high-tech systems, think of the self-providing model as just another optimized network. This is a trend that matters for the economy as a whole, and for businesses. But it is equally relevant for individuals and households, which, more and more, we should think of as little enterprises.

A shift to self-provisioning makes sense for another reason. It's a strategy for building up a new skill set among the population. While

some of the activities I've talked about can be done with relatively little training, as the transition accelerates, the complexity and ingenuity
of the sustainable economy will grow. One of its benefits, from an
economic point of view, is that certain parts of it are very knowledge-
intensive. Figuring out how to maximize productivity in a roof garden, fabricate from recycled goods, or design an energy-efficient
home are tasks that require new kinds of knowledge, much of it
gained from a study of nature itself. Right now, people are learning
in informal ways, and bioneers are adopting the apprenticeship
model that fell away in the modern era. Self-provisioning is a way to
spread the skills and practices we will need. It's especially important
because it represents a return to more widespread capacity among
the population to feed, clothe, shelter, and provide for itself. Those
are arts and skills that have atrophied substantially and that we need
to spread more widely to weather the coming economic and ecological storms. That doesn't necessarily mean a return to the ways we did
these things in the past, but it means learning how to do them so that
we can thrive in the twenty-first century.

Self-provisioning is also a spur to entrepreneurial activity. Most
people who practice it don't self-provide everything. They find some
productive activities they prefer, are more skilled at, or can do more
easily. They trade or sell what they're best at producing. We already
see this happening in some cutting-edge fields, such as home construction and permaculture. With this specialization, self-provisioning
becomes a pathway to incubating a set of small businesses that will
flourish as the sustainable economy takes off.

A last point about the economics of self-provisioning is that it
puts practitioners in the rising segment of the market. For decades,
organic foods and fibers, responsibly harvested woods, and nontoxic
alternatives have been considerably more expensive than standard
industrial products. But the green sector has moved beyond its early,
high-cost origins, and the price gap with mass production has nar-

rowed considerably, especially in the last few years. If we are able to internalize ecological costs, the differential will reverse itself. It'll be a good economic bet for those who choose it.

We are circling back, and plenitude is a synthesis of the pre- and postmodern. From the former, it borrows the vision of skilled artisans producing for their own use as well as for the market. It's a decentralized integrated production model with a less specialized division of labor compared with mass production. Total work hours are low (as they were in the precapitalist era), individuals retain more control over their time and labor, and work gives ample scope for creativity. From the postmodern period comes advanced technology and smart, ecologically parsimonious design. It's the perfect synthesis. Technology obviates the arduous and back-breaking labor of the preindustrial. Artisanal labor avoids the alienation of the modern factory and office.

Will it be enjoyable? The anecdotal evidence seems to be yes. There are challenges, to be sure, but for many, the switch from paper pushing to gardening has been welcome. Self-providers value their newfound skills, love the chance to be creative, and are getting satisfaction and security from constructing a more self-reliant lifestyle. The ability to work for oneself is highly valued. They are nourished by connection with the earth. Perhaps most important, they are rewarded by the opportunity to live without endangering others and the planet.

The Plenitude Consumer

So, you're following the program, working part-time at a new job you love, doing a bit of urban homesteading, and trying to get a small side business off the ground. But there's more to life than being productive. What about consuming, the all-American passion?

It's obvious that major changes are underfoot in the retail sector. The fast-fashion model of the last twenty years has exhausted consumers, the planet, and the forces propping it up, such as Chinese banks. Chains have gone bankrupt, retail space has been abandoned, and consumers are being cautious with their dollars. In the new paradigm, eco-impact must be significantly lower. Discretionary income will be, too.

But hold on. That doesn't mean you can't shop to your heart's content. After all, you'll have more time. Obsess about your wardrobe, or your gadgets, if it makes you happy. Decorate and redecorate your home. Plenitude suggests you should pay more, not less, attention to your consumer self.

Surprised? Old-fashioned frugality is being preached from nearly all corners these days. Critics of consumer culture have offered bromides about its superficiality and see it as poor compensation for what's missing elsewhere in our lives. Shopping and spending carry a whiff of unworthiness. But rejecting passionate consuming because the thrill of the mall is gone is about as sensible as not eating because the fast-food culture is so awful.

In fact, food shows the way. If you're reading Alice Waters, Michael Pollan, Vandana Shiva, Winona LaDuke, Frances and Anna Lappé, Carlo Petrini, José Bové, and others like them, you know they're not only critics of industrial agriculture; they are the leaders of an alternative culture of growing, distributing, preparing, and eating food. It respects the earth, nourishes the body, brings people together, fosters creativity, tastes sublime, and satisfies cravings. We should, and can, have all that for our houses, vehicles, apparel, electronics, furniture, and other consumer goods.

Let's start with stuff. There's no avoiding the fact that just as every purchase has a price in money terms, it also has an ecological impact. Some items tax the earth more, some less, but everything we buy puts carbon in the atmosphere, uses up resources, and affects the functioning of ecosystems. Cotton is pesticide-intensive and depletes the soil. Plastics are full of petroleum and toxins. Electronics use heavy metals and more toxins. Just as the alternative food movement insists on organics, local production, and sustainability, plenitude consuming must also respect the earth. In the examples above, the onus is on companies to make the transition to clean production. While that's happening, consumers can minimize impact by opting for products and companies that are already farther along that road. Choices are expanding in most categories. There are now safe household cleaners, natural and low-impact fibers for apparel and white goods, energy-saving electronics and appliances, eco-furniture, and accessories made from recycled materials. Air travel and a few other categories still lack green alternatives, although there have been some recent breakthroughs in fuel technology.

Information about how to find these items has become accessible online, if they are not locally available. Consumer friendly environmental impact information is also on its way. Products are getting carbon scores and other labels that detail ecological impacts. One new Web site allows shoppers to use their cell phones while in the store to get environmental impact scores for products. The technical information is proliferating, although there hasn't yet been convergence on a simple system of conveying this information.

Many consumers have found keeping track of ecological impacts to be a daunting task. There's a simple rule of thumb that will go a long way to simplify the challenge: moderate consumption of items that have traditionally been luxuries. (This may involve a little discussion with older generations—what *was* expensive back in the day?) Luxury status is usually caused by rarity in nature and/or the expense of bringing these products to market. Some of the most destructive consumption in recent years has occurred via the mass marketing of formerly expensive items. An early example is shrimp, whose price was driven down by farm cultivation in South and Southeast Asia that

destroyed mangroves and coastal ecosystems and undermined livelihoods for local populations. Cheap cashmere came courtesy of unsustainable expansion of herds in Central Asia, with resultant
overgrazing and desertification. Low-cost leather has been made possible by unregulated dying and tanning using dangerous chemicals
that pollute local water supplies and cause cancer in workers.
Escalating demand for gold and other precious metals and gems has
been an environmental nightmare, displacing enormous quantities
of earth and poisoning surrounding water and ecosystems. Meat is a
food that has historically been expensive and eaten sparingly, but is
now mass-marketed through an unsustainable production system.

Avoiding these disasters is essential, but not enough. We can't just
replicate what we do today with a green hue. The scale of consumption will remain too high until impact per product declines. That
means we've got to buy less, and enjoy what we do purchase more.
The first change is to shift the consumption of new items toward quality and away from quantity. It's a move to slow spending.

The Art of Slow Spending

The fast-fashion model has led to cheaper design and construction, which means that products don't last as long and are harder to
repair. Sustainable consumption entails extending product life. The
boom in shoe repair and tailoring that began with the recession is a
move in this direction, but garments and shoes have to be above a
minimum quality to make repair worthwhile. (If they cost twenty dollars at Payless or even thirty-five dollars at Macy's, they may not war-
rant a trip to the cobbler.) In many cases, sustainability entails paying
more up front. However, this is not always more expensive over the
long run. Some footwear brands will recondition their products for a

fraction of their rather steep original selling price, thereby doubling or tripling their useful life, and cutting the effective cost by a similar fraction. The longevity principle extends far beyond shoes and clothing. Policies that extend product life have advanced considerably in Europe and elsewhere through legislated producer responsibility for consumer electronics, office supplies, and vehicles. Businesses are required to take back what they have sold, so the laws build in more incentives for durability. Companies can recondition what they recapture, as many computer manufacturers already do, and some are leasing services rather than selling items. Interface, a U.S. flooring company, takes back its carpets and recycles them into new ones.

A second sustainability principle is multifunctionality. We can live comfortably with fewer products if the ones we do buy can be used in different ways. Apparel provides classic cases, such as shawls that can double as skirts, or the Indian sari, which accommodates the body's inevitable expansions and contractions. Electronics are moving in the direction of multifunctionality. Configurable seating in vehicles is another example. Innovation in multipurposing requires more design up front, which increases the initial cost, but in the long run, it delivers more service per pound of resources or financial outlay. By contrast, items with dedicated uses, whether they're kitchen appliances or specialized wardrobes, take a great ecological toll from a life-cycle perspective because they are used more infrequently.

A third principle is customization, which brings us to the retail environment that supports the plenitude spending model. It's the other end of the spectrum from the big-box store with its high turnover, low prices, and minimal service. Because the consumer is investing in fewer, more expensive items, they need to be perfect fits and remain so over time. To achieve that match, retailing should be more personal, based on communication between the designer and the consumer, and offer postpurchase product maintenance. Smaller, local stores do better with this model, in part because they can charge more (although it's not impossible for big companies). It's easy to visualize for apparel, where *fit* is literal. If you're going to spend serious money for a coat, dress, or bag, it has to be exactly what you want and need. So you begin shopping, considering various designers and styles. When you've found a concept you like, you begin working with the producer on the initial design. Once the item is made, you have a chance to adjust the fit, and over time you can go back for alterations and updates, which, depending on the initial cost of the purchase, may be free or cost a moderate amount. It's a high-involvement retail model (although for some goods it can also take place online). The consumer is investing not only money but time and emotion in the product. This helps to compensate for the less frequent pleasure of a new purchase. Jewelry provides another example. Rather than buying new pieces when styles change, consumers can (and many already do) go to local artisans who melt the precious metals, reset the stones, and create new necklaces, rings, and bracelets. Returning to the food analogy, high-involvement retail can tap human creativity, create local ties, "taste" sublime, and satisfy consumer desires. This is also the point at which the consumption side of plenitude meets self-provisioning. The people who have started to make clothes for themselves, because that's where their creative urges take them, become the designers opening the local ateliers.

So far, what I've described is a shift toward a form of retailing that can survive only with higher-priced products. Forgoing high-impact shortcuts in production and adding in services, customization, longevity, and up-front design costs money. The opposite of high volume/low margin is low volume/high margin. That means higher prices for consumers. But followers of plenitude have shorter average hours of work and less cash.

The shortfall is partly made up by the fact that the rate of purchasing new items will fall, relative to other ways of procuring goods. If the life of a product doubles, its effective yearly cost is halved. And if people are practicing self-provisioning, they've found a low-cost way to procure goods. But there's another strategy that really *is* inexpensive: the secondary market. In contrast to buying new, the recirculation of goods is an ecological and economic boon. The incremental footprint is largely the cost of transport and, if it's sold in a retail outlet, the store's costs of operation. And of course resale prices are typically far below original cost. So one can decorate and redecorate, build and divest wardrobes, accumulate, shop, and collect to one's heart's content, and still live within sensible environmental and fiscal boundaries.

The current moment presents a once-in-a-lifetime opportunity. No society in history has been rich—or reckless—enough to create so much overproduction. The silver lining of the materiality paradox is that we've racked up an enormous inventory of products that no longer have much value for their original owners. In response, economies of reuse and resale have expanded rapidly. The Web has drastically reduced the transaction costs of exchange and expanded the geographic scope of the market. In addition to well-known sites such as eBay and craigslist, there are specialized Web resellers for many items, from Harley-Davidson motorcycles to cloth diapers. Anecdotal evidence also suggests a rise in other secondary exchange practices, such as barter, regifting, and clothing, seed, plant, and craft supply swaps. In February 2008, with a nod to the global recession, IKEA organized a furniture swap in Amsterdam, at which people could come and exchange furniture, including some that the retailer donated for the event.

Ultimately, these opportunities will be limited by the inflow of items from original owners. If the retail slowdown lasts, inventories of goods for resale will shrink, and the market will stabilize at a smaller level, its size being determined by purchases in the firsthand market.

For all their newfound popularity, secondary markets do face cul-

tural barriers to expansion. The economy of resale is complex symbolic terrain. Most items lose value in resale, some gain it, and some
do both. Preowned furniture starts out as used but can cross a thresh-
old into antique, with a status premium tacked on. The size of the
initial investment can matter, but doesn't always, as today's hefty
prices for moderately priced imported furniture from the 1950s and
'60s show. Buying a preowned home carries little stigma, and charm-
ing older houses with period details command a premium. Age and
pedigree can add value to art, jewelry, watches, and other products,
but mass-produced items typically lose value in resale. With the exception of antique shops, most secondary retail outlets, such as thrift and
consignment shops, have had low status. That is beginning to change,
with the growth of designer resale in apparel and retro design shops,
which have a more affluent clientele than traditional thrift shops
(whose customers have also gone upscale in recent years). But it's a
symbolic revaluation that needs to go farther if the full potential of
secondary markets is to be realized. There's still too big a gap in the
merchandizing practices (design, decor, and layout) between new
and used retail outlets. The recent appearance of designer consignment shops in upscale malls is one promising sign. Another is the
visible promotion of the recycled lifestyle among young people and
ecologically motivated consumers.

Small Can Be Beautiful

The American love affair with the gargantuan has taken its toll
ecologically, whether we're talking houses, vehicles, televisions, or
food portions. There's no question that people have enjoyed the posi-
tives of more space and more horsepower. But with higher energy
prices, the sprawling homes of outer-ring suburban development cost

too much to heat, cool, and commute from. Just as the high gas prices of 2007 and 2008 spurred a flight into smaller cars and hybrids, the homes that will be built in coming years will not only be more energy efficient, but, on average, they will likely be smaller. Can Americans learn to love them as they have loved their McMansions?

Affordability will drive the transition. People want to own homes, but they also want them to be smart investments. There are other potential benefits to downsizing. Some argue that McMansions are just too large for optimal social connection. One housing researcher opined that these oversize homes are "good for the dysfunctional family." But a simple shrinking of homes isn't the answer. Instead, we need a repurposing driven by smart design, another quantity-to-quality shift.

If you're constrained on one dimension (square footage), optimize on others, by building multi-purpose areas and high functionality everywhere. When my family decided to fix up our seventy-plus-year-old home, we opted against the route that most renovators in our area take: blow out one side of the house to build a large kitchen and family room area. We had a small, 1920s kitchen that we did want to enlarge, but we planned to stay within the footprint of the house, to reduce our energy use. We'd also noticed that after many renovations, activity migrates to the new wing of the house, leaving much of the original space empty. In those cases, the lived-in square footage is less than the new dimensions, and people aren't getting their money's worth. Working with an architect, we chose a design that altered the configuration of rooms, created a circular flow, and integrated the space. Designers of smaller homes operate with this principle of efficient use of space. "Small is beautiful" can also be literal. The money saved by not supersizing can be used for more luxurious materials, detailing, or furniture. A 2008 survey found that more than 60 percent of potential home buyers said they would rather have a smaller house with more amenities than the converse. In our case, we got more efficient and enjoyable use of our house, and our operating costs plummeted as a result of insulation and other energy-saving renovations. We're using about half the heat we once did.

The latest generation of solar homes now being built in northern Europe is amazingly efficient, but not beyond a certain size. They use passive solar technology that relies on the sun plus the heat and energy generated by appliances and people. They require virtually no additional heating or cooling to maintain comfortable temperatures year round. They are marvels of smart design, due to tight seals and sophisticated HVAC systems that exchange warm air going out with cool air coming in, at 90 percent efficiency. They're not expensive to build, are quite comfortable, and although they can seal up tightly, they have plenty of functioning windows. But at least for now, they only work when the square footage per inhabitant is about 500. Beyond that, the heat generated by our bodies isn't sufficient to keep a whole house warm.

Smaller living spaces are getting popular. Sarah Susanka pioneered the concept with her 1998 book *The Not So Big House,* but "not so big" has been superseded by "little" (as in Shay Salomon's *Little House on a Small Planet*) and even "tiny" (à la Jay Shafer's Tumbleweed Tiny House Company, which builds structures under a hundred square feet.) At the far end of the genre are artists working on what they call "high-tech nomadic living," with teensy houses that actually walk, in homage to the peripatetic lifestyles of the Romany people. While the walking home is a curiosity, the beginnings of a trend toward ecovillages and cohousing solve the size dilemma particularly efficiently, by letting residents share spaces that are used only intermittently. Cohousing communities include guest rooms, larger spaces for entertaining, gyms, or even media rooms, pools, and other amenities that sit empty much of the time in McMansions. By combining resources, owners can obtain the benefits of large homes, but at a fraction of the cost. Recent press reports suggest the demand for small houses and living spaces is growing rapidly, given the obvious appeal of life without a mortgage, or a surfeit of stuff. The developer of one green project in Seattle that involves condos atop a Hyatt hotel is betting that the eight-hundred-square-foot size he's offering will be a winner, as others in the field write the obituary of the "big house."

The Share Solution

When I published *The Overspent American* in 1998, one sentence generated a reaction akin to outrage—my suggestion that neighbors could share expensive items that are only used periodically, such as riding mowers. Ten years later, it's not only mowers that are being jointly owned, but tractors and even vehicles. The sharing economy is taking off. The best-known example is car sharing, pioneered in the United States by Zipcar, which makes vehicles available to urban members on a short-term basis. Its founder, Robin Chase, has moved on to create GoLoco, a ride-sharing service. Freecycle.org members are committed to the reciprocity of both giving and getting. IShareStuff.com allows individuals to post items they are willing to share and to contact others who have done the same. These examples are extensions of two important movements that promote global sharing: the information commons and responsible use of common resources of land, water, and atmosphere. The ethos motivating groups such as Share the World's Resources, Creative Commons, and iCommons is equally valid for ordinary products.

Collective bicycle programs have proliferated in Europe, with London slated to begin a project in 2010. They're also taking root in the United States, and now operate in Washington, D.C.; Chapel Hill, North Carolina; Madison, Wisconsin; and Fort Collins, Colorado, among other places. North America's largest program is Montreal's

Bixi. (Negative reports on Paris's Velib program, which opened in 2007 to a great deal of fanfare, reveals a well-known fact about these programs: pure open-access models are hard to sustain. Except in certain venues, rental deposits, membership, or some other incentive against stealing is usually necessary.) Tool sharing is another collective form that has a long history, especially in low-income communities. In these examples, items are owned by an individual, company, city, or nonprofit, but they are made widely available. Another variant is shared ownership, which has started springing up in cohousing communities and other places. Households band together to buy not only small tools, but other items, including automobiles. Collective vehicle ownership is practiced in some parts of Europe, such as Scandinavia, where the logistics of insurance, damage assessment, and scheduling have been worked out.

These examples cover a variety of ownership structures (public, private, individual, collective) and financing arrangements, but they are united by a core insight: under certain conditions, sharing has clear efficiency benefits in comparison with exclusionary private possession. Sharing reduces material throughout, saves money for individuals, and builds community. Its benefits are greatest when individuals don't need the goods all the time, up-front costs are high, usage does not degrade or personalize the item, and costs of operation or depreciation can be allocated to individuals (as with cars). On the other side of the ledger, shared ownership increases what economists call transactions costs—the time and effort of creating rules, setting up scheduling, and policing problems (although the Internet has dramatically reduced these costs). When money is cheap, nature isn't counted, and time is expensive, as in the BAU economy, where incentives favor private ownership. A shift toward plenitude, which economizes on materials and is rich in time, enhances the value of sharing.

Recapitalizing the Social: Economies of Reciprocity

For the vanguard that is passionate about the sharing economy, it is a matter of more than ecological appeal. Sharing is a route to rebuilding social ties in a society that has experienced a rise in disconnection, loneliness, and individualism. Bioneers understand that reconstructing community, or recapitalizing the social, is a necessary adaptation for an economically and ecologically perilous world.

There is now a large body of research on the state of social ties among Americans. The French sociologist Pierre Bourdieu was one of the first to use the term *social capital* in the 1970s, and Robert Putnam's *Bowling Alone* documented its decline in the United States over the post–World War II period. Not only were Americans less likely to join clubs and social organizations, but they became less likely to trust one another, got together less, and retreated from the political process. While there has been debate about whether we're really bowling alone or whether we just stopped bowling and started book clubs, a broader change in social connection is well documented. (The record-setting turnout of the 2008 presidential election was a departure from this trend.) Neighborhoods have become much less important as social units, with people much less likely to interact with, or even know, their neighbors. Spending time with friends is also on the wane, according to Putnam, who found that informal socializing fell by a third from the 1970s to 2000, with an especially large decline in the 1990s. Online community is growing and filling in some of the gap. But it doesn't replicate all the functions of face-to-face interaction.

There are a variety of explanations for how we ended up here.

Historians locate the process in the eighteenth and nineteenth centuries, when the rise of capitalist production broke artisanal guilds, village solidarity, and the customs of a moral economy. These ruptures with the past were more acute in Europe. In the United States, community was always weaker, with more mobility and individualism. But some of the same factors came into play with the decline of small-town and rural America. Another school of thought blames consumer culture, a twentieth-century phenomenon, arguing that our love of things became a substitute for interacting with people. Most consumer researchers think differently, however, arguing that products fortify social bonds. These brand communities, as they call them, bring people together through a common love of, for example, a motorcycle brand, an off-road vehicle, or a media product, such as the *Star Trek* series, which has spawned a legendary fan culture. More prosaic stories emphasize geographical mobility or a growing taste for privacy.

Another explanation is that the economic function of community eroded. In the past, community was reproduced through ongoing relations of economic dependence and interdependence, or economies of reciprocity. Flows of labor and goods passed between and among people. The particulars varied with the era and the type of community, but in nearly all cases, transfers of resources were pervasive. In the distant past, people traded seeds, child care, transport, medicines, and highly skilled services such as midwifery. They helped one another to get a harvest in. Even recently, these kinds of transfers have been substantial. The stay-at-home mothers of the 1950s and '60s provided child care and transport for one another; research on poor urban African Americans in the 1970s found extensive informal exchange of labor, goods, and money.

But economic growth undermined the need for community interdependence. When people can afford to purchase services, they ask for favors less often. As people spend more time on the job, donations of labor to friends, neighbors, and extended family members decline. Prosperity itself can corrode community, by undermining our need for one another. This can be seen in the skewness of transfers across income levels. More affluent groups are less likely to engage in reciprocal labor transfers (although they do transfer money within family networks). Dependence also has its drawbacks—it can be constraining or even onerous at the same time it offers the benefits of social connection and economic assets in the form of untapped obligations.

And so we migrated to a different kind of connection, based on affinity. People were more likely to come together around products or activities they enjoy, such as following a sports team, crafting, wine tasting, or watching a TV show. These elective affinities are the kind consumer researchers study. But it's a weaker and less durable form of community, with more in-and-out movement than in geographical or family units. Its ability to get us through prolonged economic and ecological distress is questionable, in part because the economic relations that keep people together are less developed.

Sustainability activists are keenly aware of the decline of social connection and are attempting to rebuild it by creating a face-to-face economy. The local-food movement is the best known of these efforts. In urban areas, groups are organizing farmers' markets, CSAs (community-supported agriculture programs), and community gardens. The Business Alliance for Local Living Economies, a national network with more than seventy-five local chapters, supports local entrepreneurs and promotes the viability of renewed regional and local economies. Efforts to create local currencies are growing. The Berkshires area of Massachusetts has become famous for the successful launch of BerkShares, a parallel currency to the U.S. dollar that aims to create community cohesion and boost local purchasing power. Around the nation, local sustainability committees have taken up the mission of bringing their communities together for land-use planning, carbon reduction, income security, and greater self-reliance.

The vanguard of this movement is thinking long-term, spurred on by the need to wean off fossil fuels and a belief, by some, in the phenomenon of peak oil. A global movement called Transition Towns is helping small locales transform themselves to become self-reliant. The Post Carbon Cities network, which has a similar mission, is active from Spokane to Nevada City to Alachua County, Florida. There are also homegrown efforts. A few years ago, people in rural areas of Northern California began conversations to create an "off the grid" network of farms and businesses. One participant is Paul West, a maverick from a conservative Southern family who'd already been through one career as a successful public relations executive in Manhattan's fashion industry, as well as a second at an environmental NGO. West became convinced that we are moving toward a radically different economy, and in 2007 joined others in Northern California to take part in a conversation that, in his words, had already begun to "think the unthinkable." The buzz phrase was "What would you do if your money was not worth anything?" The economic system was due for a crash (they were right about that), imported energy could no longer be relied on (to be determined), and people needed to come together to start planning for very different ways of living. "It can't be one family or one ranch of 20 acres," he explained. "We need to be together and share resources." Unlike old-school neo-survivalists, many in this movement are upbeat. "I'm not motivated by fear," says West. We can "sustainably share resources. It's intoxicating."

One needn't believe in apocalyptic visions of peak oil to recognize that enhanced investment in each other, that is, in community, is good economics. The era of disconnection has left us socially undercapitalized. This is not only for the reason social scientists have traditionally identified, which is that social capital yields economic and political benefits such as better government and better economic functioning. It is also because without it, we are ill equipped to survive adverse events. Social capital is an insurance policy. The sociologist Eric Klinenberg's study of the Chicago heat wave of 1995 found that casualties shared one important characteristic: they were socially isolated. Other research shows that the denser a person's social connections are, the more likely he or she will be to receive help in a crisis. Recent work on Katrina survivors found that those with stronger predisaster support fared better after the trauma.

Economies of reciprocity are a secondary, albeit nonmonetary, banking system. People build their futures by incurring debts to others. They accrue assets in the form of unreciprocated transfers of labor, money, and goods that can be drawn on when needed. Historically, small communities have helped regulate these interpersonal flows, keeping track and punishing free riders. After all, money is only paper (or an electronic accounting), and if money is scarce, or the financial system is in crisis, it's real resources of time and nature that actually meet our needs. By letting people reclaim their daily lives, plenitude creates the means to recapitalize these diminished social economies, through our investment in one another and our common wealth and security.

Chapter Five

THE ECONOMICS OF PLENITUDE

Policies that encourage business-as-usual growth have begun to jeopardize planetary survival. It's increasingly apparent that we need to negotiate the transition from the gray (or dirty) economy to a green alternative.

Concretely, this means building a well-designed and expanding clean sector, with the right mechanisms and incentives in place to move people and resources into it. We can't just assume that what worked in the industrial economy is efficient in the green one, because it isn't. But if we manage it right, the plenitude shift will offer not just a richer, more satisfying way of life for the individuals who practice it, but significant new and widespread wealth. It's designed for efficiency, innovation, and fairness.

The plenitude principles of the previous chapter are the building blocks that speed the transition and produce the conditions for a vibrant sustainability. On the production side, these are falling hours of BAU work, an expanding army of self-provisioners and small businesses, and the reinvigoration of social capital.

Hours reductions serve multiple purposes. As hours fall in the gray sector, labor will flow into the green one. Shorter hours in both sectors also raise hourly productivity and provide livelihoods, by expanding the number of jobs. Throughout the history of capitalism, displaced workers have been absorbed in part through reductions in working hours.

The second component is the spur to self-provisioning and small businesses. This scale of enterprise, networked locally, regionally, and globally, looks more and more like the efficient model of the future. Plenitude gives individuals time to acquire skills and become entrepreneurial. It's a path with low capital requirements, which makes it available to large numbers of people. It also builds social capital, which is necessary for successful networks and local economies. On the consumption side, consumers' demand for low-impact goods and services creates the market for these enterprises.

Investment in social capital and strong economic ties among people make up the third principle, and they make possible the successful management of ecological commons through collective efforts and shared ownership. Regeneration and enhancement of ecosystems creates wealth that can be widely held and enjoyed. And of course sustainability will also require conventional solutions, such as a significant price for carbon and environmentally sound accounting.

But I begin with a dimension of the transition that has largely been ignored in discussions about sustainability: the role of knowledge and its peculiar economics. Accelerating the transition to clean production will require new ways to disseminate ecological know-how. Without getting that piece right, we'll be missing a major source of wealth and an opportunity to restore the planet.

Earth-Smart Design and the Economics of Knowledge

Efficiency is crucial to any successful economy. In the broadest terms, achieving efficient outcomes involves determining which inputs into production are plentiful and which are not, and figuring out how to remove the bottlenecks of the limiting factors. In the industrial era, labor, finance, and physical capital (i.e., machinery) have each been a limiting, or scarce, factor. By contrast, nature was treated as if it were free, that is, consumable without limits. As a result, we got resource-intensive, toxic methods of production.

Now the equation is reversed. We have global surpluses of labor. We know how to create finance through the monetary system and we can easily reproduce machinery. It's healthy ecosystems that are in short supply. This is what the sustainability conversation is mainly about. Green designers are figuring out how to use natural resources sparingly. Economists work on getting prices right, by correctly valuing nature.

The more we know about how ecosystems function, the better able we are to produce in ways that support rather than degrade them. Ecological knowledge includes the expertise to farm in earth-friendly ways, to harness the power of wind, sun, and geothermal energy, to make products without toxins or heavy metals, and to reuse materials over and over. In the industrial era, humans lost touch with much of what they knew about how to tap nature's bounty without destroying it. Moreover, we failed to make much progress in generating sophisticated new ecological knowledge, in comparison with the pace of discovery in other fields. Given the state of the planet, there is now an urgent need to develop and then spread this ecological knowledge as rapidly as possible. The best way to do this will be to move away from proprietary systems of information and technology toward open-source mechanisms of knowledge transfer. As with other aspects of plenitude, this is a shift that's already under way, because it makes economic sense.

One way to think about it is that we're heading into a world in which much of the cost of production will be the up-front brain work of ecologically driven design. Horticulturist Eric Fleisher, one of the originators of Harvard University's organic overhaul of its extensive lawns and grounds, put it succinctly: "This is not a product-based program, it's knowledge-based." Rather than purchasing fertilizers and pesticides, the caretakers learned about nitrogen cycling and organisms such as fungi and bacteria that nourish plants. The trees are thriving, the grass is lush and green, and water use has been slashed.

Lawn care is just one example. Stabilizing the climate and regenerating ecosystems will require a widespread shift into ways of producing and consuming that minimize resource use, curtail negative pollutants such as carbon dioxide, and manage without toxic substances. As I described in chapter 3, designers, architects, and technological visionaries have been busy inventing these earth-friendly ways of producing, designing, and building. But we're still at the beginning of the process. Today's hybrid vehicles, wind turbines, and organic farming are a huge leap forward from what we had been doing, but they will be seen as primitive in not too many years. Prototypes and pilots of a host of promising technologies and products are in process. Some will succeed. Others will be way stations on the road to something better. Some will just be interesting ideas that failed. We need to proliferate all of these like wildfire.

Economics has mainly been absent from this design discussion, addressing itself instead to policies that shift incentives. Its strategy is to mobilize the power of profit-oriented businesses by using government policies to price natural resources as if they were ordinary assets. Internalize the environmental externalities and let the market work. This will reduce emissions, but will it deliver a closed-loop (zero-waste) system? It seems unlikely. Unless the tax on pollution is prohibitively high, the pricing method doesn't eliminate ecological degradation; it merely results in a lower level of impact, by forcing consumers and producers to bear the costs. It has also been vulnerable to the expansion of dirty production in poorer countries. We need a better plan that does not short-change the creation and spread of ecological knowledge. In addition to funding for research and development, the usual approach, we've got to think about how innovations spread. We're facing a planetary emergency: the cost and speed with which knowledge is shared could literally determine the fate of our species and many others.

That's where the economics of knowledge, or information, comes in. The conditions for efficient production, dissemination, and ownership of knowledge are radically different from those for private goods. The standard efficiency rule for private goods is that their market price should be equal to their marginal cost, that is, the cost of making the last batch. With information, there is zero or minimal cost of producing additional, or "marginal," copies of a blueprint, code, or manual. Therefore, it is inefficient to restrict access, make proprietary, confine to the market, or otherwise establish a price above the cost of replication. New learning can only add, not subtract, from the stock of knowledge and production capability in the world. It must therefore be a net boost to wealth. The implications of this point are obviously far-reaching.

Yet the exclusion of information is widespread, through copyrights, patents, and trademarks. Why do law and public policy allow this inefficiency? One answer is that profit-making, rather than efficiency, drives policy. Companies and individuals reap the benefits of exclusive information, and have had the political power to get patent protection and other laws that maintain their ability to do that, despite the harms these policies can create. Advocates of exclusiveness have also advanced a counterargument to the standard reasoning. They argue that without restrictions, companies and individuals won't generate new knowledge, or will generate less, so that over time the economy will suffer. The reasoning is that keeping information proprietary provides more incentive for research and innovation. This point of view has dominated for much of the recent past, as copyrights and patents have been extended for longer periods of time over more things.

But exclusion has also been controversial, and it's not hard to see why. It's socially inefficient to restrict the transmission of know-how. Furthermore, the reasoning about innovation, or what is termed dynamic efficiency, goes both ways. Giving wider access to yesterday's discoveries spurs tomorrow's, because past discoveries are the building blocks for further innovation in what's called the "on the shoulders of giants" effect. Keeping market newcomers from standing on those shoulders slows down innovation. There's also the possibility that private companies can buy up and then bury discoveries because they threaten existing lines of business. The stakes are too high to leave urgent public needs to private interests. They don't always coincide. Critics of exclusion note that people invent for a variety of reasons, rather than just money, and that there are less costly ways of promoting research and development than locking up lifesaving drugs, valuable knowledge, and cost-cutting code.

In software, the controversy is partly being settled by practice. The meteoric rise of open-source platforms, with examples such as Linux, Apache, Mozilla, and Wikipedia, is eroding the rationale for costly and exclusionary information. As activity migrates to the open-access and collaboration model, the case for accessibility is strengthening. On a mass scale, individuals are collaborating and making their contributions freely available to others. Harvard University's Yochai Benkler, author of the influential *The Wealth of Networks*, argues that social sharing and exchange has become common across a wide swath of the economy—in the information, culture, education, computation, and communications sectors.

The desirability of open access is one way the economics of knowledge differs from that of ordinary private goods. Analysts of what is now called the knowledge commons have identified others, such as motivation. Widespread participation in the creation of software, online book reviews, and the posting of YouTube videos is occurring because people enjoy this work, desire peer recognition, and want to contribute to the public good, and not because they expect monetary reward. In its online form, this has been dubbed peer production, but more generally it is referred to as nonmarket, commons, or social production. One of the reasons it happens is that people devote their time off the job to these projects, in small and large chunks.

The shift to a knowledge-intensive economy has implications for the ideal structure of enterprises and how they relate to one another. The emergence of the Internet, with its radically different economic practices, has already dealt a serious blow to the dominance of large corporate ownership with restrictive access. Decentralized, or distributed, production becomes more efficient as individuals and small groups connect through voluntary networks, rather than the large command-and-control enterprises we call corporations. This is how Linux, Wikipedia, and a growing number of extraordinary products have been developed. Belief in the viability of an alternative production model is growing among the technorati, as Benkler argues: "The networked environment makes possible a new modality of organizing production: radically decentralized, collaborative and nonproprietary; based on sharing resources and outputs among widely distributed, locally connected individuals who cooperate with each other without relying on either market signals or managerial comments."

If I am right that knowledge is the scarce resource in the transition to sustainability, then it's a limiting factor in the growth of the clean sector. Overcoming that scarcity by letting green know-how flow as freely as possible will be wealth-generating and socially efficient. A collectively managed open-source process allows new knowledge to be transmitted rapidly among networked individuals and small groups who are motivated to provide value and save the planet. Innovators can be rewarded through payments for customized applications and support, as well as through public and philanthropic funds. (The competitive prize model is one popular option.) Hybrid structures that incorporate sharing and collaboration will become increasingly attractive and financially viable. There will be enhanced value in a pattern of work and leisure that gives people enough free time to participate. This isn't just a feel-good story. It characterizes a real, growing, and economically intelligent sector.

A teeming knowledge commons also allows for ongoing learning. In the Harvard lawn example, the university would post its techniques online for anyone to use. Networked individuals and firms disseminate the information and add whatever they've figured out as they adapt the methods to local conditions. Improvements are incorporated through a peer-production process that includes review. Permaculturalists and other enthusiasts promulgate the technology in the free time they have recovered by following the plenitude model. It's a parallel economy to the for-profit market. It grows alongside that market, accelerates the speed of transition, and transforms what's happening in BAU firms. After all, IBM did adopt Linux.

Plenitude practitioners have begun to apply these ideas. Factor e Farm is a group dedicated to building the "world's first self replicating self-sufficient, open source, decentralized, high-appropriate-tech resilient permaculture ecovillage." (The *e* is a reference to the transcendent mathematical constant *e* and a play on the word *factory*). Working from a converted soybean field outside Kansas City, Factor e Farm combines innovations in small-scale manufacturing with knowledge-intensive agriculture. They're using a fab lab to build what they call a Global Village Construction Set—a step-by-step guide for replicating a self-sufficient, completely sustainable community requiring minimal financial capital. With just scrap metal and plastics, the fab lab technology enables the machines to replicate themselves, obviating the purchase of costly capital equipment. They've already developed and built machines such as the Liberator 2, which makes the compressed earth bricks used to construct the buildings, and the Life Trac, a steam-powered multipurpose tractor. Both can be built at very low cost, and they will be freely replicable by others. Participants are hoping to bring these innovations to market soon, and are working on a number of other high-tech, low-materials inventions such as an egg-hatching system, raised-bed organoponic gardening, and a micro-combine, a multipurpose farming machine that can cut, thresh, and winnow. The basic machinery is highly adaptable, which allows the group to proceed with a variety of inventions. Volunteers on- and off-site take on these projects and work on them through the open-source process. The effort is a combination of high-tech innovation, self-providing, and technological diffusion. The farm's founder, Marcin Jakubowski, uses the term *neocommercialization* to describe the business model: "It means that we can both 'commercialize' a product—make it available for sale at competitive prices to others—and help others replicate the enterprise itself. We are interested not only in production, but also in business replication by others, because it's good for the world."

The Factor e Farm may or may not succeed. But it's interesting because it has zeroed in on features that can lead to a rapidly expanding green sector. It relies on open-source plans for constructing novel machinery and techniques, and on an open-dissemination mechanism once the innovations are complete. Second, the capital requirements for the innovations are low. The initial fab lab technology is relatively inexpensive, and production relies on low-cost or free materials such as scrap metal, plastics, and soil. The open source 3-D

"printer" called the RepRap, which makes objects, can almost replicate itself at minimal cost. Low capital requirements are essential,
because financing is frequently a barrier, especially with unproven
technologies. The fact that these innovations are cheap makes them
accessible to small businesses, the unemployed, and low-income
communities, as well as appropriate for diffusion in the Global South.
Given the recent performance of the centralized financial system, there's an obvious appeal to solutions that do not depend on
significant sums of money from large financial institutions or the government. Finally, the approach relies on small, decentralized units,
communicating online. Scale is one of the big questions about an
economic system that we've also got to address.

Small Is Beautiful, but Is It Efficient?

The twentieth century was unquestionably the era of bigness. The
mass production model was pioneered in automobiles, and then expanded across manufacturing. Companies installed dedicated, or
single-purpose, machinery capable of churning out enormous numbers of cheap products. As the decades passed, the assembly lines
moved faster and the companies got larger. Farms, mines, retail outlets, and other service-sector entities also expanded. Manufacturing
eventually shifted to vast factory complexes in Asia.

When mainstream economists have addressed scale, they tended
to interpret the growth in the size of production facilities and companies as evidence of superior efficiency, or what are termed economies of scale. This perspective typically ignored environmental
impacts, such as the emissions associated with long-distance transport. If there was a worry, it was about such large concentrations of
market and political power, one consequence of which is the "too big

to fail" dilemma that has resulted in taxpayer bailouts of reckless financial institutions and failing automobile companies.

Beginning in the late 1970s, a productivity slowdown and squeeze on corporate profitability led to questions about whether the mass production model had outlived its usefulness. Two MIT political economists, Michael Piore and Charles Sabel, began studying small-scale manufacturing, including a group of advanced, design-intensive manufacturing firms in the Emilia Romagna region of Italy that were achieving impressive results. One dimension of their success was computerized, multipurpose machinery that obviated the hugely expensive dedicated-capital equipment of the mass production era. These machines allowed for more flexible responses to market demand than did the industrial behemoths, so the model was termed flexible (rather than mass) production. To overcome some of the drawbacks of small size, the companies formed networks to share functions such as training, research and development, and marketing. Piore and Sabel predicted an industrial future of these small but networked production units. As they envisioned, start-ups and small firms, clustering in geographical proximity, have been remarkably successful in information technology, biomedical, and other fields.

So the era of "bigger is better" may have finally ended. Certainly the presumption in favor of bigness is harder to defend now than it was fifty years ago. There's a growing constituency for small, including adherents of the network model, a hybrid that transcends the simple large-versus-small dichotomy.

The literature on size and economic performance does not speak with one voice. Results are often industry-specific, and vary by time period, country, and the variable being measured. It's difficult for researchers to keep up with the pace of technological development as software and multipurpose manufacturing machines revolutionize small-scale production. We do know that small businesses have been at the forefront of innovation and employment growth. In recent years, nearly two thirds of all jobs have been created by firms with fewer than five hundred employees. And recession-induced job loss has become more prevalent in large than small companies.

This history provides a prima facie case that the emerging green sector will be powered by small and medium-size firms, with their agility, dynamism, and entrepreneurial determination. The rising cost of energy will favor more local and regional economies made up of smaller firms. The export-led, fossil-fuel-dependent globalization of the last few decades has relied on artificially cheap long-distance transport, and that is unlikely to continue. The economic collapse of 2008 and its aftermath also highlighted the vulnerabilities associated with centralization. As the system came crashing down, it was apparent how much damage a few institutions could wreak on the whole. If it is true that there will be heightened instability on account of climatic, ecological, and market fluctuations, decentralization should create more resilience and containment of adverse events. Biologists' findings that more diverse systems are more resilient and adaptable are relevant to economies as diversity is nurtured through local adaptation.

The counterargument is that big firms can move expeditiously. When Wal-Mart decided to reduce its footprint, it was able to affect its suppliers' practices quickly. This may be the most compelling argument in favor of large size. When the big actors do decide to move mountains, they bring enormous resources to the table. Conversely, that power can be deployed to block progress, as we have witnessed with ExxonMobil and other large companies regarding climate change.

Whatever the ultimate fate of the large corporations, there's enormous potential in the plenitude model. Practitioners are freed up to start new production, either as individuals or in groups, especially in areas such as energy, food, culture, software, information, and light manufacturing. Over time these entities can become a sizable sector of low-impact enterprises, which form the basis of animated local communities and provide livelihood on a wide scale. Such a vision of revitalized local economies anchored in a dense network of small and medium-size businesses is at the heart of cutting-edge sustainability thinking.

Will the large corporations absorb, neutralize, or even destroy these upstart competitors? There's no simple answer to that question. If small is more efficient, as I think it can be, that gives it an edge, although there's always the threat of buyout. The political-economic context is also relevant. The giants are favored on account of their enormous political power, which in turn yields government subsidies. It'll be crucial to cut off the flow from that spigot and move policy in the direction of promotion and protection of small firms. The more the small sector can organize itself to push for fair, or even preferential, treatment, the more secure its future will be.

If starting an economic revolution from individuals and small-scale activities sounds unrealistic, it's worth remembering that the first industrial revolution in Britain developed in just this manner. What became the powerhouse companies in textiles, potteries, shoes, and other manufactures began from individual craftspeople working on a small scale, in workshops and homes. Enterprising, strategic, and lucky ones, like Josiah Wedgwood, remain known even today.

Natural Assets and Shared Ownership

As national and global economies attempt to emerge from the slowdown, they are faced with the question of where replacements for disappearing jobs and businesses will come from. In the wealthy countries, much of the thinking centers on alternative energy, services, software, and high tech. But there's another source of jobs and value that should be front and center in our planning: the restoration of natural assets. Nature is an input into all production, and its degradation raises costs. Less fertile soil leads to less food production. Cleaning up toxins in brownfields and waterways, nourishing depleted forests, replenishing water supplies, and enhancing biodiversity all generate wealth. Pollution-induced asthma, cancers, and birth defects result in expensive health care. Provided climate change doesn't spiral out of control, wreaking havoc on ecosystems in its wake, restoration is a smart strategy. The next economic era needs to be devoted to restoring the capacity of the earth to support humans and other life forms.

Ecological regeneration is also a solution to another of the most pressing economic problems we face: extreme inequality and poverty. More than half the world's population lives on less than $2.50 a day. As the climate warms, that fraction will rise, due to declining crop yields, further collapse of fish stocks, loss of coastline, water scarcity, and higher energy prices. Even in the wealthy United States, a large portion of the population is without economic assets. In 2004, 30 percent of households had less than twelve thousand dollars in net worth. The bottom 90 percent owned only 29 percent of total net worth, compared with the 34 percent going to just the top 1 percent. (Financial wealth is even more unequally distributed.) Since the downturn, the picture has worsened as millions have been pushed out of the middle class, poverty has accelerated, and households are being stripped of decent livelihoods. Most of the attention has been focused on income, but long-term earning power, financial stability, and well-being depend on access to economic assets.

Some of the most important environmental economic research in the last decade has studied the impacts of regenerating natural assets. Pioneered by researchers such as University of Massachusetts economist James Boyce, Indian environmentalists Anil Agarwal and Sunita Narain, and others, this work has found that income and human well-being expand when degraded land, water, and ecosystems are cleaned up and repurposed by the people who live on and around them. An array of case studies from around the world show that converting a vacant lot into urban businesses, planting a marketable crop on an abandoned field, installing a water-harvesting system to raise agricultural yields, and reforestation are ways to lift people out of poverty, empower communities, and heal the earth.

Part of the economic potency of this strategy is that it transforms unowned or devalued nature into community-managed, income-producing property. In impoverished tribal areas in India, villages in water-scarce regions have come together for watershed management and rainwater collection, and begun to share water fairly. This in turn has led to higher crop yields, the expansion and harvesting of grasses with cash value, and the chance to enhance animal husbandry. (Some villages have been able to shift from goats to more lucrative milk-producing buffalo.) In other cases, degraded and worthless government-owned land has been transferred to poor villagers who have planted restorative crops that they've then sold. Areas that once resembled moonscapes now support trees.

Boston's pioneering Dudley Street Neighborhood Initiative gained title to unused urban lots through eminent domain and from the city government, and the land was used to revitalize a blighted neighborhood. They began with an intensive community planning process, and have succeeded in converting more than half the abandoned lots to new uses, including housing, community centers, parks, playgrounds, schools, a greenhouse, and an orchard, as well as a town common. They've got a community land trust and are fulfilling their dream of creating a lively urban village.

The case studies reveal that ecological regeneration can create assets that yield ongoing income streams, which can be held by either communities or individuals. Giving community members secure access to land for cultivation creates the potential to produce food and income. Other elements of success include mobilizing surplus time among the un- and underemployed, a transparent, democratic process for participation, and a legal and policy framework that ensures benefits flow to participants, rather than being siphoned off by private interests or the government. These cases chronicle not just double dividends, but triple wins, lifting people out of poverty, building natural capital, and giving political voice to disenfranchised groups. The natural-assets literature also highlights a new type of ecological property that can be created: shares in the atmospheric commons. If polluters were charged for emissions, and citizens had rights to those revenues, it would be the equivalent of creating a new ecological asset in atmosphere. The Sky Trust proposal put forward by Peter Barnes calls for the revenue collected from greenhouse gas emitters to be returned to citizens, on a per capita basis, like the Alaska Permanent Fund.

Enhancements to natural capital generate returns for decades, even centuries, and can be used to support communities. Ecological historians have found that prior human investments in ecosystems, sometimes mistakenly considered "natural," have yielded long-term benefits. Ancient farmers stirred charcoal residues into soil and created the superrich, superfertile dark earth (*terra preta*) that is believed to cover 10 percent of the Amazon basin. Valuable forest islands within West African savannas were once thought to be remnants of forested areas, but are now known to be nineteenth-century human constructions situated within grasslands to conserve water and provide shade and timber. Today's investments include such examples as the regeneration of prairie in Nebraska, cleanup of the Hudson River, and dam removal in the Pacific Northwest. The shift from monocropping to diversified farming rebuilds a local-food system and provides livelihoods for the farmers and small businesses that connect to it. Enhancing crop diversity improves the soil and can support heirloom varieties with high market value. Remodeling an abandoned factory or mill provides living space, shops, restaurants, and offices that serve a regional economy.

Natural-asset projects have been centered in low-income communities. But the strategy is more broadly relevant, and can be used to invest in an array of productive ecological assets, including those that are not severely degraded. Plenitude is key to this process. Research on the management of natural assets shows that social capital is a condition for success. Plenitude lifestyles reclaim time, so people can reinvigorate their social connections, build community, and work together on investments in local and regional ecosystems. Sustainability groups operating at the local and regional levels are already part of networked efforts to influence economic development, pushing for community investments with public payoffs.

A commonwealth approach is a departure from the usual debates about inequality, which center on income rather than assets, and redistribution rather than expansion of wealth. After-the-fact taxation that redirects skewed market outcomes was once the dominant approach to inequality, but it has become less popular as its drawbacks surfaced. Neoliberal ideology has predisposed many to view market outcomes as natural or even fair, and has obscured the underlying biases, subsidies, and distortions associated with current market rules and structures. Interventions that create more equality in the initial distribution of assets or restructure flawed rules are more likely to yield fairer market outcomes that need less ex post facto tinkering.

These examples also raise issues of how to own and manage commons. History provides sophisticated examples of hybrid property rights regimes, including shared property systems that incorporate elements of both private and collectively held systems, and take us beyond simplistic debates over private versus state ownership. The Boston College economic historian Prasannan Parthasarathi has described how in eighteenth-century South India, agricultural groups shared the risk and bounty of each season, as in a common property system, but also maintained individual, transferable property rights to future harvests. Similar arrangements can be found in cooperatives, partnerships, and other modern economic enterprises. The beauty of these systems is that on a small enough scale they produce incentives for productivity and sustainable use of resources.

Natural asset regeneration projects can also benefit the knowledge economy. An active open-source process can lead to a great upskilling of green knowledge. New forms of skill acquisition are already under way. Community-based environmental justice groups such as Sustainable South Bronx, Green for All, and Green Worker Cooperatives have begun to train low-income and minority individuals in river restoration, installations of green roofs, home insulation, hazardous-waste removal, and related activities. A National Science Foundation–funded "GreenFab" collaboration between Sustainable South Bronx and New York University has been teaching low-income and minority high school students about fab lab technology and its applications to sustainability.

These initiatives will create pressure within markets for a more equal income distribution, because wages flow in significant part from skill levels. The more widely these new knowledges and skills are dispersed, the less skewed the distribution of wages will be. A green upskilling will begin to reverse the growing inequality that has characterized the labor market over recent decades, and reduce the need for redistributive policies to correct excessive inequality generated by market processes.

An informal education network has developed to foster permaculture, agroforestry, and biodynamic farming; cob, earthen, straw-bale, and other alternative construction; and solar and wind energy, biofuels, and other new ways of creating livelihood and meeting basic needs. Much of the skill transmission happens in short courses and workshops, under the auspices of a growing number of institutes, hands-on classes, and collaborative learning communities.

Master practitioners pass on what they have learned. Skills are also being transmitted by books, videos, and open-source online information. There's a lot of learning by doing, including efforts to get the techniques to more sophisticated levels. Some of the recently founded institutes have begun offering degrees. There is still relatively open access to these emergent skill sets, a feature that it is essential to retain.

It's difficult to overstate the importance of this skill acquisition. It will make possible the expansion of high-productivity self-provisioning and spur novel sources of livelihood that develop into successful businesses. Wider access to nature-complementing skills is also the basis of a fairer distribution of property, income, and, by extension, political and social power.

Jobs and Hours: The Shorter-Hours Imperative

U.S. companies have been shedding labor at a dizzying rate. By October 2009, 8 million jobs had already been destroyed and one in six workers was unemployed or underemployed. To put these people back to work and accommodate a growing population, the economy would have to generate an astounding half million jobs every month for the next two years. That will not happen. With the exception of exports and stimulus funds, there are few bright spots in the employment picture. Anemic consumer demand, ongoing technological change, outsourcing, and global competition will slow job creation.

Even in normal times, the economy must continually reabsorb workers whose jobs are lost due to technological advances. When productivity rises, a given level of production can be achieved with fewer workers. The classic case is agriculture, which now employs only about 1.4 percent of the American workforce, while it once comprised roughly three quarters. The history of manufacturing is similar. Productivity growth has dramatically reduced the person-hours required to make a car, television, or computer. The auto companies, for all their failures, have shed labor at a rapid rate. In recent years, companies in the service sector have been able to use technology to get rapid productivity growth as well, whether it's in the areas of customer service, data management, or calculation. Since 1973, productivity has almost doubled in the nonfarm business sector. And there are two technological revolutions now in view: continued labor displacement from the use of information technology and the beginnings of the shift to eco-efficiency. Jobs will be lost in outmoded energy sectors, as well as other failing industries and companies. Where will all these people go, and how will they get employment?

For at least 150 years, the market economy has used growth to absorb the labor that it sheds through technological change and industrial decline. Displaced farmhands found jobs in northern auto factories. Out-of-work autoworkers found positions in hospitals and educational institutions. New companies, products, and industries develop and pull in some of the jobless. Existing businesses expand by taking over their failed competitors. More than half a century ago, economists debated whether it would be possible to maintain enough jobs for all who needed them, but over time, the market has displayed a remarkable capacity to draw the unemployed back into its orbit.

This solution is no longer available in the way that it has been historically. Bumping up against planetary boundaries means that BAU growth as the way out of unemployment, at either the national or the global level, is folly. Much of it would be growth in name only. Furthermore, economic globalization also means that the new job opportunities may not be located where the unemployed live. That's especially likely in the United States, where wages are high. This means the amount of extra GNP needed to create an additional job is greater than in the past, making growth a less efficient generator of jobs.

So we need to use productivity growth differently and reduce the number of hours associated with each job. This allows businesses to innovate without laying off personnel, cushions declines in sales, and results in more positions when demand expands. Reducing hours per job may sound slightly exotic, but it's what happened in response to the technological change of the nineteenth and twentieth centuries. Hours of work in the United States began to decline after about 1870, at which point they were nearly 3,000 a year. By 1929 hours had fallen by more than 600, to 2,342. In 1973 hours stood at 1,887, 1,077 below where they had been a century earlier. This is the equivalent of a half-time job, on the assumption of a forty-hour week. (Forty hours for a full year is 2,080 hours.) If hours hadn't fallen, structural unemployment would have grown even before the 1930s Depression.

The experience of other wealthy countries was similar. Between 1870 and 1973, the United Kingdom experienced a decline of 1,065

FIGURE 5.1 Historical Changes in Working Hours, 1870 to 1973

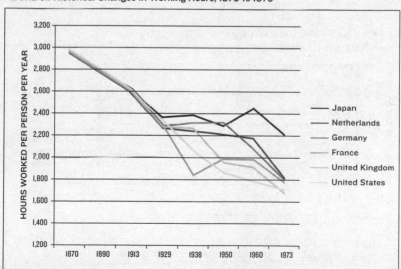

Source: Maddison (1987), "Table A-9: Hours Worked Per Person Per Year," p. 686

hours, France 922, Germany 1,071, the Netherlands 1,141, and Japan 779. Reducing hours in tandem with productivity growth allowed prosperity to be broadly shared and helped build the middle class. The grueling schedules of the nineteenth century undermined health and prevented people from achieving what we now call quality of life. For much of the industrial age, it hasn't only been growth that accounted for the reabsorption of surplus labor. Falling hours have been roughly as important a contributor to employment.

Despite this history, economists' focus is almost solely on growth as a mechanism for job creation. Reductions in hours are usually ignored, or opposed on grounds that they impair competitiveness or are not desired by workers. (According to the conventional model, if people wanted shorter hours, they'd already have gotten them, because markets are assumed to operate "perfectly.") The question of competitiveness is an important one, but it's hourly costs that matter, or more accurately, labor costs per unit of production, not the total number of hours worked by each person. Some of the most efficient and competitive manufacturing sectors in the world, such as Germany,

FIGURE 5.2 Recent Changes in Working Hours, 1973 to 2007

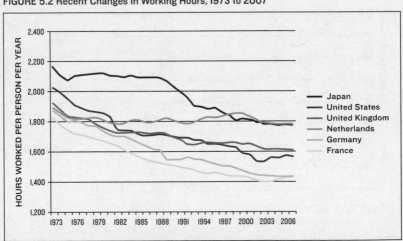

Source: Groningen Total Economy Database (2008), Annual Hours Worked

the Netherlands, and Sweden, have short hours but high productivity per hour worked. In fact, long hours can be a sign of inefficiency. Typically, reductions in daily hours are associated with a rise in productivity per hour, as work is done more intensively and intelligently. So shorter hours are also a wealth-creating, as well as a wealth-sharing, solution.

In the 1970s, the United States veered off its historical trajectory, in contrast to other wealthy nations. According to one widely used data source, between 1973 and 2007, the continental countries of France, Germany, and the Netherlands reduced annual hours in the neighborhood of 400 hours. (The figures are 453, 437, and 389 hours respectively.) The United Kingdom had a decline of 306, Japan 381. Most wealthy countries followed a similar trajectory. But the United States was different. U.S. hours barely fell between 1973 and 2000 (32 hours). They have declined 78 hours since then, due in part to the two downturns of the twenty-first century, yielding a total decline of 110 since 1973. (This data understates the case, in comparison to other sources, such as the household data I presented in the previous chapter. That measure includes multiple job-holding and self-employment, and shows that since 1973 work time has risen by 204 hours.)

In the United States, the hours-reduction process stalled out for a number of reasons, including ballooning health care costs (which are an incentive to keep head count down and hours up), rising inequality, intensified demands from employers, and the erosion of purchasing power among hourly workers. According to the household surveys, in the last half century the only interval in which U.S. hours actually fell was 1967–1973, now a distant memory.

This history makes the task of achieving a viable economy much harder. If we don't reengage the process of reductions in hours, it's likely that unemployment will grow, as the available work is concentrated in too few jobs. One hopeful sign is that many employers responded to the downturn by reducing hours and instigating furloughs. The key is to maintain a flexible structure of hours, and support shorter schedules as the economy begins to revive. This is the work-sharing dimension of hours reduction. If average hours per job fall, then for any given level of production, more workers will be needed.

The other reason we need to get back on the shorter-hours path is ecological, a point that sustainability advocates increasingly recognize. Along with economic revival will come productivity growth—the ability to produce a given amount of output with fewer inputs. Some of it will be growth in the productivity of natural assets achieved by the switch to clean tech. Labor productivity will also increase, especially in the early phases of the recovery. If the freed-up hours are used to expand output, they'll cause more ecological degradation. The alternative is to produce the same amount in less time, which puts less pressure on the planet. It's a far cry from austerity, because it doesn't involve doing with less, only forgoing additions to income, an important distinction.

Beyond Physophilia

In the last three decades, pressures for economic growth have intensified as a result of what has been called the financialization of the United States economy: the expanding reach and power of Wall Street and other financial entities, relative to the nonfinancial businesses that provide goods and services. When companies borrow money, or become more highly leveraged, they need bigger profits, because they have to use them not only to improve productivity but also to pay off their bankers. As financialization has proceeded, Wall Street has applied more pressure to deliver short-term results and higher profits. It is now widely recognized how detrimental this has been to the economy, by undermining the ability of companies to invest for the long run, to manage a sustainable rate of growth, and to act in ways that preserve the larger human and natural environments they need to survive. Finance-mandated expansion has been a destructive force that has decimated and bankrupted many once-healthy companies.

The process of financialization raises larger questions about economic policy. Data on the state of planetary ecosystems and the arithmetic of the IPAT formulation that I reviewed in chapter 3 suggests that the imperatives of achieving a safe climate target and a reversal of ecosystem degradation will be hard, if not impossible, to reconcile with current growth aspirations. But there's a widespread belief that a market, or capitalist, economy must grow. It's a point of view that's often held without much thought. However, when we look more closely, the growth imperative is on less solid ground than is generally realized. There's not much in economic theory that actually requires growth. The measure used to determine when growth is occurring is widely acknowledged to be badly flawed. And there's now a voluminous literature casting doubt on the once-sacrosanct link between income growth and well-being. It's time to become far more discriminating, and reframe the debate to figure out what needs to grow and what needs to shrink.

To unpack the growth imperative, we can start by differentiating among households, firms, and the economy as a whole. Households (or individuals) are the easiest case. In its most abstract form, mainstream economic theory centers on the idea that people maximize their well-being, and that they do so through exchanges with others. The influential formulations of Gary Becker and the Chicago school hold that this economic approach to human behavior can be applied to anything. People can decide that what matters most to them is preserving nature, raising children, or having a leisurely work environment. Income growth is in no way integral to or even implied by the model. Evidence of widespread downshifting, or voluntary trade-offs of money for time, makes clear that maximizing income is by no means a universal desire.

While "human nature" is often invoked as an explanation for maximally acquisitive behavior, the evolutionary psychology literature supporting this position falls short of being convincing. There is strong evidence that humans, like other species, engage in status competitions. However, status markers differ across times and places, and human societies exhibit widespread differences in their predilection to compete over consumer goods and income. The extent of consumption-based competition appears to vary with the distribution of income, for example, which is hardly an evolutionary variable. Decades of research show a decline in materialist values in a range of countries. Indeed, as the maximal growth model is increasingly shown to be courting ecological disaster, one might argue that simplicity has become an evolutionarily superior trait.

The growth imperative is assumed to operate more strongly for firms, and "grow or die" is a common mantra. But here, too, it's worth parsing the logic. In the standard model, which assumes competitive markets, what matters for companies is their productivity and per-unit costs. Efficient companies survive and thrive. Inefficient ones fail. Efficiency and size are related, of course, but not linearly. Some firms are too small to take advantage of the lower unit costs, or economies of scale, they could achieve if they grew. Others get too big and bureaucratic to be wieldy. Bigness can also result in market power that becomes a rip-off of consumers.

It may be difficult to conceive of a company prospering without growing, but consider the situation of a small mom-and-pop operation. Each year it has costs and revenues, and the difference between the two is profit (or loss). The owners can use their profits to upgrade their machinery or software, or lower costs in other ways. But they don't face a growth imperative. If the business is generating a decent living, it can operate at the same size for years. Productivity improvements, rather than size itself, are the key to success. That logic applies to many kinds of businesses, far more than people realize. While many argue that business expansion is necessary to retain market share, the logic behind that view is not compelling. Leaving aside market power, competitors are successful when they offer better quality for a given price. To keep up, they need to reinvest their profits in order to upgrade operations and reduce costs. Over time, competitive position is mainly a matter of productivity growth and efficiency. Once a business is large enough to achieve economies of scale, the growth imperative dissipates. If I am right that the optimal size of the firm is falling, the economy would be better served with a larger number of smaller firms. Many companies have operated profitably and successfully at a more or less stable size for years and even decades.

There's also a large sector of businesses that are not subject to the profit imperative on account of their ownership structure. The University of Maryland political economist Gar Alperovitz has studied employee-owned companies, cooperatives, and credit unions and notes that in 2003, there were more than 48,000 cooperatives, 11,000 firms with employee stock ownership plans, nearly 4,000 community development corporations, and countless business ventures owned and operated by states, municipalities, and nonprofits.

Not coincidentally, these are entities that are less reliant on Wall Street and big banks. Financialization boosts the required growth rate of an economy, in order to pay both bankers and shareholders. But rather than accept a finance-dominated economy as a natural state, we'd do well to remember that this shift has been relatively recent (post-1980), and it has been a key factor in the hollowing out of much of the manufacturing base of the nation. Popular anger against Wall Street may be partly reflecting this understanding. In any case, returning to a world in which profits fund investment and business expansion is likely to be not only ecologically beneficial but also a route to a healthier domestic economy.

The dangers of an exaggerated sense of urgency about growth have been recognized by the Slow Money movement. The movement's founder, Woody Tasch, a venture capitalist and entrepreneur, argues that we need to bring our fast financial system "down to earth" in order to reconnect money with soil, sustainable food systems, and local businesses. In a Slow Money regime, people invest where they live, for the long term, and in ways that enrich the soil, communities, and human welfare. Participants in the Slow Money movement are values investors, cousins of the growing number of conscious consumers who seek out and pay a bit more for products that are fair trade, sweat-free, organic, or local.

Will savers really accept lower returns than they can get from large corporations? The socially responsible investment sector provides a real-world affirmative answer. (Although it's also true that socially responsible investing can be more, not less, profitable.) But there's another reason that a shift to slower paybacks could happen. Now that Keynes is back in vogue, we may remember that not only did he believe in deficit financing, but he understood that investors were psychological beings whose expectations of returns were socially adaptable. He anticipated that over time, market economies would gravitate to slower rates of growth, and as a consequence, investors would reduce the returns they were looking for. There is no magic, or "natural," rate of return that must be paid.

The bottom line on firms is that in a market economy, some expand while others do not. If we transition to a smaller scale of production, there will be less pressure to grow for growth's sake. If we transition to a less centralized financial system and the power of Wall Street abates, the mandate to grow, especially in risky ways, will also abate. And if we transition to a Slow Money system, we can mobilize the power of finance to regenerate our food systems, local economies, and communities. Then we'll be growing with intelligence, expanding the things that truly give us health and benefit, and shifting out of destructive activities.

Finally, do we need what economists call aggregate growth, which is usually defined as the expansion of GDP? GDP itself is a seriously distorted measure, as has been recognized for decades and was reemphasized in late 2009 in a major study led by the Nobel Prize–winning economists Joseph Stiglitz and Amartya Sen. GDP measures only marketed activity. It leaves out reductions in the stocks of natural capital. It ignores changes in leisure time. If air pollution is impairing the health of a population, it counts their medical expenditures as an addition, but fails to add a corresponding negative tally for their deteriorating health status. It's an increasingly antiquated metric, which is why alternatives, such as the Human Development Index, the World Bank's genuine saving estimates, the genuine progress indicator, and the ecological footprint have been developed. If we do need aggregate growth, it has to be measured by something far more defensible.

Measurement aside, there are two reasons aggregate growth might matter. The first is to create jobs to assimilate the unemployed and anticipate increases in population. The second is to improve living standards. Economic logic does not require overall expansion to achieve either of these objectives. An expanding labor force can be accommodated if hours of work fall. And it's productivity growth, rather than the overall size of the economy, that drives improvements in living standards. It may seem counterintuitive, but consider for a moment that productivity is a measure of how much can be produced in an hour of work. The size of the economy is, roughly, that measure times the total number of hours worked. Getting bigger doesn't necessarily yield wealth; improving productivity does. This is one of the fundamental insights of economic thinking that curiously has almost dropped out of the conversation as economists, politicians, and the public got swept up in the physophilia, or love of growth, of the post–World War II era. Productivity-driven improvements in well-being can be attained in a number of ways: by gaining leisure, by changing the mix of products, by saving natural resources. Indeed, if we define aggregate growth in ecological, rather than dollar, terms, the link between expansion and living standards is even more tenuous, and may be negative.

But can we slow down painlessly, without disruption to employment and incomes? That's a question environmentalists and even some economists are beginning to pay attention to. In 2008, the first International DeGrowth Conference was held in Paris under the auspices of the European Society for Ecological Economics. Modeling exercises on this question remain scarce, but the ecological economist Peter Victor used a conventional model of the Canadian economy to figure out whether a planned reduction in growth would be feasible. He found one thing we know already. A simple cessation of growth is a disaster, as unemployment and poverty soar, and income per person falls. That's not too far from what happened in the United States and elsewhere in 2008. But with a modest amount of policy tinkering, much better outcomes emerge. If working hours fall, unemployment declines and free time rises. Poverty can even be reduced, if the government transfers some income to the poor. What may be most surprising is the validation of the point I made above: income per head can improve without expansion of the overall size of the economy, through higher investment. This in turn raises productivity and well-being. It's how efficiently we produce, not how much we produce, that determines how well off we are. Victor also worked through scenarios for taxing carbon, and showed that emissions can fall even as the economy produces rising GDP per person, declining unemployment and poverty, and a reduction in government debt.

Victor's model doesn't incorporate a shift out of polluting energy and our industrialized food system. If it did, the results would be even stronger, because nature-saving technologies and patterns of consumption open up additional possibilities for achieving well-being without fast growth. The green economy yields more employment per unit of GDP. A recent study finds that investments in alternative energy produce 3.2 times the employment per dollar spent than in the capital-intensive fossil fuel sector. The logic is similar for small-scale and organic agriculture and local businesses, which are more labor-intensive.

While this has been an important conversation, the rhetoric of degrowth or the steady-state economy obscures a key point about the road to sustainability. The nub of the problem is the transition from a dirty to a clean sector. How that plays out on average will change depending on where we are in the journey. At the moment, BAU is so large that aggregate growth is on balance destructive. Over time, as the balance between the two sectors changes, growth *could* have a net positive impact on the environment. But we're a long way from there.

For now, a global perspective trumps the national one. The wealthy countries, and particularly the United States, have an ethical duty to abandon BAU growth. They're the carbon-legacy nations that have created a problem that has the potential to devastate the planet. Between 1750 and 2006, the United States accounted for 28 percent of global carbon emissions. No other nation has had a comparable impact. Not the United Kingdom (6 percent), Japan (4 percent), Russia (8 percent), Germany (7 percent), or even the remainder of Europe (18 percent). China is accountable for only 8 percent. Poor countries deserve what's left of the globe's ecological space to improve their living standards, reduce poverty, and catch up to the wealthy. If that means slowing down in the Global North, while we phase out fossil fuels and destructive production, it's the only fair way to proceed. That may seem harsh, or unachievable. But plenitude suggests that far from being painful, doing what's right may feel good after all.

Plenitude and Well-being

Debates about sustainability often feature the idea that protecting the planet requires austerity of one kind or another. Trade-off economists warn that there will be lost income and unemployment. Environmentalists get pegged as hair-shirters who want to deny the good life to worthy populations. (It's a charge with a grain of truth—there is a subset who argue for a rhetoric of sacrifice in wealthy countries.)

The counterargument is that protection costs less than degradation. For climate change, we've learned that a vigorous response will reduce emissions and raise income relative to no response. The accumulating data on ecosystems points to a similar conclusion. Natural capital yields benefits that ordinary accounting ignores.

But there's another problem with the sacrifice view. It lags behind social science findings on how income and time use affect well-being. In rich countries, for all but the poor, growth in income yields less value to people than is typically assumed. Trade-off economists make the mistake of overestimating the value of additional income, as, apparently, do people themselves. Similarly, the time-use literature suggests that spending time outside the market is highly satisfying. The idea behind plenitude is that it moves us from a mix of incentives and imperatives that are no longer particularly efficient at delivering well-being (growth, work-and-spend, ecological degradation) to a way of living that a growing body of findings suggests will really make us better off.

The research on income and happiness is now enormous, and

casts considerable doubt on a simple translation of income into well-being, once a certain level of income has been reached. Poor people and poor countries do benefit from higher consumption. But then things get complicated. Studies find the surprising result that a number of wealthy countries, including the United States, the United Kingdom, and Japan, have flatlined in well-being for decades, as income has risen significantly. Survey data suggests that China's rapid growth in material prosperity has led to less, not more, satisfaction among its population.

Within countries, lower-income households are worse off than wealthier ones. But once a household is out of poverty and into the middle class, more income isn't too effective in raising well-being. The British economist Richard Layard found that across the globe, the average happiness score of a country stops rising when its per capita income reaches $26,000 in today's dollars. Economist Richard Easterlin, who got this debate started in the 1970s, has also found that across a group of people born at roughly the same time, happiness is almost wholly unresponsive to increases in income.

There are a number of explanations for these counterintuitive findings. The first is that people adapt to higher incomes by raising their expectations. Last year's luxury becomes this year's necessity. A few studies have found that between 35 and 60 percent of incremental income falls victim to this adaptation effect. If earnings rise by $10,000, between $3,500 and $6,000 comes to be seen as "required," and no longer a boon to well-being.

A second explanation is social comparison. The more people care about their own position vis-à-vis others, the more general increases in consumption fail to yield additional well-being. There is a growing body of evidence showing that people care a great deal about these positional effects. One study of U.S. localities found that a person's happiness declines when his or her neighbors' incomes rise, and that the drop is large. The well-known treadmill effect occurs when people try to raise their incomes by working harder, but find that they aren't getting ahead because others are doing the same.

So why don't we learn, and hop off the treadmill? It does happen. Downshifters have figured out that money doesn't buy contentment. But researchers are finding there's a widespread tendency to anticipate that additional income will yield more happiness than it does. The existence of this projection bias leads people to overvalue income and consumption, relative to what will make them feel best. People think money will make them happier, but it mostly fails to deliver.

For many people, earning additional money requires working longer hours. Evidence that longer hours of work are associated with lower happiness is accumulating, as is the more general point that how people spend their time is strongly related to well-being. In a series of studies, the psychologists Tim Kasser and Kennon Sheldon found that being time-affluent is positively associated with well-being, even controlling for income. In some of their studies, time trumped material goods in importance. Kasser and Kirk Brown found that working hours are negatively correlated with life satisfaction. The study on neighbors' incomes cited above had a similar finding. The Nobel laureate Daniel Kahneman and his Princeton colleague Alan Krueger, using a sample of working women in Texas, report that the three activities most likely to elicit a bad mood are the evening commute, work, and the morning commute. A study among European Union countries found that the higher the working hours, the lower the happiness level, again controlling for other variables. Data from a large-scale German survey also found a negative relationship between working hours and happiness. Another notable finding is that income is positional, but leisure time is not. The benefits of more vacation days or shorter hours are durable, remaining even when others also gain free time.

So if it's the case that in wealthy countries, income and long hours won't yield much additional well-being, what will? No surprises here. Spending more time with family and friends. Spending more time in intimate relations. Spending more time eating and exercising.

Nature itself is also a source of well-being. Environmental psychologists and others have found numerous benefits to humans from contact with the outdoors. Parks and gardens help people relax and restore; proximity to plants and green space reduces stress and promotes emotional balance. Being in nature can reduce blood pressure and improve muscular health. Patients recover faster when they are exposed to plants, flowers, and trees. Workers' productivity and well-being improve with natural light and access to the outdoors. Residential complexes with more greenery yield benefits for dwellers.

Looking back on the experience of the last few decades, an increasing number of people are coming to the conclusion that the same market forces that propel the economy are driving ecological degradation, time poverty, the decline of community, and the collapse of social connection. Measures broader than GDP tell a similar story. The New Economics Foundation's Happy Planet Index incorporates ecological footprint, life satisfaction measures, and life expectancy into a single metric that measures how efficiently nations are using natural resources to produce happy lives (or "happy life years"). Costa Rica tops the list, with its 99 percent renewable energy, life expectancy of 78.5 years, and average satisfaction score of 8.5 out of 10. (It also has one of the lowest poverty rates in the developing world, is reforesting its land, and abolished its army in 1949.) By contrast, the United States clocks in at a dismally inefficient 114th, largely because its ecological footprint is so high relative to "happy life year" results that are about average for wealthy countries.

Plenitude aims to transcend this inefficiency. If we manage it, the question of well-being will begin to solve itself. In addition to, and perhaps more important than, the question of whether we are better or worse off in a quantitative sense—the issue to which the literature is addressed—we will discover that we are different. We will have brought our way of living into alignment with what most of us care about most, promoting health and well-being for humans, other species, and the planet.

Plenitude Emerging

Many of the elements of plenitude are beginning to take shape as the catalyst of economic collapse has been added to an already expanding sustainability movement. Urban and suburban gardening are burgeoning. Individuals are planting vegetable plots, community gardens are sprouting, and in a number of major cities, efforts to grow healthy organic food for inner-city residents are thriving. Detroit, Milwaukee, and Chicago all have large-scale organizations that are reshaping residents' food habits. Farmers' markets, community-supported agriculture, local sourcing by restaurants, Slow Food chapters, schoolyard gardens, and related initiatives are on the rise. Practices are expanding from simple vegetable plots to urban homesteading. People are growing mushrooms, keeping bees, and raising livestock. A chicken underground has sprung up in cities with laws against backyard poultry, and urban poultry households stretch from Los Angeles to South Portland, Maine. Backyard livestock has become so popular that some locales have even spawned mobile slaughtering businesses, trucks that move through neighborhoods to kill the animals on-site. A similar phenomenon is happening with energy. People are installing solar collectors and corncob and wood pellet stoves. They're opting into green energy sources available from their utilities. Some are going off the grid, or tapping into wind and geothermal power. They're insulating their homes, installing LEDs, downsizing their spaces, and designing smart buildings that take advantage of free cooling and heating from nature through wind, sun, and shade. They're microgenerators rejecting the inevitability of fossil fuels.

Local to global networks are emerging to solve problems of economics, energy, and ecology. The Transition Town movement, which began in Totnes, England, has spread rapidly to other countries. It has a lot in common with plenitude. It is optimistic, self-reliant, and confident that there is a way forward that is better for humans and the earth. It advocates re-skilling, food sufficiency, renewable energy, and the forging of social bonds at the community level. It's a decentralized movement, without a blueprint other than a process it recommends for communities that take up the challenge.

New ways of living are proliferating in the United States and around the world, both at the household level and, more important, as people come together in community. These centers, or ecovillages, are pioneering earth-friendly ways of growing food, harvesting water, getting energy, healing the body, and making products, as well as democratic and collaborative methods for human interaction. Many are primarily learning, or living and learning, centers. The Farm in Tennessee teaches low-impact, high-satisfaction living, with education in solar building, permaculture, food forestry, rainwater harvesting, water filtration, and many other topics. They manage a wilderness area, operate a forest mushroom-laying ground, and grow temperate bamboo species. In Colorado, the Earth Restoration Corps is spawning trainers who are spreading indigenous knowledge for healing and protecting the earth. A group in Philadelphia associated with the Business Alliance for Local Living Economies is aiming to incubate sustainable businesses, restore urban land, and provide hundreds of new jobs. There are ecovillages from Wisconsin to Georgia.

The Center for Alternative Technologies in Wales is teaching local methods of green woodworking, as well as how to build wind turbines, solar water heaters, and self-constructed homes. Eco-communities in Italy and Germany teach the healing arts, conflict resolution, and crafts, along with earth-friendly technologies for daily life. Similar endeavors can be found in Australia, throughout Central and South America, and in sub-Saharan Africa. Vandana Shiva's Bija Vidyapeeth (Earth Citizenship) center in northern India combines an innovative organic farm operating in community with nearby villages with courses taught by Indian and international sustainability leaders. Also in India, the eco-city of Auroville hosts people from around the world to learn building techniques, medicinal plant cultivation, alternative technologies, and other subjects. Schumacher College in Devon, England, where I have spent considerable time, offers participants vegetarian meals, a daily routine of classes on cutting-edge practices and analyses, meditation, and training in deep ecology and holistic sciences. The Global Ecovillage Network, to which many of these examples belong, connects thirteen thousand diverse communities around the world. They are dedicated to practicing, teaching, and disseminating not just sustainability, but "sustainability plus," a way of living that gives more back to the earth than it takes.

As we look forward into the future, there is much to be fearful about. Two thousand and nine ended without a meaningful global climate deal. There's a narrow window remaining, but the coal, oil, and fossil fuel lobby launched a sophisticated advertising and lobbying effort that has undermined the political momentum for a solution. The U.S. Senate remains a formidable obstacle to a treaty. Failure could be catastrophic. The recession led to an unprecedented flow of funds to alternative energy and green jobs programs, but its continuing legacy of joblessness, reduced incomes, and insecurity has narrowed the political space for a rise in the price of fossil fuel energy, a necessary step in achieving reductions in greenhouse gas emissions.

Progressive solutions, such as the Sky Trust proposal, which would benefit lower-income households through rebated revenues from polluters, have been kept off the table by powerful corporate interests. Environmental politics hasn't yet escaped the dead end of unpalatable trade-offs.

But there are also hopeful developments. The planet has begun to communicate in ways that more and more of us are understanding. People are responding by planting, growing, saving, sharing, recycling, making, and caring. They are taking responsibility in individualized ways, advocating for their new lifestyles in a language of sustainability. More and more of us are acting at the local level, getting carbon commitments from mayors and state governments, fighting for the right to keep chickens or hang laundry on a clothesline, and teaching others how to garden, can, and preserve. Climate activism and even civil disobedience aimed at stopping the expansion of the coal economy is expanding. A few miles from my home in Newton, Massachusetts, college students are refusing to sleep in dorms, apartments, and houses powered by dirty energy and are camping out in the Boston Common instead. They're demanding that the state pledge to achieve 100 percent clean energy by 2020. They may just get it: they recently earned a meeting with the governor.

Throughout the country and the across the globe, millions are already following the path of plenitude—whatever they call it—creating a twenty-first-century economy that has the potential to restore the earth. They see that it's a smart strategy, which it must be if it is to work. It is attuned to the monumental shifts now taking place in the global economy, to the declining power of the BAU model, and to the rising potential in small-scale, time-abundant, low-impact ways of producing and consuming. In Cleveland, they're building clean, cooperative businesses that offer jobs and long-term wealth creation to local residents. In Worcester, Massachusetts, they're investing in biodiesel. From the wreckage of the Great Recession, an economically savvy, alternative model is gaining legitimacy and adherents.

But plenitude is not thriving only because it is fiscally intelligent. It is also growing because it repairs our fractured lives, heals our souls, and can make us truly wealthy in ways that have little to do with money and consumption. And as it does, it begins to build, step by step, a better way of human being. In the process, it promises to restore the bounty and beauty of our miraculous planet and all its inhabitants. We should settle for nothing less.

Acknowledgments

Because I have been thinking about and working on the issues raised in this book over many years, I have incurred many debts.

My first foray into environmental issues began at the World Institute for Development Economics Research, in the late 1980s, for a project whose core question was how the macro-economy would differ if we were to take ecological limits seriously. It proved to be a challenging question. Tariq Banuri and Stephen Marglin were central to that project, and they have both influenced my thinking over many years. Andrew Glyn, who is very much missed, took the lead on that conference and volume, which was published as *The North, The South and the Environment*.

A few years later, in the mid-1990s, I was fortunate to be invited onto the founding board of the Center for a New American Dream, a nonprofit devoted to making American lifestyles socially and eco-logically sustainable. Through that work I met a number of the most important sustainability thinkers of our era, and was introduced to their movement. A series of conversations that spanned the early years of the Center were especially formative for me, and I would especially like to thank the members of the original group: the late Donella (Dana) Meadows, Betsy Taylor, Robert Engelman, Alan Durning, Vicky Robin, and Paul Gorman, as well as other early board members Peter Forbes, Liz Barratt-Brown, Dick Roy, Jacqueline Hamilton, and Alan Atkisson. Over the years wonderful new colleagues joined the board and Center staff, and I am grateful to current and former board colleagues Eleanor Sterling, Wendy Philleo, Chris Jordan, Michael Totten, Alicia Gomez, Julie Gorte, Alan Balch, Daesha Ramachandran, Gay Nicholson, and Jeffrey Baer, as well as current and former Center staff Sean Sheehan, Dave and Monique Tilford, Franca Brilliant, Lisa Wise, Eric Brown, Chris O'Brien, and Bob Ferris. I have learned from each of them.

I have also been privileged to teach at Schumacher College, a world-renowned center of much of the alternative thinking that I discuss in this book. I have learned so much from Satish Kumar, Stephan Harding, Vandana Shiva, and Brian Goodwin, who, sadly, died recently. I would also like to thank Roy Cherian for a special meeting on these issues in November 2007, at which many of the most innovative thinkers on economic alternatives came together to try and work out a new vision. (Members of that group predicted the following year's financial crash, by the way.)

A number of people have been especially important in steering my thinking on these issues, through their writings and friendship. I am grateful to Gus Speth, Stephen Marglin, and Bill McKibben. My enormous debt to Fritjhof Bergmann should be obvious from chapter 4. Paul Hawken's work has been a special source of inspiration. And my largest thank-you is to Betsy Taylor, who invited me into her world and shared many types of wisdom, including how to communicate about these issues, at a time when few had figured that out.

I have incurred a number of more direct debts in the production of this book. I am especially grateful to economists Frank Ackerman of the Stockholm Environment Institute, Gerald Epstein of the University of Massachusetts, and Lawrence Goulder of Stanford University. They read large portions of the manuscript and gave me detailed and extremely useful comments. They bear no responsibility for the final product, other than improving it significantly. S. Krishnan Dasaratha read and commented on the manuscript. Prasannan Parthasarathi read numerous drafts and helped me with the historical literature. For materials and data I thank David Kotz, Gerald Epstein, Edward Wolff, and especially Stephan Lutter of SERI. Robert Costanza and Paul West kindly agreed to be interviewed for the book, and I thank them for their generosity.

The research in chapter 2 was prompted by an invitation from Bill McKibben to speak at Middlebury College. I was there the night the United States invaded Iraq, which was the occasion for my first paper on the role of cheap resources and goods in the consumer culture. I developed that theme in a keynote address to the U.S. Society for Ecological Economics, at their 2003 annual meeting. I also presented parts of this book in its various stages at a number of universities, including Harvard University, New York University, Oxford University, the University of Manchester, the University of Minnesota, the University of Massachusetts Amherst, Drexel University, Villanova University, the Fashion Institute of Technology, the University of Linz, the Institute for Social Ecology, the Pocantico Conference Center of the Rockefeller Brothers Fund, and Boston College, as well as a number of conferences, including the American Sociological Association and the Eastern Sociology Association annual meetings, and the Consumer Culture Theory Conference. I am grateful for discussions and input from many colleagues at those schools and meetings, including Douglas Holt, Craig Thompson, Randy Hodgson, Dalton Conley, Nancy Folbre, Jim Boyce, Deepak Bhargava, and Marina Fischer-Kowalski, among others.

I have a number of debts to Boston College, where I have been since 2001. The College of Arts and Sciences gave me two semesters of sabbatical to write this book, when I was entitled to only one. Colleagues in the department of sociology have been an ongoing source of intellectual engagement and collegiality. I am grateful to my graduate students and especially Anders Hayden, whose work has taught me a lot about the question of economic growth in the context of debates on climate change. A number of undergraduate research assistants worked with me on the collection of the material volumes and unit data over a number of years. They include Christa Martens, Amanda Buescher, Margaret Ford, and Dominic Kim. Most important, Margaret Willis was a fantastic research assistant and worked on this book for months. I am exceptionally grateful for her superb work.

I would like to thank Melanie Jackson, agent extraordinaire, for her role in all aspects of this process, as well as for sticking with me through false starts too numerous to count. It meant a lot to me that she never lost confidence. Ann Godoff's exquisite editorial work on this book has been a special gift. I feel blessed to have found her. I am also grateful to Lindsay Whalen for her excellent editorial help. From Penguin, I would like to thank Veronica Windholz and Sarah Hutson. Finally, Don McDonnell did an outstanding copy-edit on the manuscript.

My children, Krishna and Sulakshana, have been enthusiastic, as always, about this project. I hope we can act quickly enough to ensure their futures. I would also like to thank my family—James, Jonathan, David, and Sharon, and especially M.S. and Indira Partharasathi and Bernard and Louise Lown for their love and support.

After I had settled on the title *Plenitude*, I found that the consumer anthropologist Grant McCracken, whose work I admire a great deal and cite in chapter 4, had used it for a 1996 book about luxury. In addition, an influential inventor and participant in the world of information technology, Rich Gold, wrote a book called *The Plenitude* that was posthumously published in 2007. I thank them both for their work.

Twenty-five years ago I had a transformative conversation about ecological limits and global distribution with Prasannan Parthasarathi. As a new assistant professor in the department of economics at Harvard, I took a position typical of the discipline, which was that global poverty could be solved, not by Americans sharing the planet's ecological resources more equitably but through technological change that allowed everyone else to live like us. He led me to recognize how wrongheaded that view is. This proved to be the first step on my path to a more fundamental critique of economics, and eventually to this book. Thank you, Prasannan, for that, for your many contributions to this book, and for all the other ways you have changed how I think and who I am.

Notes

CHAPTER 1

1 $50 trillion of wealth was erased: Asian Development Bank Study, Loser (2009).

1 safe operating zones for the earth's complex systems: Rockström et al. (2009).

2 A body of research, writing, and practice on economic alternatives: Ecological economists Herman Daly, Robert Costanza, and Hazel Henderson, economist James Boyce, physicist and activist Vandana Shiva, entrepreneur Paul Hawken, political economist Thomas Princen, environmental writers, researchers and activists Gus Speth, Alan Durning, Bill McKibben, and Van Jones, development economist David Korten, and members of the International Forum on Globalization, as well as many others, including sustainability activists noted below.

2 the larger movement for sustainability: In addition to those named above, one thinks of Wendell Berry, David Suzuki, Amory Lovins, Hunter Lovins, Terry Tempest Williams, Joanna Macy, Janine Benyus, Satish Kumar, Gunter Pauli, William McDonough, Majora Carter, and Fritjof Capra, among many others, in the U.S. context.

3 relevant for lower-income households in poor countries: The key difference is that a reduction in labor hours is not typically a viable strategy for this group.

7 only 53 percent of adults would agree: Rasmussen Reports (2009).

7 $453 billion for imported oil: United States Bureau of Economic Analysis (2009).

8 oceans were rising: Macabrey (2009).

8 Drought conditions were spreading: IPCC report by Bates et al. (2008).

8 World emissions were sharply up in 2007: National Oceanic and Atmospheric Association (2009) shows a continued increase in greenhouse gas emissions during the economic crisis (data through the end of 2008), and Environmental Protection Agency (2009) reports on emissions and sinks through 2007.

8 James Hansen . . . told Congress: Hansen (2008).

8 By February 2009, the news was worse: See Lydersen (2009), Kintisch (2009) on the 2009 Copenhagen Climate Congress, and Climate Adaptation Science and Policy Initiative (2007).

8 levels beyond 350 ppm are incompatible: Hansen et al. (2008).

8 only 6 percent, or $52 billion, of the stimulus: Gallagher (2009), who calculates the $52 billion by tallying figures from ICF International (2009).

9 General Motors and Chrysler were handed $30 billion: Associated Press (2009).

9 Dead zones are proliferating rapidly in the oceans: Diaz and Rosenberg (2008).

9 Biodiversity is shrinking: World Wildlife Fund (2008). For a popular account of anthropogenic mass extinction, see Kolbert (2009).

9 oceans will be devoid of fish: Jackson (2008).

9 primary source of animal protein for a billion people: Tidwell and Allan (2001).

9 not to say that economists were intellectually stuck: The postcrash reaction of professional economists is discussed by Cohen (2009).

10 A declining fraction of the population considered appliances: Morin and Taylor (2009).

10 "goodbye *homo economicus": Context-Based Research Group and Carton Donofrio Partners (2008).

10 Surveys I worked on as early as 2004: Widmeyer Research and Polling (2004).

10 some notable exceptions: Examples of those who did see the crisis coming are Paul Krugman of Princeton, Nouriel Roubini of New York University, Robert Shiller of Yale, Jane D'Arista of the Financial Markets Center, and James Crotty and Gerald Epstein of the University of Massachusetts.

10 "slept comfortably": Uwe Reinhardt (2009).

10 "groupthink": Shiller (2008). In response to a query from Queen Elizabeth about why economists failed to see what was happening, a group of U.K. economists attributed the failure to the "feel-good" factor and a failure of the "collective imagination." See Stewart (2009).

11 body of research that attests to human adaptability: See the section on the relation between income and happiness in chapter 5.

11 behavioral economics, cultural evolution, and social networking: An introduction to behavioral economics is Kahneman and Tversky (2000). For cultural evolution, see Bowles and Gintis (2004). On social networking, see Christakis and Fowler (2007).

11 human evolution . . . more compressed: Hawks et al. (2007), or for a summary see Keim (2007).

12 Some of the most important economic research . . . shows that a single intervention: See the literature on natural assets, including Boyce and Pastor (2001), Harper and Rajan (2004), Stanton and Boyce (2005), Agarwal and Narain (2000), and Boyce and Shelley (2003).

15 fossil fuels will be smaller and less profitable: Of course, the profitability of the oil industry has long been associated with high degrees of market concentration (monopoly power) and government protection and subsidies. There is an especially strong political dimension to their economic returns.

15 the fatal flaw of the current growth regime: For the theory of periodic restructuring of growth regimes, in which each growth regime develops a profit-eroding flaw, or contradiction, and the transition out of the "Golden Age" of capitalism, see Marglin and Schor (1990).

15 the human and economic costs: The estimate of 315, 000 deaths and $125 billion in losses from climate change is from Global Humanitarian Forum (2009). A recent estimate of some of the direct health and other costs of burning coal and oil in the United States, which excludes all costs associated with global warming, as well as a number of other major effects, was $120 billion a year (National Research Council 2009).

17 Some historians now argue . . . fossil fuel resources: Wrigley (1990) and Fischer-Kowalski and Haberl (2007).

17 "Fossil fuels were a one-time gift": McKibben (2007).

17 Europe and Asia deforested in order to grow: Richards (2003) and McNeill (2000).

17 first national study to assess . . . overstatement of growth: Repetto et al. (1989).

17 The situation is even starker in China: GDP overstatement of 8–13 percent in 1990s is from Smil and Yushi (1998); 25 percent now is from Thampapillai, Wu, and Sunderaj (2007)

17 deforestation . . . at $2 trillion to $5 trillion a year: Sukhdev and European Communities (2008).

18 Bureau of Economic Analysis . . . environmental accounts: For a discussion of this history, see Wagner (2001).

18 net loss of $28.2 billion: This and other profitability data is from Repetto and Dias (2006).

19 renewable-energy sector ground to a halt: Galbraith (2009).

19 Hybrid vehicles emit less carbon, but their batteries are toxic: HybridCars.com (2006) and Union of Concerned Scientists (2005).

19 The prices of food and energy: Food and energy prices fell dramatically in the second half of 2008. Food (excluding beverages) declined 29 percent, and energy, including petroleum, fell 48 percent. Author's calculations from International Monetary Fund (2009).

19 The index of primary commodities . . . Food prices: The index of primary commodities rising 23 percent per year from 2003–2007 and food prices 9 percent are from Askari and Krichene (2007).

19 most explanations crediting strong demand: However, see Taibbi (2009) for an intriguing argument that unrealistic speculation, rather than supply and demand factors, was behind the rapid increase in oil prices.

CHAPTER 2

25 **gross domestic product devoted to personal consumption stood at 61.5 percent:**
Economic report of the president (2009), table B-1, p. 282, author's calculation.

25 **Expenditures per person hit a peak:** *Economic report of the president* (2009), table
B-31, p. 321, per capita consumption expenditures in current dollars, 2007.

25 **global average income of only $8,500:** The figure $8,579 is from World Bank
(2009a), Global National Income in 2008. More than half earning less than a
thousand dollars annually is the author's calculation from Chen and Ravallion
(2008), table 5.

26 **In 1960 the average person consumed just a third:** *Economic report of the president*
(2009), table B-31, p. 321, per capita consumption expenditures in 2000 dollars,
author's calculation. 1960–2008:3.

26 **inflation-adjusted per-person expenditures have tripled for furniture and
household goods:** *Economic report of the president* (2009), table B-17, p. 305, author's
calculation of per capita changes from aggregate expenditures, 1990–2008:3.

26 **Overall, average real per-person spending increased 42 percent:** *Economic report
of the president* (2009), table B-31, p. 321, per capita consumption expenditures in
2000 dollars, author's calculation, 1990–2008:3.

26 **Since 2000, nearly half, or 47 percent, of the nation's entire income:** Mishel,
Bernstein, and Shierholz (2009), table 1.7, p. 61.

26 **income inequality was worse than . . . since the end of the 1920s:** The U.S.
Census Bureau's historical data on Gini coefficients shows the 2006 Gini of 47 as
the highest since 1967, the earliest reported by the Census. See United States
Census Bureau (2009). The Gini in 1929 is estimated at 41 as reported by Brenner,
Kaelble, and Thomas (1991), p.199. The share going to the top 1 percent was not
quite at 1929 levels (Saez [2008]). See also Mishel, Bernstein, and Shierholz
(2009), figure 1K, p. 64.

26 **Broader measures showed erosion in well-being :** United Nations Development
Programme (2007) for 1980–2005. The U.S. plunge to number fifteen is from
Conley (2009).

26 **The nonstop upscaling of lifestyles was arguably contributing:** For discussions
of how rising expenditures can fail to improve quality of life, see Schor (1992)
and Schor (1998).

26 **trade deficit of $719 billion:** *Economic report of the president* (2009), table B-24, p. 312,
balance on current account, 2007.

26 **nearly $14 trillion in household indebtedness:** Federal Reserve Statistical Release
(2009), debt outstanding by sector.

28 **clothing can now be purchased by weight:** Where I live, dollar-a-pound clothing
can be found at Garment District (2009).

28 **In the West, apparel has been expensive:** Lemire (2006). See also Roche
(1994).

28 **Apparel also traversed social hierarchies:** A classic, albeit contested, work on the

origins of the consumer revolution in Britain describes this process. McKendrick, Brewer, and Plumb (1982).

28 clothing . . . as an alternative currency: Lemire (2006), chapter 4.

29 Global surpluses of labor: The exploitation of workers in garment factories has received extensive attention in recent years, and activists have tried through various means to improve wages and working conditions. See Ross (1997), Ross (2004), and Rosen (2002). See Schor (2002) for more detail on these points.

29 In 1991 Americans bought an average of: Annual apparel purchases for various years are author's calculations, using data from the U.S. Census Bureau (2005 and earlier years) and, for 2007, American Apparel & Footwear Association (2009).

30 a shift out of what the industry calls basics . . . to fashion: Abernathy et al. (1999). For a popular account from an industry insider, see Lee (2003). *McFashion* is her term.

31 "the aestheticization of everyday life": Featherstone (2007).

33 measures such as the actual number of items: More detail on this research, including information on sources and methods of calculation, is contained in Schor (2008).

34 Products come into the country in four main ways: Data on imports comes from two sources, each of which contains two methods of importation. Goods arriving or departing by sea and air are from WISERTrade (2009). Goods arriving or departing by rail and truck are from the Department of Transportation TransBorder Freight Data (Research and Innovative Technology Administration [2009]), which began in 1993. Imports are constructed by summing these four importation methods. Final goods weights do not include the other materials used in production, a topic to which I turn in the next section. Data on Domestic Production is from the U.S. Census, Annual Survey of Manufactures, various years.

34 I've compiled the data from 1998 until 2007: The years 1998 and 2007 were chosen because 1998 was the first available year online, and 2007 is the latest year for which all data was available and was also the last year of the boom.

35 domestically produced furniture . . . rose 25 percent: This likely understates the increase, because furniture prices have fallen. It's possible that the prices of domestic but not imported furniture rose, but this information is not available.

35 Consumer electronics are also exhibiting a fashion cycle: In value, or dollar, terms, domestically produced electronics consumed fell by 27 percent. However, the prices of these goods collapsed over this period, by much more than 27 percent. Computer prices fell to a tenth of their original price. Television prices fell from 60.0 to 18.4, although industry data shows only a small (1.8 million units) increase in television sales (Environmental Protection Agency [2008], table 2.1, p. 8). Because the price decline for the category is likely larger than the reduction in domestic dollar values, the net contribution of domestic production (by units or weight) is likely positive.

36 Industry data shows that total purchases of computers rose: Environmental Protection Agency Office of Solid Waste (2008), table 3.2, p. 20.

36 The weight of imported ceramics rose by 83 percent: A fashion-cycle explanation would postulate that the availability of cheap dishes and other ceramic items at chic but inexpensive retailers such as Target accounts for the large increase in this category, and that the trend is due to households replacing their dishes more frequently than in the past. However, examination of the detailed unit categories shows that although units of imported table and kitchenware have increased, the rise is modest in comparison to the increases in bathroom fixtures and tiles. Given the housing boom and sharp increase in bathrooms per home, as well as the popularity of kitchen remodeling during this period, the increases in these categories are not surprising. To some extent, kitchen remodeling can be thought of as fashion driven because older kitchens and bathrooms have gone out of style. However, there is also a scale effect, as the number of bathrooms per home and the size of kitchens have grown. The domestic value data shows a decline of 38 percent over the period; however, we do not have details on which types of ceramics are domestically produced. The category from the consumer price data is non-electric cookware and tableware, but only from 2003. The index fell very slightly, from 92.1 in February 2003 to 91.8 in February 2007, indicating that a considerable portion of the domestic decline is likely real (rather than a price effect), and that import substitution is occurring; however, we cannot say to what extent.

37 The growth in domestic production was in addition to: In dollar terms, domestic production, subtracting exports, fell 0.9 percent for the group of twenty-four commodities and rose 24 percent for the entire sector. Because goods prices fell, the volume of domestically produced consumption appears to have risen.

38 new homes have gotten much larger: Median and average square feet of floor area in new one-family houses completed by location, in United States Census Bureau (2007). See also Dwyer (2007), p. 363.

38 National Association of Professional Organizers: http://NAPO.net (2009).

38 One in ten households now rents storage space . . . 20.8 square feet: Self Storage Association (2008). See also Mooallem (2009).

38 140 million cell phones . . . to only 19 million in 1999: Environmental Protection Agency Office of Solid Waste (2008), table 3.2, p. 20.

38 Two hundred and five million computers and peripherals . . . compared with 124 million in 1999: Environmental Protection Agency Office of Solid Waste (2008), table 3.1, p. 20.

38 1.2 billion computers and televisions . . . with another 235 million: Environmental Protection Agency Office of Solid Waste (2008), table 3.4, p. 25.

39 373 million . . . arrived at EOL in 2007: Environmental Protection Agency Office of Solid Waste (2008), table 6.1, p. 34. 1.2 per American is the author's calculation.

39 The secondhand clothing industry has been estimated to exceed one billion dollars: Fernandez (2004).

39 316 million pounds . . . 1.1 billion: United Nations Statistics Division. Regression analyses were done with Kristen Heim, then a Ph.D. candidate in the department of sociology, Boston College, using data from United Nations Statistics Division (2005).

39 textiles made up approximately 4.7 percent of the municipal waste stream of 254 million tons: This figure and seventy-eight pounds are the author's calculations from Environmental Protection Agency (2008).

39 data on exports of used or secondhand merchandise . . . increased 66 percent: WISERTrade (2009), air weight plus vessel weight, 1998–2005, author's calculation of used or secondhand merchandise data.

40 theorists of consumer society: These include Baudrillard (2001), Ewen (1988), Lash and Urry (1994), Ritzer (2005), and Gottdiener (2000).

41 theorists of dematerialization: Weizsäcker, Lovins, and Lovins (2001), McDonough and Braungart (2002), and Pauli (2000). For the application of postindustrial ideas to services, see Gershuny (2000).

41 Raymond Williams's famous quip: Williams (1996).

42 The field is still in its infancy: Material flows are not direct measures of environmental consequences, although there are beginning to be efforts to combine materials data with environmental measures. However, flows are far superior to dollar metrics for measuring the ecological impacts of economic activity.

42 40 billion metric tons: This and subsequent data on materials flows comes from Sustainable Europe Research Institute (2009b) and the SERI database, available at www.materialflows.net.

43 a hundred or more tons of earth: Perlez and Johnson (2005).

43 the global average was about 8.8 metric tons: Sustainable Europe Research Institute (2009b). In 1980 it was 8.9.

44 17.9 billion metric tons: Data provided to the author by Stephan Lutter, from the Sustainable Europe Research Institute.

44 average American emitted 19.7 tons of CO_2: This figure and other countries' per capita emissions are from United Nations Statistics Division (2009).

44 United States households are responsible for less than half of all emissions: Frank Ackerman, private communication. CO_2 emissions from fossil fuel combustion are the largest source of greenhouse gas emissions in the United States. In 2007, residential end use (heating, cooling, lighting, etc.) accounted for 21 percent of these emissions, while industrial and commercial use accounted for 27 percent and 18 percent, respectively, of CO_2 emissions (Environmental Protection Agency [2009], p. 8). These figures include the emissions from fossil fuel combustion in the generation of electricity as well. Transportation accounted for 33 percent of CO_2 emissions from fossil fuel combustion, but this includes both personal vehicle use and heavy-duty vehicles and aircraft.

44 how food is produced and consumed in the United States: See discussions in Steinfeld et al. (2006), Pollan (2006), Lappé and Lappé (2002), and Nestle (2002).

44 1,800 miles of driving: Fiala (2009).

45 Americans eat more beef: U.S. beef consumption of ninety-four pounds in 2005 is from United States Department of Agriculture (2006), p. 20.

45 in comparison to asparagus: Fiala (2009).

45 an estimated 40–50 percent of U.S. food is wasted: From an eight-year study detailed in Jones (2004).

45 The average single-family dwelling . . . had expanded 45 percent: United States Census Bureau (2007), "Median and Average Square Feet of Floor Area in New One-Family Houses Completed by Location," p. 363. 95 percent with two or more bathrooms is from "Number of Bathrooms in New One-Family Houses Completed," p. 32; 90 percent with air-conditioning is from "Presence of Air-Conditioning in New One-Family Houses Completed," p. 4; 19 percent had three-car or larger garages is from "Type of Parking Facility of New One-Family Houses Completed," p. 387.

45 United States and Canada increased their materials use by 54 percent: Organization for Economic Cooperation and Development (2008b).

46 650 pounds a year: World Resources Institute (2007). One hopeful sign is that there has been a decline in the last few years, after a large rise in the 1990s.

46 America accounts for a third of paper consumption: Worldwatch (2008).

46 Western Europe has done much better than North America: North American and European materials consumption from 1980–2005 is from Organization for Economic Cooperation and Development (2008b), "Materials Mix by OECD Region," p. 40.

46 wealthy countries have been off-loading: Hertwich and Peters (2009) calculate carbon footprints accounting for global trade patterns. That the United States outsourced 20 percent of emissions is from Ghertner and Fripp (2007).

48 a synthetic gas called nitrogen trifluoride: NF_3 and televisions is discussed in Weiss et al. (2008) and Udell (2008).

50 their book sensation, *The Limits to Growth:* Meadows et al. (1972).

50 *The Limits to Growth* asked what would happen over the long run: The most pessimistic of the scenarios is discussed in Meadows, Randers, and Meadows (2005), p. xi.

51 "brazen . . . impudent nonsense": Beckerman (1972), p. 327.

51 Nordhaus . . . argued that the *Limits* model failed to incorporate: Nordhaus's first paper is Nordhaus (1973). See also Nordhaus, Stavins, and Weitzman (1992), for his response to Meadows, Randers, and Meadows (1992).

52 The no-adaptation . . . scenario . . . a point the systems dynamics researchers understood: The *Limits* school had done quite a bit of work modeling alternative paths, but the economists' critiques tended to focus on the doomsday predictions of the standard run, the one in which there is, by definition, no adaptation.

52 The debate didn't progress in the way one might have hoped: For Dennis

Meadows's reflections on the *New York Times* review of the book, see Meadows (2005). The review was by Peter Passell, M. Roberts, and L. Ross, and ran on April 2, 1972.

52 **seen as prima facie evidence:** Price trends cannot be assumed to simply represent the balance of supply and demand at a point in time, a point I return to in chapter 3. They also incorporate market participants' views about the future and the state of knowledge. For example, climate-change denial affects energy prices.

53 **Beckerman dismissed it as a scare story:** Beckerman (1972). 5 percent improvement in world output is from Nordhaus (1982), p. 242. Even a decade later, Nordhaus (1991) concluded that "climate change is likely to produce a combination of gains and losses with no strong presumption of substantial net economic damages" (p. 993). There is now a significant literature on the indefensibility of Nordhaus's assumptions, which I discuss in chapter 3.

53 **ecosystem indicators such as biodiversity were showing sharp declines:** World Wildlife Fund (2008).

53 **"human beings and the natural world are on a collision course":** Union of Concerned Scientists (1992).

53 **half the world's population will be facing serious food shortage:** Battisti and Naylor (2009). The more pessimistic assessment is from Romm (2009).

53 **Early warnings about BAU growth:** Meadows, Randers, and Meadows (2004) argue that the 1972 model is fairly accurate for early twenty-first-century predictions. Turner (2008) has similar findings.

53 **An international collaboration . . . to define safe operating zones:** Rockström et al. (2009).

55 **The official word from two thousand scientists who gathered in Copenhagen:** Key message 1 on climate trends from the Climate Change: Global Risks, Challenges & Decisions conference. Copenhagen Conference on Climate Change (2009).

55 **Oceans are less absorptive now:** Evidence of less carbon uptake in the North Atlantic is from Schuster and Watson (2007); less uptake in the Southern Ocean is from Le Quéré et al. (2007).

55 **heat waves have already begun to reduce photosynthesis:** Ciais et al. (2005).

55 **the Greenland ice sheet is melting twice as fast:** Rignot and Kanagaratnam (2006).

55 **Sea levels are rising, with some predictions of at least two meters by century's end:** Hansen (2008). See also Hansen et al. (2008).

55 **the power of feedback loops is still being debated:** Not all scientists have shifted to the view that feedback loops will be strong. See Revkin (2009) for a discussion of this debate.

56 **a two-degree Celsius . . . rise:** Hansen (2008). His 350 ppm target is gaining acceptance.

56 **an influential 2006 report by Nicholas Stern:** BAU yielding 550 ppm by 2035 and other figures are from Stern (2006), chapter 7, pp. 169–170.

56 **Others are predicting as much as 1,000 ppm by 2100:** Romm (2008).

56 **MIT . . . predicts a catastrophic rise of five degrees Celsius:** Sokolov et al. (2009).

56 **Disaster scenarios are being spun:** Lovelock (2006) and Lynas (2008).

56 **climate destabilization causing famines, droughts, and storms:** Intergovernmental Panel on Climate Change (2001).

56 **At a minimum, a one-degree Celsius warming:** Stern (2006), Executive Summary, p. 3.

56 **a growing international movement to make 350 ppm the target:** See www.350 .org, the organization founded by Bill McKibben. Rajendra Pachauri, the chair of the IPCC, has now personally endorsed 350 ppm.

56 **emissions rose four times faster:** This figure and that for growth in atmospheric concentrations are from Global Carbon Project (2008).

56 **emissions per dollar of GDP have fallen...total emissions are expanding:** "Inventory of US Greenhouse Gas Emissions and Sinks: 1990–2007," from Environmental Protection Agency (2009).

57 **Early reports are that the economic crash has reduced global emissions:** Harvey (2009).

57 **Hansen reports that arid subtropical climate zones are expanding:** Hansen (2008), p. 2.

57 **compared present-day New England flora and fauna:** Willis et al. (2008).

57 **The southwestern United States is at risk of becoming a permanent dust bowl:** Solomon et al. (2009).

57 **A major study by the International Union for the Conservation of Nature:** International Union for the Conservation of Nature (2009), p.17.

57 **A U.S. report on birdlife:** North American Bird Conservation Initiative, U.S. Committee (2009).

57 **main drivers of species decline:** World Wildlife Fund (2008), p. 5.

58 **Living Planet Index . . . has declined by 30 percent:** These figures are from World Wildlife Fund (2008), pp. 2, 8.

58 **role of species in ecosystem functioning:** Daily (1997).

58 **A comprehensive assessment of the state of the world's ecosystems:** Millennium Ecosystem Assessment (2005): "rapidly and extensively," p. 2; the fifteen of twenty-four (60 percent) figure and nonlinearities, p. 1; "established, although incomplete evidence," p. 1; systems in decline, p. 7.

58 **Stocks of large open-ocean fish have plummeted:** Jackson (2008), p. 11461.

58 **Coral reefs may be completely gone:** Jackson (2008), p. 11462.

59 **scientists found 405 oceanic dead zones, in comparison with 49:** Diaz and Rosenberg (2008).

59 **ocean habitats turn into the equivalent of algal deserts:** Jackson (2008) p. 11461.

59 **learning about ecocide can be demoralizing or overwhelming:** Findings that

information about ecosystems can be destabilizing or lead people to tune out, shut down, or become hopeless is from Norgaard (2006a, 2006b); see also Macy and Young Brown (1998).

59 an evocative metric: Ecological footprint data is available in World Wildlife Fund (2008) and also at the Global Footprint Network Web site (www.footprintnetwork .org). The national figures, with the exception of Brazil, are from the 2009 Data Tables, available at http://www.footprintnetwork.org/en/index.php/GFN/page/ ecological_footprint_atlas_2008/m (accessed November 25, 2009). (The Brazilian figure is from the previous year, 2008 data.)

59 For the household, it takes into account how far food travels: Households can calculate their own ecological footprints at the Global Footprint Network site, http://www.footprintnetwork.org/en/index.php/GFN.

60 a continual process of refinement and improvement: The treatment of carbon sequestration is one of the footprint's controversial features. For criticisms and refinements of the footprint, see Venetoulis and Talberth (2008) and the comprehensive treatment in Kitzes et al. (2009).

60 Between 1961 and 1995, measured biocapacity . . . Global Footprint Network 2009 data tables.

61 the world first reached its limits in 1986 . . . 40 percent above biocapacity: A summary of overshoot can be found at the Global Footprint Network site (www .footprintnetwork.org).

62 Between 1961 and 2005, the U.S. footprint has risen: Changes in per-person footprints from 1961 are from Ewing et al. (2008), appendix table 7. Per capita incomes, corrected for purchasing power parity, are from Organization for Economic Cooperation and Development (2008).

63 Privatization . . . threatens equitable solutions: Barlow (2002).

63 the number of people living in water-stressed areas may increase dramatically: Bates et al. (2008), figure 3.3 and p. 45.

63 The water footprint shows how much: Water footprints are from Hoekstra and Chapagain (2007).

64 2,000 liters of water to produce one T-shirt: Global averages for products and water footprint data are from Hoekstra and Chapagain (2007), table 2 (p. 41) and table 3 (p. 42) respectively.

65 Now we've got twin crises: Thomas L. Friedman connected the two crises in a *New York Times* column entitled "Mother Nature's Dow," on March 28, 2009.

CHAPTER 3

68 most rejected the need for vigorous collective action on climate: Geoffrey Heal, another leading environmental economist, makes this point in his review of the economics of climate change. See Heal (2009).

69 an interdisciplinary group called the Society for Ecological Economics: It is now a worldwide group. The infeasibility of infinite growth in a physical world is a guiding principle. On this point, see Daly (1977, 1996, 2005). See also Beddoe et al. (2009), Costanza, Graumlich, and Steffen (2007), Ayres (1993, 1996), Victor (2008), and Schor (1991). For a comprehensive account of the development and history of ecological economics, see Røpke (2004, 2005).

69 **to cannibalize its very conditions of existence:** Sociologists have also made this point. See Schnaiberg (1980) and Gould, Pellow, and Schnaiberg (2008).

69 **resulted in a literal externalization:** Environmental economics has suffered from its relative isolation in that it has been slow to incorporate theoretical innovations from other parts of the discipline and outside, most notably the shift to evidence-driven models of decision-making pioneered by behavioral economics, and new research on the relation between well-being and income.

69 **Environmental economics has also been closely intertwined with energy economics:** The National Bureau of Economic Research has a joint environmental and energy-economics program.

71 **"most of my economist colleagues have always known . . .":** Beckerman (1972), p. 327.

71 **discipline has historically tended to optimism:** Partha Dasgupta, one of the world's top environmental economists, makes this point in Dasgupta (2005), p. 106.

71 **a sixth of the world's population . . . already hungry:** Food and Agriculture Organization of the United Nations (2009). 1.4 billion people living on less than $1.25 per day is from World Bank (2009b).

71 **Nordhaus said climate change might even end up improving well-being:** Nordhaus (1982); his on-balance positive conclusion is from Nordhaus (1991). Nordhaus also took the view that until now, man's activities had affected our hospitable environment "negligibly," in contrast to a growing literature in environmental history that draws quite different conclusions. For recent contributions, see McNeill (2000) and Diamond (2005).

72 **Lower oil prices in the 1980s and falling food and other commodity prices:** See the discussion in Nordhaus, Stavins, and Weitzman (1992).

72 **ready substitutes for nature:** See Nordhaus (1973) and Nordhaus, Stavins, and Weitzman (1992), which emphasize substitution.

73 **Cornucopians have tended to be political:** There is also an influential nonpolitical version of this argument, which is that population growth leads to more geniuses, which in turn spurs innovation and wealth; however, it has not been applied to natural resource issues. See Kremer (1993).

73 **Whatever the merits of the Kuznets model:** The Environmental Kuznets Curve belongs to a larger class of seemingly commonsensical but deeply flawed modernization models. The most famous may be Maslow's hierarchy-of-needs tale. Maslow argues that the poor are motivated by basic survival and can only attend to "higher" needs such as spiritual development or self-actualization once incomes rise. (How to explain India, then, with its high levels of religiosity and poverty?) By contrast, those with higher incomes are more fully developed and actualized

individuals. Although still widely taught, Maslow has been rejected by contemporary scholarship. Another version of this nineteenth-century paradigm was imperialist ideology, which held that white Westerners had attained a higher level of civilization than primitive, backward peoples in the colonies. Development economics itself has mainly been a modernizing enterprise, designed to help backward others become more like an advanced, superior West. All "stage" theories have come in for withering criticism in recent decades, and rightly so.

73 **the Kuznets model . . . was applied to the environment:** Early versions of the EKC are from Grossman and Krueger (1993, 1995). See also Frankel and Rose (2005).

74 **the Environmental Kuznets Curve findings haven't held up well:** Recent studies of the EKC that do not find support for it include Bagliani, Bravo, and Dalmazzone (2008) and Caviglia-Harris, Chambers, and Kahn (2009). Romero-Ávila (2008) analyzes a number of econometric problems with existing estimates, and reviews the literature on problems with earlier studies, for both CO_2 and single pollutants. For a cautionary discussion, see Arrow et al. (1995). See also Gallagher (2004) on the Mexican experience.

74 **greenhouse gas emissions . . . do not decline at any level:** The standard view holds that this is due to the global nature of the problem and the lack of a global government to enforce a solution, unlike with the release of gases that have local or national effects.

75 **If investors have a bias toward good news:** Keynes famously discussed investor bias in *The General Theory*. See Keynes (1936).

75 **most people . . . have tended toward denial about climate change:** For accounts of denial about climate change, see Norgaard (2006a,b).

75 **Massive government subsidies:** For a discussion of studies estimating U.S. government subsidies to fossil fuels, see Koplow and Dernbach (2001) and Koplow (2007). A number of the larger estimates include the damage associated with CO_2 emissions, as well as the cost of defending oil in the Persian Gulf. A 2006 estimate of annual direct fossil fuel subsidies by Koplow was $49 billion (Koplow, 2007).

76 **Environmental economics frequently operates in the realm of trade-offs:** For critiques of trade-off economics, see Goodstein (1999) and Ackerman (2006). Of course, not all environmental economics is about trade-offs.

77 **The closer one hews to orthodox economic thinking:** While it's not representative of most economists, there is a strong version of this argument that still has adherents. It is summed up in a blog post by the George Washington University economist Steve Suranovic, who claims that it is a "fiction" to believe that green technologies can create new jobs. "In order to do one thing—i.e., clean the environment—we must not do other things." Then he took the point even further, arguing that government policy already reflects the will of the people, and whatever level of protection has been enacted to date is optimal. "Currently people do not value environmental cleanup as much as they value the other

goods and services they demand and buy. If they did, there would be no need for government to intervene to change what people choose. Government tax and regulatory policies to combat climate change will force people to change to what the government, or environmental advocates, want them to choose . . . Most Americans, and probably most in the world, do not really want to change much of what they do to combat climate change. If they did, they would welcome higher gasoline prices." This view relies on a number of faulty assumptions, including the claim that government policy is an accurate reflection of a unified public interest, that the public is fully informed about the impacts (including "costs and benefits") of climate change and policies to reduce emissions, and that people believe the burden of higher prices will be fairly shared. Quote from Suranovic (2007).

77 **It exists, therefore it must be optimal:** Reinhardt (2009).

78 **Nordhaus . . . "optimal" response:** Nordhaus uses a linguistic sleight of hand to call his optimal path "reduction," in which the word refers to staying below a hypothetical path of steep increases, when his optimal policy actually calls for an expansion of emissions. On action being too costly, see Nordhaus (2008), chapter 1, pp. 13–19. Nordhaus estimates that lower targets will cost $17 trillion (p. 15), but his damage functions are considerably out of date, incorporating data from the third IPCC assessment, rather than the fourth, which was already out of date when published in 2007. Current thinking is much more pessimistic than the 2007 report.

78 **larger class of mainstream economic models built around trade-offs:** Other leading integrated modelers include Richard Tol and Robert Mendelsohn.

78 **They take climate change seriously, but . . . suggest doing almost nothing:** On this point, see Ackerman et al. (2009). By contrast, the Stern model suggests vigorous action. See below.

78 **Economists . . . who have studied them:** Economists who have studied the effect of changing assumptions in IAMs include Ackerman and Finlayson (2006), Sterner and Persson (2008), Ackerman, Stanton, and Bueno (forthcoming), and Ackerman et al. (2009). See also Heal (2009) on this point. Stern (2006) is a major statement on climate modeling. Dell, Jones, and Olken (2008) offer another approach, with different results. See DeCanio (2005) on modeling strategies. Heal (2009) and Goulder and Pizer (2008) are good reviews of climate-change economics.

78 **The best known of these controversies concerns the discount rate:** For discussions of discounting, see Stern (2006), Heal (2009), Nordhaus (2008), and Ackerman et al. (2009). There are actually two discount rates. One is called the pure rate of time preference, which compares the welfare of present and future generations. Many economists argue this rate should be zero, an egalitarian solution, although some say that future generations should be worth less. The second, which I discuss in the text, is the consumption discount rate, and it adjusts current

and future dollars to a common metric. The standard practice in IAMs has been to discount future dollars on the grounds that people will be richer in the future. The argument is that the marginal utility (or benefit) of consumption will fall so that a dollar tomorrow is worth less than a dollar today. However, if climate change reduces growth and consumption, by this logic, tomorrow's dollars will be worth more than today's, and the consumption discount rate should be negative. Different IAMs use different consumption discount rates, which are a main driver of results. High discount rates have other analytic problems, because they are inconsistent with various types of observed financial behavior, such as the behavior of equity prices. The IAMs appear to be lagging behind in both science and economic theory. Stern set his discount rate very low, which was the part of his report most contested by those advocating relative inaction.

79 much of the world's population lives in places that are already too hot: On the temperature assumptions of DICE, see Ackerman and Finlayson (2006). The 2007 version of DICE changed its treatment of this assumption, after it was pointed out by this paper in the previous year.

79 higher temperatures will substantially reduce the incomes of the global poor: Dell, Jones, and Olken (2008).

79 preventing 2.5 degrees of warming . . . is worth only $5 billion to the American public: See Ackerman and Finlayson (2006), p. 515, for the $5 billion figure. As Ackerman and Finlayson note, this is about fifty-four dollars per household to save humans and all other species from catastrophe. It's a bizarre calculation, rendered even more puzzling given that studies show Americans have been willing to spend more than that to save a variety of individual species. Americans spent eight times that on their pets in 2007 ($41 billion), as reported by Brady and Palmeri (2007).

79 attributing lesser value to the residents of poor countries: On valuations across geographic regions through the use of Negishi weights, see Stanton, Ackerman, and Kartha (2009), pp.10–11, who note that Nordhaus and other IAM modelers are inconsistent when they discount the incomes of richer future generations but fail to do so for richer populations in the present.

80 arbitrary estimates of how damages will develop: Stanton, Ackerman, and Kartha (2009), pp. 6–8, and Ackerman et al. (2009).

80 simplistic projections of technological change: For a comprehensive analysis of more sophisticated treatments of technological change, see Edenhofer et al. (2006).

80 failure to take uncertainty seriously: An influential contribution on the treatment of uncertainty is Weitzman (2009).

81 nature's far more important role is as an input into production: On the inability of the standard production-possibility curve to take into account the relationship between nature and income, see Goodstein (1999).

81 methods to value nature as capital . . . beginning to make headway: There is now a large literature on natural-capital valuation. See Daily (1997), Daily et al. (2000), and Costanza et al. (1997).

81 **when climate models include ecosystem services, the case for urgent action is much stronger:** Sterner and Persson (2008).

81 **standard cost-benefit analysis . . . has tended to use a partial accounting:** For a critique of cost-benefit analysis, see Ackerman and Heinzerling (2004).

81 **systematic bias . . . to overestimate costs and underestimate benefits:** For a discussion of the literature on the accuracy of cost-benefit studies, see Ackerman (2006).

81 **environmental protections that have been far less burdensome than opponents expected:** For a discussion of a major chemical protection law and its light costs, as well as a more general discussion of this point, see Ackerman (2006).

82 **innovation is more rapid and less costly than initially assumed:** See Edenhofer et al. (2006) for a discussion of technological change in climate models.

82 **Nicholas Stern . . . game-changing report:** Stern (2006).

82 **2 percent price tag:** Jowit and Wintour (2008).

82 **it would cost a mere $1.8 trillion a year:** Sachs's estimates of $1.8 trillion a year are based on a combination of plug-in hybrids and carbon-capture-and-sequestration technology and assume a cost of thirty dollars per ton of avoided emissions. Sachs assumes that world output will be six times higher in 2050, so that sum won't be a burden. Of course, CCS is not a functioning technology, and many believe it will not be viable even by 2050. Estimates of climate-change costs are from Sachs (2008), pp. 103–105.

83 **an update concluded it would be possible to reduce emissions 70 percent below BAU by 2030:** McKinsey assumes that carbon is priced at fifty dollars a ton, and the target is a three-gigaton reduction in emissions. The amount saved would be enough to fund the more expensive abatements necessary to get to the target. McKinsey & Company (2007, 2009).

83 **Cutting emissions is an insurance policy:** The risk-aversion argument is from Weitzman (2009).

83 **Double-dividend thinking is evident in proposals:** See Goulder (2002) on double dividends when tax policies are assumed to create inefficiencies.

83 **Climate change is the most serious market failure in human history:** The possibly obvious point that climate change is the most serious market failure in history was made in the Stern Review. See also Foley (2007) for a lucid discussion.

84 **McKinsey assumes a doubling of gross world product by 2030:** McKinsey & Company (2007, 2009).

84 **Sachs assumes output will expand six times by 2050:** Sachs (2008).

84 **Nordhaus assumes a quadrupling in per capita consumption by 2105, plus more than an additional 2 billion people:** Nordhaus (2008).

84 **enormous progress in the first stage of a sustainability revolution:** On the new paradigm, see Weizsäcker, Lovins, and Lovins (1998), Hawken, Lovins, and

Lovins (2000), McDonough and Braungart (2002), and Benyus (2002). More than a decade ago, Hawken (1997) sketched out some of the inventions coming on-stream: "Down the road we'll have quantum semiconductors that store vast amounts of information on chips no bigger than a dot; diodes that emit light for 20 years without bulbs; ultrasound washing machines that use no water, heat, or soap; hyperlight materials stronger than steel; deprintable and reprintable paper; biological technologies that reduce or eliminate the need for insecticides and fertilizers; plastics that are both reusable and compostable; piezoelectric polymers that can generate electricity from the heel of your shoe or the force of a wave; and roofs and roads that do double duty as solar energy collectors."

85 **resource savings will at least pay for the cost of the innovation:** Amory Lovins has been particularly influential on this point.

85 **A classic example is creating an energy-efficient workplace:** William McDonough, the nation's leading green architect, designed a factory for chair maker Herman Miller that had these impacts. McDonough and Braungart (2002).

86 **Friedman . . . looking to clean tech:** Friedman (2008).

86 **In the McKinsey studies, the reigning assumption was to calculate emissions reductions without behavior change:** The 2009 report did add some estimates for behavior change.

86 **the pure efficiency properties of a technology . . .** On this point, see *Forces of Production*: Noble (1986).

88 **Daniel Khazzoom and Leonard Brookes . . . analyze the gains in energy efficiency of the 1970s:** Khazzoom (1980) and Brookes (1978).

88 **Researchers have not definitively settled on quantification of these effects:** Estimates of rebound effects in home heating and cooling and automobiles are from Sorrell (2007), chapter 3. See also Hertwich (2005) and Holm and Englund (2009). Indirect effects and the U.K. estimate of 26 percent rebound is from Sorrell (2007), chapter 4 and pp. 59–60.

89 **Some analysts believe energy is particularly potent in boosting profits and economic growth:** Sorrell (2007), chapter 5.

89 **The U.S. experience over the last few decades:** Rubin and Tal (2007). On the complex politics of global warming in the United States, see Luedicke, Thompson, and Giesler (2010).

91 **The U.K. debate between those advocating a purely technology and pricing approach and those who think growth needs to be curbed:** The study is by Anders Hayden, one of my Ph.D. students. See Hayden (forthcoming).

91 **"carbon crazy":** Makower (2007).

91 **this approach is known as ecological modernization:** Ecological modernization was pioneered by Arthur Mol. See Mol (1995, 1996) and Mol and Spaargaren (2000).

93 **levels of production were about a tenth of what they are today:** Gross world product in 1960 of $6.855 trillion (in 1990 dollars) is from DeLong (1998).

The 2008 gross world product of $61.22 trillion is from Central Intelligence Agency (2009).

93 **nature is truly of infinite value:** Goulder and Kennedy (forthcoming) and Heal (2009).

94 **The answer was a definite maybe:** Arrow et al. (2004). The authors' term was "tentative," rather than "definite."

94 **One reason for uncertainty was the lack of data for key environmental resources:** The paper relied on important new estimates from the World Bank, but they capture only some types of natural capital. See Hamilton et al. (2006).

94 **accounting framework developed by . . . Paul Ehrlich . . . and . . . John Holdren:** Ehrlich and Holdren (1971).

95 **more complex formulations have been developed:** For different functional forms, see York, Rosa, and Dietz (2003).

95 **medium scenario is that population will peak at 9.1 billion in 2050:** United Nations (2009).

95 **world population is growing at just under 1.2 percent per year:** Central Intelligence Agency (2009).

95 **Reductions in carbon emitted per dollar of income under BAU will be 1.2 percent:** McKinsey and Company (2009), p. 24.

96 **5–7 percent annual improvements in decarbonization alone:** McKinsey & Company (2009), p. 26. See Speth (2008) for a discussion of these issues.

96 **improvements in technology have to be even larger:** For a new study of the economics of 350 ppm, see Ackerman et al. (2009).

96 **From 1980 to 2005 . . . 30 percent on a worldwide basis:** Sustainable Europe Research Institute (2009b), p. 23. Forty-five percent increase in total materials use from p. 10.

96 **decoupling in North America has only been about 25 percent:** Author's calculations from Organization for Economic Cooperation and Development (2008b), table on p. 40.

96 **per capita annual income is already . . . $47,200:** 2008 figure from the *Economic report of the president* (2009), table B-31, p. 321.

CHAPTER 4

101 **Formalized in the 1960s by the Chicago economist Gary Becker and others:** The original paper on the theory of time allocation was Becker (1965). See also Lancaster (1966).

102 **people are devoting less unpaid labor time to community work:** See, for example, Putnam (2000). On the exception of seniors, see Goss (1999).

104 **The neuropsychiatrist Peter Whybrow . . . The filmmaker John de Graaf:** Whybrow (2005) and De Graaf, Wann, and Naylor (2001).

104 **competing sources of data collected at different points in the business cycle:** Studies that rely on time diaries do not correct for business cycle effects, which

are strong. The time-diary studies are from a mixture of strong and medium growth and recession years.

104 **Employees with low educational attainment have suffered:** Data on differences in working-hours trends by education is from Jacobs and Gerson (2005).

104 **But *all* sources show . . . hours of market work have risen:** Time-diary researchers have disputed the finding of growth of working hours. A comprehensive study of diary data is Aguiar and Hurst (2007), table 2. Comparing a series of time diaries, a data collection method in which individuals identify their activities throughout a day, they find an increase of 2.5 hours per week in core market work (paid labor) and a decline of 2 hours in unpaid household work between 1975 and 2003. This data is weekly, and understates the increase because weeks worked per year have risen. Women's hours have gone up much more than men's. Studies that claim leisure is increasing often derive their findings from a drop in market work between 1965 and 1975 in the time diary surveys, the shortcomings of which are discussed in Leete-Guy and Schor (1992). The data I discuss below, which only covers paid work, uses a recall method, in which people are asked how many hours they worked last week (or in a usual week) and how many weeks they work in a year.

105 **the average working person was putting in 180 more hours of work:** The figure of 180 more hours is from Mishel, Bernstein, and Shierholz (2009), table 3.2, p. 128. Hours for married couples are the author's calculation from Mishel, Bernstein, and Shierholz (2009), table 1.21, p. 92. Data is from the March Current Population Survey. The increase is in weeks worked per year, not hours per week. This data from the Current Population Survey shows rising hours, while data from employers (discussed in the next chapter) does not. The difference is that the latter data represents paid hours per job, not per person. A significant number of people hold more than one job, which is one source of difference. Unpaid but worked hours are also excluded from the employer estimates.

105 **Many more men are working schedules in excess of fifty hours per week:** Kuhn and Lozano (2008).

105 **the fraction of the population employed . . . rose from 60 percent in 1985 to 63 percent in 2007** Employment-to-population ratio from *Economic report of the president* (2009), table B-35, pp. 326–27.

105 **American schedules are striking:** International hours data from Conference Board and Groningen Growth and Development Centre (2008). U.S. hours exceeding other countries' by an average of 270 is the author's calculation.

106 **A 2004 study found that 44 percent:** These and subsequent findings are from Galinsky et al. (2004).

106 **Adverse effects of long hours, stress, and overwork have been found:** Studies include Kleppa, Sanne, and Tell (2008), Virtanen et al. (2009), Artazcoz et al. (2009), and Golden and Wiens-Tuers (2008).

106 **An international study from the 1990s used walking speed:** Levine (1997). The

United States was not so highly ranked on two other measures (how fast a postal clerk gives a customer change and the accuracy of bank clocks), but walking speed is probably a better indicator of the pace of life.

107 **For the individual, a sensible response is to work fewer hours:** These responses are the substitution and income effects discussed in chapter 3 in reference to energy prices. Here the issue is the "purchase" of leisure time. A decrease in the wage rate causes people to substitute out of paid employment, but the fall in income leads them to work more. Standard economic theory is agnostic about which effect will dominate.

107 **signs that a culture shift toward shorter hours and lower-impact living has begun:** The 1996 survey on downshifters is in Schor (1998), chapter 5, and Schor (2000). Data for 2004 is from Widmeyer Research and Polling (2004).

107 **New Yorkers' famously fast pace of life stopped accelerating:** Wiseman (2007) conducted a ten-year follow-up to Levine's earlier study and found that New Yorkers' walking speeds did not change.

108 **17 percent of the labor force was working part-time:** The author's calculation from United States Bureau of Labor Statistics (2008), table A-7.

108 **31 percent of the labor force was working in nonstandard employment:** Nonstandard work at 30.6 percent of the workforce is from Mishel, Bernstein, and Shierholz (2009), table 4.7, p. 253.

108 **People who make these changes report being very satisfied:** Attitudes toward downshifting come from Schor (1998, 2000) and Widmeyer Research and Polling (2004).

108 **In the first year of the recession, many businesses avoided layoffs:** Richtel (2008).

108 **one study of large firms found that 20 percent:** Luo (2009).

110 **Even lower-income nations such as Malaysia:** Countries with universal health care can be found at Wikipedia. See Universal health care (2009) and Healthcare in Malaysia (2009).

110 **pensions are more generous and reliable:** The greater generosity of pension systems in other countries is from Organization for Economic Cooperation and Development (2007), especially chapter 4.

110 **United States lags behind comparable nations in social spending:** Estimates of both gross spending and corrections for tax and other indirect effects in the OECD are from Adena and Ladaique (2005).

111 **the fraction of health care costs attributed to administration . . . has been estimated to be as high as 31 percent:** Woolhandler, Campbell, and Himmelstein (2003).

112 **psychologists Kirk Brown and Tim Kasser measured the ecological footprints of four hundred people:** Brown and Kasser (2005).

112 **A simple graph shows that countries:** The original graph of the ecological footprint versus hours, using data from earlier years, is from Schor (2005).

113 A fuller model: Hayden and Shandra (2009).

113 A study by David Rosnick and Mark Weisbrot: Rosnick and Weisbrot (2006).

113 The most obvious effect is through scale: The relation between ecological footprint and consumption expenditure is analyzed in Lenzen and Murray (2001) and Weidmann et al. (2006).

114 A Finnish study of the material intensity of time: Jalas (2002), table 1, pp. 115–16.

114 A French study found that . . . households with longer working hours: Devetter and Rousseau (2009).

116 one in five Americans said they were making plans to plant a garden: Morin and Taylor (2009).

116 service-oriented businesses . . . experienced a decline in business: Rampell (2009).

116 An annual expo called Maker Faire: See http://www.makerfaire.com. Attendance quadrupling is from Krieger (2009).

117 Fourteen percent of additions to solar capacity were in off-the-grid installations: Author's calculation from Solar Energy Industries Association (2009), p. 5.

117 followers of the visionary Egyptian architect Hassan Fathy: The Adobe Alliance and Swan's home can be found at http://www.adobealliance.org See Swan (2009).

117 Tom and Renee Elpel built a solar slipform house: Elpel (2008).

118 a visionary philosopher named Frithjof Bergmann: A discussion of the New Work system and its relation to ecology can be found in Bergmann (2000). Other information on Bergmann is from personal communications with the author.

121 the Hypercar and other superefficient options: See the discussion in Hawken, Lovins, and Lovins (2000) on the Hypercar. Bergmann has also been involved with portable electricity generators that run on biomass.

121 Led by the physicist Neil Gershenfeld: The creation of the fab lab is discussed by Gershenfeld (2005). Fab lab technology is the opposite of the dedicated (one-purpose) machinery used in older industrial production. The machines are infinitely adaptable, an extreme case of a late twentieth-century industrial paradigm called flexible specialization, which many successful smaller manufacturing companies have been practicing for some time. On this shift, see Piore and Sabel (1986) and the discussion in chapter 5.

122 the initial setup with machines and supplies was only about twenty thousand dollars: Gershenfeld (2005), p. 12. More recent estimates, of more elaborate systems, are in the range of fifty thousand dollars.

125 just another optimized distributed network: For the economics of networks, see Benkler (2006). I take up this discussion in chapter 5.

127 The anecdotal evidence seems to be yes: See Crawford (2009) for one man's story of the joys of abandoning academia for motorcycle mechanics.

128 There's no avoiding the fact: Some recent books on the ecological impacts of consumer goods are Pearce (2008), Halweil et al., (2004), and Dauvergne (2008).

129 **One new Web site allows shoppers:** The Good Guide site, founded by the University of California professor Dara O'Rourke. The site, still in beta, is at http://www.goodguide.com. The iPhone application is discussed by Furchgott (2009). An early site of this type is http://www.newdream.org/marketplace/index.php.

129 **Many consumers have found keeping track of ecological impacts to be a daunting task:** Connolly and Prothero (2008) and Seyfang and Elliott (2009).

129 **Some of the most destructive consumption in recent years:** On shrimp, see Johnston, Soderquist, and Meadows (2000). On cheap cashmere production, see Moyers (2001). On toxic tanning, see Wickens (2008). On gold, see Perlez and Bergman (2005). On meat, see Steinfeld et al. (2006).

130 **Sustainable consumption entails extending product life:** For a discussion of these principles, applied to apparel, see Schor (2002).

130 **Some footwear brands will recondition:** European shoe companies such as Mephisto, Birkenstock, and Finn Comfort provide this service.

133 **IKEA organized a furniture swap:** Van den Broek (2008).

134 **The economy of resale is complex symbolic terrain:** For an interesting discussion of the role of patina, or evidence of age, in the value of used goods, see McCracken (1990), chapter 2, pp. 31–43.

134 **thrift shops . . . have also gone upscale in recent years:** Ferla (2009). This trend began before the current downturn.

135 **"good for the dysfunctional family":** Fletcher (2004), quoting Gopal Ahluwahlia, director of research for the National Association of Home Builders.

135 **A 2008 survey found more than 60 percent:** National Association of Home Builders survey, cited in Bender (2009).

136 **the latest generation of solar homes now being built in northern Europe:** Described in Rosenthal (2008).

136 **Smaller living spaces are getting popular:** There have been a number of press accounts of the small-house movement. See Bender (2009) and Kurutz (2008). See also Resources for Life (2009).

136 **Cohousing communities:** For a list of cohousing groups, which in early 2009 numbered 113, see http://www.cohousing.org/directory. There are currently nineteen ecovillages in the United States.

136 **Recent press reports . . . green project in Seattle . . . the obituary of the "big house":** Bender (2009).

137 **Freecycle.org members are committed:** Lawrence (2008) and Nelson, Rademacher, and Paek (2007).

139 **Spending time with friends is also on the wane:** Putnam's findings of declining socializing are from Putnam (2000), p. 107. Analyses of data from the General

Social Survey by sociologists from the University of Arizona and Duke recorded a precipitous drop in the size of the average close friendship network (number of people who were available to talk to about important matters) from three to two between 1985 and 2004. See McPherson, Smith-Lovin, and Brashears (2006), although Fischer (2009) has raised questions about the reliability of this data.

140 **Most consumer researchers think differently:** On brand communities, see Muniz and O'Guinn (2001). On *Star Trek* fans, see Jenkins (1992).

140 **the economic function of community eroded:** For a recent treatment of the erosion of community by the market, see Marglin (2008).

140 **research on poor urban African Americans in the 1970s:** Stack (1983).

141 **More affluent groups are less likely to engage in reciprocal labor transfers:** For extensive treatments of transfers, see Sarkisian, Gerena, and Gerstel (2006) and Sarkisian and Gerstel (2004).

141 **the successful launch of BerkShares:** For the philosophy and history of Berk-Shares, see http://www.berkshares.org.

142 **Post Carbon Cities Network:** See its list of actions at http://postcarboncities.net/actions/table?sort=desc&order=Population.

142 **economic and political benefits such as better government:** On the relationship between good government and better economic functioning, see Putnam, Leonardi, and Nanetti (1994).

142 **Eric Klinenberg's study of the Chicago heat wave:** Klinenberg (2003)

143 **the denser a person's social connections:** On the relation between social connection and receiving help in crises, see Hurlbert, Haines, and Beggs (2000).

143 **Recent work on Katrina survivors:** Lowe, Chan, and Rhodes (forthcoming).

CHAPTER 5

148 **"This is not a product-based program":** Fleisher quoted in Raver (2009).

148 **Economics has been mainly absent:** There is, of course, a conversation about clean energy technology transfer between south and north as part of the global climate conversation.

149 **vulnerable to the expansion of dirty production in poorer countries:** Larry Summers's infamous memo on the optimality of sending toxic waste to Africa pointed out this perverse logic in the operation of the current market system. On the rich countries' ecological footprints and carbon footprints being generated in poor nations, see Ghertner and Fripp (2007) and Hertwich and Peters (2009).

149 **That's where the economics of knowledge, or information, comes in:** The difference between the economics of information and knowledge is discussed by Foray (2006). I am using the two interchangeably, given the level of generality of my treatment.

149 **The implications of this point are obviously far-reaching:** For a general treat-

ment of the economics of information, see Foray (2006). For an excellent introduction to the information commons, and the complexities and possibilities for managing it, see Hess and Ostrom (2006), chapter 1.

150 **as copyrights and patents have been extended:** For a critique of intellectual property in the global context, see especially the work of Vandana Shiva on biopiracy (Shiva 1999).

150 **the "on the shoulders of giants" effect:** The phrase comes from Isaac Newton, who famously noted, "If I have seen far, it is by standing on the shoulders of giants." For discussions of the "on the shoulders of giants" effect, see Scotchmer (1991), Caballero and Jaffe (1993), and Benkler (2006). This is one reason even market-oriented economists often support government funding of basic research and subsidies even for applied research.

151 **a wide swath of the economy:** The list of sectors where information sharing is becoming common is from Benkler (2006), p. 121.

151 **In its online form, this has been dubbed peer production:** *Peer production* is Benkler's term. See also Bauwens (2005).

151 **Decentralized, or distributed, production:** The literature differentiates between decentralized and distributed production, with the former having mandatory hubs, which are absent in the latter. See Bauwens (2005). I am collapsing the two here.

151 **"The networked environment":** Benkler (2006), p. 60.

152: **Factor e Farm is a group dedicated to:** On open-source ecology's mission, see Statement of Aims from http://factorefarm.org/content/factor-e-farm-weblog.

153 **They've already developed and built machines:** For the list of Factor *e* Farm projects, see http://factorefarm.org/view/projects/all.

153 **The farm's founder, Marcin Jakubowski, uses the term *neocommercialization*:** Jakubowski (2008). He continues, "The concept of neo-commercialization embodies both our own ability to produce and earn from the products, as well as our interest to disseminate the products via open franchising. Open franchising means that our products and production processes are under an unrestricted, open license, where users are free to decide for themselves as to how they will use, develop, or market the technologies. There are no strings attached. It is our private interest to have people contribute back to open production capacity, but we are not interested in policing the use of our creations. We are interested in maximum dissemination, because we believe that our products have a beneficial contribution to society. People are free to make living [*sic*] from our products, and modify them how they choose."

153 **The Factor e Farm may or may not succeed:** The organization and the farm may fall prey to the limitations of the founders. Some conflicts have emerged. See for example Lippincott (2009).

154 **the RepRap, which makes:** Discussion and video at Jakubowski (2009). The RepRap cannot make its own metal parts or wiring, but replicates its plastic components.

155 **a productivity slowdown and squeeze on corporate profitability:** For an analysis of the slowdown and the mass production model, see Marglin and Schor (1990) and Schor and You (1995).

155 **Two MIT political economists:** Piore and Sabel (1986).

155 **The literature on size and economic performance:** Recent discussions of size and economic performance include Benkler (2006) and Shuman (n.d.)

156 **nearly two-thirds of all jobs . . . job loss has become more prevalent in large than small companies:** Helfand, Sadeghi, and Talan (2007).

157 **the heart of cutting-edge sustainability thinking:** For arguments in favor of local economies, see work from the International Forum on Globalization, including Cavanagh and Mander (2004); Shuman (2006); and the Business Alliance for Local Living Economies, at http://www.livingeconomies.org.

158 **More than half the world's population lives on less than $2.50 a day:** Chen and Ravallion (2008), table 6, p. 32.

158 **In 2004 30 percent of households had less than twelve thousand dollars:** This and other wealth statistics are from Mishel, Bernstein, and Shierholz (2009), table 5.4, p. 270 (twelve thousand dollars); bottom 90 percent and 34 percent from table 5.1, p. 265, using the research of New York University economist Edward Wolff.

158 **Some of the most important environmental economic research:** Boyce and Pastor (2001), Harper and Rajan (2004), Stanton and Boyce (2005), Agarwal and Narain (2000), and Boyce and Shelley (2003).

159 **community-managed, income-producing property:** For a pioneering discussion of commons management, see Elinor Ostrom (1990), who received the 2009 Nobel Prize in economics for this work. See also Parthasarathi (2002) for a discussion of the history and sustainability principles of common property.

159 **In impoverished tribal areas in India:** Indian case studies are from Agarwal and Narain (2000).

160 **The Sky Trust proposal:** Barnes (2001).

160 **prior human investments in ecosystems:** Information on Amazon *terra preta* and West African savannas comes from Stanton and Boyce (2005).

161 **social capital is a condition:** On the conditions for successful commons management, see the work of Ostrom (1990). See also Hess and Ostrom (2006), chapter 1.

161 **in eighteenth-century South India:** Parthasarathi (2002).

162 **A National Science Foundation–funded "GreenFab" collaboration:** Program information is at http://itestlrc.edc.org/greenfab-sustainable-design-through-engineering-and-technology.

162 **An informal education network:** In the United States, examples include the Solar Living Institute, the Farm, the Permaculture Institute, Yestermorrow, the Regenerative Design Institute, and others. See discussion of the Global Ecovillage Network below for more examples.

163 **U.S. companies have been shedding labor:** The estimates of 8 million jobs lost, one in six under- or unemployed, and necessary job growth of half a million per month for two years are from Shierholz (2009). The monthly figure for job growth is 573,000.

163 **The classic case is agriculture:** The three-quarters share of the labor force in agriculture is from Margo (2000), table 5.3, p. 213. The 1800 figure is 74.4 percent. The 1900 figure is 36 percent. The 2009 1.4 percent figure is from United States Bureau of Labor Statistics (2009b).

164 **Since 1973, productivity has almost doubled:** *Economic report of the president* (2009), table B-49, p. 342.

164 **economists debated whether it would be possible:** The historical debate is discussed by Hunnicutt (1988).

165 **Hours of work in the United States began to fall after about 1870:** All data from 1870 and 1929 is from Maddison (1987), table A-9, p. 686. Data from 1973 is from Conference Board and Groningen Growth and Development Centre (2008). In the United States, hours fell from 2,964 to 2,342 between 1870 and 1929.

166 **if people wanted shorter hours:** See Schor (1992) for a critique of the argument that workers get the hours they desire.

166 **Some of the most efficient and competitive manufacturing sectors in the world:** Hourly productivity in manufacturing is from United States Bureau of Labor Statistics (2009c), table 1, Output per hour in manufacturing.

167 **reductions in daily hours are associated with a rise in productivity per hour:** On working hours, costs, and competition, see the discussion in Schor (1992). Germany and the Netherlands are examples of high-productivity, low-hours economies. See Burgoon and Baxandall (2004) and Hayden (2006) for discussions of the political economy of hours reductions.

167 **According to one widely used data source:** All data for 1973 through 2007 is from Conference Board and Groningen Growth and Development Centre (2008).

167 **This data understates the case:** The cross-national data from Groningen is from employers, and is calculated per job. The data in the previous chapter is per person, from the Current Population Survey. Work time rising by 204 is from Mishel, Bernstein, and Shierholz (2009), table 3.2, Trend in average wages and average hours, 1967–1973, p. 128.

168 **reducing hours and instigating furloughs:** Dewan (2009) and Luo (2009).

168 **sustainability advocates increasingly recognize:** Speth (2008), Victor (2008), and, earlier, Hayden (2000).

168 **the financialization of the United States economy:** Epstein (2006) and Epstein and Schor (1990).

169 **The influential formulations of Gary Becker:** Becker (1978).

170 **the evolutionary psychology literature . . . falls short:** Saad (2007) and Miller (2009). For example, the evolutionary argument predicts strong sex differentiation in consumption patterns; however, recent trends are toward convergence, as

in cosmetics and other consumer purchases. A compelling treatment is Whybrow (2005).

170 **consumption-based competition appears to vary with the distribution of income:** For the influence of income inequality on hours and income, see Bowles and Park (2005).

170 **a decline in materialist values:** Inglehart (1989, 1997).

171 **Gar Alperovitz has studied employee-owned companies:** Alperovitz (2005).

172 **Slow Money movement:** Tasch (2008).

172 **Conscious consumers who . . . pay a bit more for products:** On the conscious-consumer movement, see Willis (2009), Willis and Schor (n.d.), Seyfang and Elliott (2009), and Schor (forthcoming).

172 **investors would reduce the returns:** Keynes (1936).

172 **There is no magic, or "natural," rate of return:** Neoclassical economic theory has used the concept of "natural" rates, for example, the "natural" rate of unemployment. In the case of profit, the reasoning relies on a flawed theory of aggregate capital. This issue was the subject of the famous Cambridge capital controversy in the 1950s, between economists in Cambridge, England, and Cambridge, Massachusetts. Rather than representing some "natural" rate, profit is distributed to owners of capital from the overall surplus generated in the economy.

173 **a major study led by Nobel Prize–winning economists:** Stiglitz, Sen, and Fitoussi (2009). For a discussion of some of the initiatives currently under way to revise GDP or go "beyond growth," particularly in Europe, see Abdallah et al. (2009), pp. 16–18.

173 **The second is to improve living standards:** There is a third argument for growth, which is that historically it has been the grease that keeps distributional conflicts from getting too intense, through the "rising tide lifts all boats" mechanism, as Friedman (2005) and others have argued. This justification is less powerful now, when growth is also associated with more, not less, inequality in many countries. When growth has other negative consequences, direct attention to distribution is a more efficient way to address the problem.

173 **Getting bigger doesn't necessarily yield wealth; improving productivity does:** Taking productivity growth in the form of leisure is a strategy that will reach its limits (when hours fall so far that additional leisure time is not useful). However, by the time we get to that point, production may be sufficiently "clean" that growth is not environmentally degrading.

174 **the first International Degrowth Conference:** Other groups addressing this question include the New Economics Foundation, Redefining Progress, the Schumacher Society, the Association for the Steady-State Economy, Shrinking Economies in the Developed World, and the International Forum on Globalization, as well as individuals within the International Society for Ecological Economics.

174 **ecological economist Peter Victor:** Victor (2008), chapter 10. Other critiques of growth include Daly (1996) and Schor (1998), epilogue.

175 **investments in alternative energy produce 3.2 times the employment:** The employment impacts of different types of energy are from Pollin, Heintz, and Garrett-Peltier (2009), table 4, p. 28, and figure 1, p. 30.

175 **The United States accounted for 28 percent of global carbon emissions:** This figure and subsequent countries' shares are from Monastersky (2009).

175 **Poor countries deserve:** A pioneering study of how this could happen is Sachs, Loske, and Linz (1998). See also Schor (1991, 1995, 2005) on this topic.

176 **a rhetoric of sacrifice in wealthy countries:** On the environmental politics of sacrifice, see Maniates and Meyer (forthcoming).

176 **The research on income and happiness is now enormous:** Recent studies and reviews include the influential volume by Kahneman, Diener, and Schwarz (1999), Clark and Oswald (1996), Layard (2005), Easterlin (2003), Di Tella and MacCulloch (2006), Loewenstein, O'Donoghue, and Rabin (2003), Kahneman and Krueger (2006), Kahneman et al.(2006), Frey and Stutzer (2002), and Van Praag and Frijters (1999). For dissenting findings, see Stevenson and Wolfers (2008a, 2008b).

177 **China's rapid growth in material prosperity has led to less, not more, satisfaction:** Kahneman and Krueger (2006), figure 4.

177 **British economist Richard Layard found:** Figure of $20,000 from Layard (2005), p. 33, updated to today's prices by author.

177 **happiness is almost wholly unresponsive:** Easterlin (2003, 2004).

177 **explanations for these counterintuitive findings:** For a discussion of whether the results are an artifact of measurement, a possibility that has received a good deal of attention, see Kahneman and Krueger (2006).

177 **35 to 60 percent of incremental income falls victim:** Van Praag and Frijters (1999), who report 35–60 percent increases in "required" income across countries (table 2). See also Stutzer (2003).

177 **people care a great deal about these positional effects:** See Frey and Stutzer (2002) for a review of the findings on positionality. See Solnick and Hemenway (1998) for survey evidence. For an argument about positionality as a driver of consumption behavior, see Schor (1998).

177 **One study of U.S. localities:** Luttmer (2005). Luttmer found that the impact of neighbors' income rising is equivalent to a similarly sized fall in one's own income.

178 **anticipate that additional income will yield more happiness ... projection bias:** On overvaluing income, or projection bias, see Loewenstein, O'Donoghue, and Rabin (2003); on the related concept of the focusing illusion, see Kahneman et al. (2006).

178 **In a series of studies, the psychologists Tim Kasser and Kennon Sheldon:** Kasser and Sheldon (2009).

178 **Kasser and Kirk Brown found that working hours:** Kasser and Brown (2003).

178 Nobel laureate Daniel Kahneman and his Princeton colleague: Kahneman and Krueger (2006), table 2.

178 A study among European Union countries: Alesina, Glaeser, and Sacerdote (2005), table 15.

178 Data from a large-scale German survey: Pouwels, Siegers, and Vlasblom (2008).

178 income is positional, but leisure time is not: Vacations and shorter hours not being positional is from Solnick and Hemenway (1998). See also Frank (1985).

179 No surprises here: Activities that yield well-being are from Kahneman and Krueger (2006), table 2.

179 numerous benefits to humans from contact with the outdoors: See the review of findings by Kellert (2005). Many of the studies are from the field of environmental psychology. In addition to Kellert, see the work of Terry Hartig and Rachel and Stephen Kaplan.

179 The New Economics Foundation's Happy Planet Index: Abdallah et al. (2009). The Costa Rica discussion is on p. 28; the United States' rank is from the HPI results table, p. 61.

180 urban homesteading: Coyne and Knutzen (2008).

180 chicken underground: Block (2008).

181 The Transition Town movement: See http://transitiontowns.org/Transition Network/TransitionNetwork and, for the United States, http://transitionus .ning.com.

181 New ways of living are proliferating: A description of the Global Ecovillage Network (GEN), its living and learning philosophy, and more detail on these and other examples from around the world can be found at http://gen.ecovillage.org

182 thirteen thousand diverse communities: Global Ecovillage Network (2009).

184 a better way of human being: In 2007, Paul Hawken published a study of "the largest movement in the world," a largely unrecognized convergence of millions who are working for the environment, social justice, and indigenous peoples, which includes more than one hundred thousand groups contributing to these efforts. See Hawken (2007) and the database and community associated with the project, at http://www.wiserearth.org.

References

Abdallah, Saamah, Sam Thompson, Juliet Michaelson, Nic Marks, and Nicola Steuer. 2009. *The un-happy planet index 2.0: Why good lives don't have to cost the earth*. London: New Economics Foundation. Available from http://www.happyplanetindex.org/public-data/files/happy-planet-index-2-0.pdf (accessed September 7, 2009).

Abernathy, Frederick H., John T. Dunlop, Janice H. Hammond, and David Weil. 1999. *A stitch in time: Lean retailing and the transformation; Lessons from the apparel and textile industries*. New York: Oxford University Press.

Ackerman, Frank. 2006. The unbearable lightness of regulatory costs. *Fordham Urban Law Journal* 33 (4) (May): 1071–96.

Ackerman, Frank, Stephen J. DeCanio, Richard B. Howarth, and Kristen Sheeran. 2009. Limitations of integrated assessment models of climate change. *Climatic Change* 95 (April 2): 297–315. Available from http://www.springerlink.com.proxy.bc.edu/content/c85v5581x7n74571/fulltext.pdf (accessed June 30, 2009).

Ackerman, Frank, and Ian J. Finlayson. 2006. The economics of inaction on climate change: A sensitivity analysis. *Climate Policy* 6: 509–26.

Ackerman, Frank, and Lisa Heinzerling. 2004. *Priceless: On knowing the price of everything and the value of nothing*. New York: The New Press.

Ackerman, Frank, Elizabeth A. Stanton, and Ramon Bueno. Forthcoming. Fat tails, exponents, and extreme uncertainty: Simulating catastrophe in DICE. *Ecological Economics*.

Ackerman, Frank, Elizabeth A. Stanton, Stephen J. DeCanio, Eban Goodstein, Richard B. Howarth, Richard B. Norgaard, Catherine S. Norman, and Kristen A. Sheeran. 2009. *The economics of 350: The benefits and costs of climate stabilization*. Economics for Equity and the Environment Network. Available from http://www.e3network.org (accessed October 10, 2009).

Adena, Willem, and Maxime Ladaique. 2005. *Net social expenditure 2005 edition: More comprehensive measures of social support*. Paris: OECD.

Agarwal, Anil, and Sunita Narain. 2000. *Redressing ecological poverty through participatory democracy: Case studies from India.* PERI Working Paper Series #36. Amherst, Mass.: Political Economy Research Institute. Available from http://www.peri.umass .edu/fileadmin/pdf/working_papers/working_papers_1-50/WP36.pdf (accessed July 23, 2009).

Aguiar, Mark, and Erik Hurst. 2007. Measuring trends in leisure: The allocation of time over five decades. *The Quarterly Journal of Economics* 122:3: 969–1006.

Alesina, Alberto, Edward Glaeser, and Bruce Sacerdote. 2005. *Work and leisure in the US and Europe: Why so different?* NBER Working Paper 11278. Cambridge, Mass.: National Bureau of Economic Research.

Alperovitz, Gar. 2005. *America beyond capitalism: Reclaiming our wealth, our liberty, and our democracy.* Hoboken, N.J.: Wiley.

American Apparel & Footwear Association. 2009. *Trends: An annual statistical analysis of the U.S. apparel & footwear industries, annual 2008 edition.* Available from http:// www.apparelandfootwear.org/UserFiles/File/Statistics/trends2008Annual.pdf (accessed August 1, 2009).

Arrow, Kenneth, Bert Bolin, Robert Costanza, Partha Dasgupta, Carl Folke, C. S. Holling, Bengt-Owe Jansson, et al. 1995. Economic growth, carrying capacity, and the environment. *Science* 268 (April 28): 520–21.

Arrow, Kenneth, Partha Dasgupta, Lawrence Goulder, Gretchen Daily, Paul Ehrlich, Geoffrey Heal, Simon Levin, et al. 2004. Are we consuming too much? *Journal of Economic Perspectives* 18 (3): 147–72.

Artazcoz, L., I. Cortès, V. Escribà-Agüir, L. Cascant, and R. Villegas. 2009. Understanding the relationship of long working hours with health status and health-related behaviours. *Journal of Epidemiology and Community Health* 63 (7): 521–27.

Askari, Hossein, and Noureddine Krichene. 2007. *Inflationary trends in world commodities markets: 2003–2007.* Occasional Paper Series, Center for the Study of Globalization, The George Washington University. Available from http://gstudynet.org/spot light/workingpapers/InflationaryTrendsinWorldR1_Askari.pdf (accessed June 15, 2009).

Associated Press. 2009. Government to give GMAC $7.5B in new aid. National Public Radio [database online]. Available from http://www.npr.org/templates/story/ story.php?storyId=104420777 (accessed May 22, 2009).

Ayres, Robert U. 1996. Limits to the growth paradigm. *Ecological Economics* 19 (2) (November): 117–34.

———. 1993. Cowboys, cornucopians, and long-run sustainability. *Ecological Economics* 8 (3) (December): 189–207.

Bagliani, Marco, Giangiacomo Bravo, and Silvana Dalmazzone. 2008. A consumption-based approach to environmental Kuznets curves using the ecological footprint indicator. *Ecological Economics* 65: 650–61.

Barlow, Maude. 2002. *Blue gold: The fight to stop the corporate theft of the world's water.* New York: New Press.

Barnes, Peter. 2001. *Who owns the sky? Our common assets and the future of capitalism.* Washington, D.C.: Island Press.

Bates, Bryson C., Zbigniew W. Kundzewicz, Shaohong Wu, and Jean P. Palutikof. 2008. *Climate change and water: Technical paper of the intergovernmental panel on climate change.* Geneva: IPCC Secretariat. Available from http://www.ipcc.ch/ipccre ports/tp-climate-change-water.htm (accessed June 1, 2009).

Battisti, David S., and Rosamond L. Naylor. 2009. Historical warnings of future food insecurity with unprecedented seasonal heat. *Science* 323 (January 9): 240–44.

Baudrillard, Jean. 2001. *Selected writings.* Edited by Mark Poster. Stanford, Calif.: Stanford University Press.

Bauwens, Michel. 2005.The political economy of peer production. CTheory [database online]. Available from http://www.ctheory.net/articles.aspx?id=499 (accessed April 30, 2009).

Becker, Gary. 1978. *The economic approach to human behavior.* Chicago: Chicago University Press.

———. 1965. A theory of the allocation of time. *Economic Journal* 75: 493–517.

Beckerman, Wilfred. 1972. Economists, scientists, and environmental catastrophe. *Oxford Economic Papers* 24 (3): 327–44.

Beddoe, Rachael, Robert Costanza, Joshua Farley, Eric Garza, Jennifer Kent, Ida Kubiszewski, Luz Martinez, et al. 2009. Overcoming systemic roadblocks to sustainability: The evolutionary redesign of worldviews, institutions, and technologies. *PNAS* 106 (8) (February 24): 2483–89. Available from http://www .uvm.edu/giee/publications/Beddoe%20et%20al%202009pnas.pdf (accessed June 25, 2009).

Bender, Kristen. 2009. Small is better: Big houses are out and downsizing is in. Independent Media Institute [database online]. Available from http://www.alter net.org/environment/139839/small_is_better%3A_big_houses_are_out_and_ downsizing_is_in/?page=entire (accessed May 29, 2009).

Benkler, Yochai. 2006. *The wealth of networks: How social production transforms markets and freedom.* New Haven, Conn.: Yale University Press.

Benyus, Janine M. 2002. *Biomimicry: Innovation inspired by nature.* New York: Harper Perennial.

Bergmann, Frithjof. 2000. Ecology and New Work: Excess consumption and the job system. In *The consumer society reader,* edited by Juliet B. Schor and Douglas B. Holt. New York: The New Press, 488–502.

BerkShares, Inc.: Local currency for the Berkshire region. 2009. BerkShares, Inc. [database online]. Available from http://www.berkshares.org (accessed September 7, 2009).

Block, Ben. 2008. U.S. city dwellers flock to raising chickens. Worldwatch Institute [database online]. Available from http://www.worldwatch.org/node/5900?emc =el&m=216150&l=6&v=8fa3fab31a (accessed March 19, 2009).

Bowles, Samuel, and Herbert Gintis. 2004. The evolution of strong reciprocity:

Cooperation in heterogeneous populations. *Theoretical Population Biology* 65 (1): 17–28.

Bowles, Samuel, and Yongjin Park. 2005. Emulation, inequality and work hours: Was Thorsten Veblen right? *The Economic Journal* 115: 397–413.

Boyce, James K., and Manuel Pastor. 2001. *Building natural assets: New strategies for poverty reduction and environmental protection.* Amherst, Mass.: Political Economy Research Institute. Available from http://www.peri.umass.edu/fileadmin/pdf/research_brief/RR3.pdf (accessed June 9, 2009).

Boyce, James K., and Barry G. Shelley, eds. 2003. *Natural assets: Democratizing environmental ownership.* Washington, D.C.: Island Press.

Brady, Diane, and Christopher Palmeri. 2007. The pet economy. *BusinessWeek,* August 6. Available from http://www.businessweek.com/magazine/content/07_32/b40-45001.htm (accessed July 7, 2009).

Brenner, Y. S., Hartmut Kaelble, and Mark Thomas. 1991. *Income distribution in historical perspective.* New York: Cambridge University Press.

Brookes, L. G. 1978. Energy policy, the energy price fallacy and the role of nuclear energy in the UK. *Energy Policy* 6 (2): 94–106.

Brown, Kirk Warren, and Tim Kasser. 2005. Are psychological and ecological well-being compatible? The role of values, mindfulness, and lifestyle. *Social Indicators Research* 74: 349–68.

Burgoon, Brian, and Phineas Baxandall. 2004. Three worlds of working time: Policy and politics in work-time patterns of industrialized countries. *Politics and Society* 32 (December): 439–73.

Business Alliance for Local Living Economies (BALLE). The Business Alliance for Local Living Economies: 20,000 entrepreneurs building the new economy. Available from http://www.livingeconomies.org (accessed September 7, 2009).

Caballero, Ricardo J., and Adam B. Jaffe. 1993. How high are the giants' shoulders: An empirical assessment of knowledge spillovers and creative destruction in a model of economic growth. *NBER Macroeconomics Annual* 8: 15–74.

Cavanagh, John, and Jerry Mander. 2004. *Alternatives to economic globalization: A better world is possible.* San Francisco: Berrett-Koehler.

Caviglia-Harris, Jill L., Dustin Chambers, and James R. Kahn. 2009. Taking the "U" out of Kuznets: A comprehensive analysis of the EKC and environmental degradation. *Ecological Economics* 68 (4): 1149–59.

Central Intelligence Agency. 2009. The world factbook. Available from https://www.cia.gov/library/publications/the-world-factbook/geos/xx.html (accessed August 3, 2009).

Chen, Shaohua, and Martin Ravallion. 2008. *The developing world is poorer than we thought, but no less successful in the fight against poverty.* Policy Research Working Paper 4703. World Bank. Available from www-wds.worldbank.org/.../2008/...20080519094812/.../wps4621.pdf (accessed July 23, 2009).

Christakis, Nicholas S., and John H. Fowler. 2007. The spread of obesity in a large social network over 32 years. *New England Journal of Medicine* 357: 370–79.

Ciais, Ph., M. Reichstein, N. Viovy, A. Granier, J. Ogee, V. Allard, M. Aubinet, et al. 2005. Europe-wide reduction in primary productivity caused by the heat and drought in 2003. *Nature* 437 (September 22): 529–33.

Clark, Andrew, and Andrew Oswald. 1996. Satisfaction and comparison income. *Journal of Public Economics* 61 (3): 359–81.

Climate Adaptation Science and Policy Initiative. 2007. *Evidence of accelerated climate change.* The University of Melbourne for the Climate Institute. Available from http://www.climateinstitute.org.au/images/stories/CI056_EACC_Report_v1.pdf (accessed June 1, 2009).

Cohen, Patricia. 2009. Ivory tower unswayed by crashing economy. *The New York Times,* March 4. Available from http://www.nytimes.com/2009/03/05/books/05deba .html?emc=eta1 (accessed March 6, 2009).

Cohousing Association of the United States. 2008. Cohousing directory. Available from http://www.cohousing.org/directory (accessed February 8, 2009).

Conference Board, The, and Groningen Growth and Development Centre. 2008. Total economy database. Available from http://www.conference-board.org.proxy.bc .edu/economics (accessed March 15, 2009).

Conley, Dalton. 2009. America is #. . . 15? *The Nation,* March 4. Available from http://www.thenation.com/doc/20090323/conley?rel=hp_currently (accessed March 29, 2009).

Connolly, John, and Andrea Prothero. 2008. Green consumerism: Life politics, risks and contradictions. *Journal of Consumer Culture* 8 (1): 117–45.

Context-Based Research Group and Carton Donofrio Partners, Inc. 2008. *Grounding the American dream: A cultural study on the future of consumerism in a changing economy.*

Copenhagen Conference on Climate Change: Global Risks, Challenges & Decisions. 2009. *Key messages from the congress.* Available from http://climatecongress.ku.dk/ newsroom/congress_key_messages (accessed March 27, 2009).

Costanza, Robert, Ralph D'Arge, Rudolf De Groot, Stephen Farber, Monica Grasso, Bruce Hannon, Karin Limburg, et al. 1997. The value of the world's ecosystem services and natural capital. *Nature* 387 (May 15): 253–60.

Costanza, Robert, L. J. Graumlich, and W. Steffen, eds. 2007. *Sustainability or collapse? An integrated history and future of people on earth.* Dahlem Workshop Report 96. Cambridge, Mass.: MIT Press.

Coyne, Kelly, and Erik Knutzen. 2008. *The urban homestead: Your guide to self-sufficient living in the heart of the city.* Port Townsend, Wash.: Process Publishers.

Crawford, Matthew B. 2009. The case for working with your hands. *The New York Times Magazine,* May 21. Available from http://www.nytimes.com/2009/05/24/ magazine/24labor-t.html (accessed September 7, 2009).

Daily, Gretchen C. 1997. *Nature's services: Societal dependence on natural ecosystems.* Washington, D.C.: Island Press.

Daily, Gretchen C., Tore Soderqvist, Sara Aniyar, Kenneth Arrow, Partha Dasgupta, Paul R. Ehrlich, Carl Folke, et al. 2000. The value of nature and the nature of value. *Science* 289 (5478) (July 21): 395–96.

Daly, Herman E. 2005. Economics in a full world. *Scientific American* 293 (3) (September): 100–107.

———. 1996. *Beyond growth: The economics of sustainable development.* Boston: Beacon Press.

———. 1977. *Steady-state economics: The economics of biophysical equilibrium and moral growth.* San Francisco: W.H. Freeman.

Dasgupta, Partha. 2005. A measured approach. *Scientific American* 293 (3) (September): 106.

Dauvergne, Peter. 2008. *The shadows of consumption: Consequences for the global environment.* Cambridge, Mass.: MIT Press.

DeCanio, Stephen J. 2005. Descriptive or conceptual models? Contributions of economics to the climate policy debate. *International Environmental Agreements* 5: 415–27.

De Graaf, John, David Wann, and Thomas Naylor. 2001. *Affluenza: The all-consuming epidemic.* San Francisco: Berrett-Koehler.

Dell, Melissa, Benjamin F. Jones, and Benjamin A. Olken. 2008. *Climate shocks and economic growth: Evidence from the last half century.* Working Paper 14132. Cambridge, Mass.: National Bureau of Economic Research. Available from http://indiaenvironmentportal.org.in/files/climate_shocks%5B1%5D.pdf (accessed July 29, 2009).

DeLong, J. B. 1998. Estimating world GDP, one million B.C.–present. Available from http://econ161.berkeley.edu/TCEH/1998_Draft/World_GDP/Estimating_World_GDP.html (accessed July 7, 2009).

Devetter, F. X., and S. Rousseau. 2009. *Working hours and sustainable development.* Unpublished; provided privately to author.

Dewan, Shaila. 2009. A slowdown that may slow us down. *The New York Times*, March 1. Available from http://www.nytimes.com/2009/03/01/weekinreview/01dewan.html (accessed September 7, 2009).

Diamond, Jared. 2005. *Collapse: How societies choose to fail or succeed.* New York: Viking Penguin.

Diaz, Robert J., and Rutger Rosenberg. 2008. Spreading dead zones and consequences for marine ecosystems. *Science* 321 (5891) (August 15): 926–29. Available from http://www.sciencemag.org/cgi/content/abstract/321/5891/926?ijkey=Lk77Ef I/7oLkY&keytype=ref&siteid=sci (accessed April 2, 2009).

Di Tella, Rafael, and Robert Macculloch. 2006. Some uses of happiness data in economics. *Journal of Economic Perspectives* 20 (1): 25–46.

Dwyer, Rachel E. 2007. Expanding homes and increasing inequalities: U.S. housing development and the residential segregation of the affluent. *Social Problems* 54 (1): 23–46.

Easterlin, Richard A. 2004. *Diminishing marginal utility of income: A caveat.* University of Southern California Law School, Law and Economics Working Paper Series No. 5. Available from http://ideas.repec.org/p/bep/usclwp/usclwps-1004.html (accessed July 14, 2009).

———. 2003. Explaining happiness. *PNAS* 100 (19): 11176–86.

Economic report of the president. 2009. Washington, D.C.: United States Government Printing Office. Available from http://www.gpoaccess.gov/eop/2009/2009_erp .pdf (accessed July 6, 2009).

Edenhofer, Ottmar, Kai Lessmann, Claudia Kemfert, Michael Grubb, and Jonathan Kohler. 2006. Induced technological change: Exploring its implications for the economics of atmospheric stabilization; Synthesis report from the innovation modeling comparison project. *The Energy Journal,* Endogenous Technological Change and the Economics of Atmospheric Stabilisation Special Issue: 57–107.

Ehrlich, Paul R., and John P. Holdren. 1971. Impact of population growth. *Science* 171 (3977) (March 26): 1212–17.

Elpel, Thomas J. 2008. Sustainable living skills. Available from http://www.hollowtop .com/cls_html/cls.html (accessed August 12, 2009).

Environmental Protection Agency. 2009. *Inventory of US greenhouse gas emissions and sinks: 1990–2007.* EPA 430-R-09-004. Washington, D.C.: Environmental Protection Agency. Available from http://epa.gov/climatechange/emissions/usinventoryre port.html (accessed March 29, 2009).

———. 2008. *Municipal solid waste in the United States: Facts and figures.* Washington, D.C.: U.S. Environmental Protection Agency. Available from http://www.epa.gov/osw/ nonhaz/municipal/msw99.htm (accessed November, 24, 2009).

Environmental Protection Agency Office of Solid Waste. 2008. *Electronics waste management in the United States.* EPA 530-R-08-009.Washington, D.C.: Environmental Protection Agency. Available from http://www.epa.gov/epawaste/conserve/ materials/ecycling/manage.htm (accessed July 2, 2009).

Epstein, Gerald A. 2006. *Financialization and the world economy.* Cheltenham, U.K.: Edward Elgar.

Epstein, Gerald A., and Juliet B. Schor. 1990. Corporate profitability as a determinant of restrictive monetary policy: Estimates for the postwar United States. In *The political economy of American monetary policy,* edited by Thomas Mayer. New York: Cambridge University Press.

Ewen, Stuart. 1988. *All consuming images: The politics of style in contemporary culture.* New York: Basic Books.

Ewing, B., S. Goldfinger, Mathis Wackernagel, M. Stechbart, S. M. Rizk, A. Reed, and Justin Kitzes. 2008. *The ecological footprint atlas 2008.* Oakland: Global Footprint Network.

Factor e farm: Site projects. 2009. Open Source Ecology [database online]. Available from http://factorefarm.org/view/projects/all (accessed April 29, 2009).

Factor e farm weblog. 2009. Open Source Ecology [database online]. Available from http://factorefarm.org/content/factor-e-farm-weblog (accessed April 29, 2009).

Featherstone, Mike. 2007. *Consumer culture and postmodernism*. 2nd ed. London: Sage.

Federal Reserve Statistical Release. 2009. *Flow of funds accounts of the United States*. Available from http://www.federalreserve.gov/releases/z1/Current/z1r-2.pdf (accessed April 7, 2009).

Ferla, Ruth. 2009. Look who's shopping Goodwill. *The New York Times*, June 10. Available from http://www.nytimes.com/2009/06/11/fashion/11goodwill.html?scp=21&sq=second%20hand&st=cse (accessed September 7, 2009).

Fernandez, Bob. 2004. Cast-off clothing fuels a surge in thrift business. *The Philadelphia Inquirer*, December 20.

Fiala, Nathan. 2009. The greenhouse hamburger. *Scientific American* (February): 72–75.

Fischer, Claude S. 2009. The 2004 finding of shrunken social networks: An artifact? *American Sociological Review* 74 (August): 657–69.

Fischer-Kowalski, Marina, and Helmut Haberl, eds. 2007. *Socioecological transitions and global change: Trajectories of social metabolism and land use*. Northampton, Mass.: Edward Elgar.

Fletcher, June. 2004. The dysfunctional family house. *The Wall Street Journal*, March 26.

Foley, Duncan K. 2007. *The economic fundamentals of global warming*. Prepared for the Workshop on the Economics of Global Warming, Schwartz Center for Economic Policy Analysis. Available from http://homepage.newschool.edu/~foleyd (accessed November, 24, 2009).

Food and Agriculture Organization of the United Nations. 2009. 1.02 billion people hungry: One sixth of humanity undernourished—more than ever before. FAO United Nations [database online]. Available from http://www.fao.org/news/story/en/item/20568/icode (accessed October 12, 2009).

Foray, Dominique. 2006. *The economics of knowledge*. Cambridge, Mass.: MIT Press.

Frank, Robert. 1985. *Choosing the right pond*. New York: Oxford University Press.

Frankel, Jeffrey A., and Andrew K. Rose. 2005. Is trade good or bad for the environment? Sorting out the causality. *The Review of Economics and Statistics* 87 (1) (October): 85–91.

Frey, Bruno S., and Alois Stutzer. 2002. What can economists learn from happiness research? *Journal of Economic Literature* 40 (2): 402–35.

Friedman, Benjamin M. 2005. *The moral consequences of economic growth*. New York: Alfred A. Knopf.

Friedman, Thomas L. 2009. Mother Nature's Dow. *The New York Times*, March 29. Available from http://www.nytimes.com/2009/03/29/opinion/29friedman.html?_r=1 (accessed March 29, 2009).

————. 2008. *Hot, flat and crowded: Why we need a green revolution and how it can renew America.* New York: Farrar, Straus and Giroux.

Furchgott, Roy. 2009. App of the week: Rating your shopping basket's conscience. *The New York Times* Gadgetwise Blog, April 7. Available from http://gadgetwise.blogs .nytimes.com/2009/04/07/app-of-the-week-goodguide-rates-your-shopping-baskets-conscience (accessed June 10, 2009).

Galbraith, Kate. 2009. Dark days for green energy. *The New York Times*, February 3. Available from http://www.nytimes.com/2009/02/04/business/04windsolar .html?_r=1&ref=business (accessed June 11, 2009).

Galinsky, Ellen, James T. Bond, Stacy S. Kim, Lois Backon, Erin Brownfield, and Kelly Sakai. 2004. *Overwork in America: When the way we work becomes too much.* Executive Summary. New York: Families and Work Institute.

Gallagher, Kevin. 2009. Bursting the carbon bubble. *The Guardian*, May 5. Available from http://www.guardian.co.uk/commentisfree/cifamerica/2009/may/04/ economy-green-shoots-environment-climate-change (accessed May 5, 2009).

————. 2004. *Free trade and the environment: Mexico, NAFTA, and beyond.* Stanford, Calif.: Stanford University Press.

Garment District, The. 2009. Dollar-a-pound clothing. Available from http://www .garmentdistrict.com/dollar_lb/dollar_a_pound.htm (accessed March 17, 2009).

Gershenfeld, Neil. 2005. *Fab. The coming revolution on your desktop; From personal computers to personal fabrication.* New York: Basic Books.

Gershuny, Jonathan. 2000. *Changing times: Work and leisure in post-industrial society.* New York: Oxford University Press.

Ghertner, D. Asher, and Matthias Fripp. 2007. Trading away damage: Quantifying environmental leakage through consumption-based, life-cycle analysis. *Ecological Economics* 63: 563–77.

Global Carbon Project. 2008. *Carbon budget and trends 2007.* Available from http://www .globalcarbonproject.org/carbonbudget/07/index.htm (accessed July 1, 2009).

Global Ecovillage Network. 2009. Global Ecovillage Network [database online]. Available from http://gen.ecovillage.org (accessed July 21, 2009).

Global Footprint Network. 2008. *Ecological footprint and biocapacity, 2005.* National Footprint Accounts. Available from http://www.footprintnetwork.org/en/index .php/GFN/page/ecological_footprint_atlas_2008.

Global Footprint Network. 2009. *The ecological footprint atlas 2009.* Available from http:// www.footprintnetwork.org/atlas (accessed November 25, 2009).

Global Humanitarian Forum. 2009. *Human impact report: Climate change—the anatomy of a silent crisis.* Available from http://www.ghf-geneva.org/OurWork/RaisingAwareness/ HumanImpactReport/tabid/180/Default.aspx (accessed July 27, 2009).

Golden, Lonnie, and Barbara Wiens-Tuers. 2008. Overtime work and wellbeing at home. *Review of Social Economy* 66 (1): 25–49.

Goodstein, Eban. 1999. *The trade-off myth: Fact and fiction about jobs and the environment.* Washington, D.C.: Island Press.

Goss, Kristen A. 1999. Volunteering and the long civic generation. *Nonprofit and Voluntary Sector Quarterly* 28: 378–415. Available from http://nvs.sagepub.com/ cgi/content/abstract/28/4/378 (accessed October 9, 2009).

Gottdiener, Mark, ed. 2000. *New forms of consumption: Consumers, culture, and commodification.* Lanham, Md.: Rowman and Littlefield.

Gould, Kenneth A., David N. Pellow, and Allan Schnaiberg. 2008. *The treadmill of production: Injustice and unsustainability in the global economy.* Boulder, Colo.: Paradigm.

Goulder, Lawrence H., ed. 2002. *Environmental policy making in economies with prior tax distortions.* Cheltenham, U.K.: Edward Elgar.

Goulder, Lawrence H., and Donald Kennedy. Forthcoming. Interpreting and estimating the value of ecosystem services. In *The theory and practice of ecosystem service valuation in conservation,* edited by Gretchen C. Daily, Peter Kareiva, Taylor Ricketts, Heather Tallis, and Steven Polasky. New York: Oxford University Press.

Goulder, Lawrence H., and William A. Pizer. 2008. The economics of climate change. In *New Palgrave dictionary of economics,* 2nd ed., edited by Steven N. Durlauf and Lawrence E. Blume. Basingstoke, U.K.: Palgrave Macmillan.

GreenFab: Sustainable design through engineering and technology. 2009. NSF ITest: Education, Employment & Community Programs [database online]. Available from http://itestlrc.edc.org/greenfab-sustainable-design-through-engineering- and-technology (accessed May 6, 2009).

Grossman, Gene, and Alan Krueger. 1995. Economic growth and the environment. *Quarterly Journal of Economics* 110 (2) (May): 353–77.

———. 1993. Environmental impacts of a North American free trade agreement. In *The U.S.-Mexico free trade agreement,* edited by Peter Garber. Cambridge, Mass.: MIT Press.

Halweil, Brian, Lisa Mastny, Erik Assadourian, Christopher Flavin, Hilary French, Gary Gardner, Danielle Nierenberg, et al. 2004. *State of the world 2004: Special report—the consumer society.* New York: W.W. Norton.

Hamilton, Kirk, Giovanni Ruta, Katharine Bolt, Anil Markandya, Suzette Pedroso, Patricia Silva, M. Saeed Ordoubadi, Glenn-Marie Lange, and Liaila Tajibaeva. 2006. *Where is the wealth of nations?* Washington, D.C.: World Bank. Available from http://siteresources.worldbank.org/INTEEI/Home/20666132/WealthofNations conferenceFINAL.pdf (accessed August 3, 2009).

Hansen, James. 2008. Twenty years later: Tipping points near on global warming. *The Guardian,* June 23. Available from http://www.guardian.co.uk/environment/ 2008/jun/23/climatechange.carbonemissions (accessed June 1, 2009).

Hansen, James, Makiko Sato, Kharecha Pushker, David Beerling, Robert Berner, Valerie Masson-Delmotte, Mark Pagani, Maureen Raymo, Dana L. Royer, and James C. Zachos. 2008. Target atmospheric CO_2: Where should humanity aim? *Open*

Atmospheric Sciences Journal 2: 217–31. Available from http://arxiv.org/ftp/arxiv/papers/0804/0804.1126.pdf (accessed June 1, 2009).

Harper, Krista, and S. Ravi Rajan. 2004. *International environmental justice: Building the natural assets of the world's poor.* Amherst, Mass.: Political Economy Research Institute. Available from http://www.peri.umass.edu/fileadmin/pdf/working_papers/working_papers_51-100/WP87.pdf (accessed June 9, 2009).

Harvey, Fiona. 2009. Recession results in steep fall in emissions. *Financial Times*, September 20. Available from http://www.ft.com/cms/s/0/a0f0331c-a611-11de-8c92-00144feabdc0,_i_email=y.html (accessed September 20, 2009).

Hawken, Paul. 2007. *Blessed unrest: How the largest social movement in history is restoring grace, justice, and beauty to the world.* New York: Viking Press.

———. 1997. Natural capitalism. *Mother Jones* (March 1).

Hawken, Paul, Amory Lovins, and L. Hunter Lovins. 2000. *Natural capitalism: Creating the next industrial revolution.* Boston: Little, Brown and Co.

Hawks, John, Eric T. Wang, Gregory M. Cochran, Henry C. Harpending, and Robert K. Moyzis. 2007. Recent acceleration of human adaptive evolution. *PNAS* 104 (52) (December 26): 20753–58. Available from http://www.pnas.org/content/104/52/20753.full.pdf+html (accessed June 10, 2009).

Hayden, Anders. 2006. France's 35-hour week: Attack on business? Win-win reform or betrayal of disadvantaged workers? *Politics and Society* 34: 502–42.

———. Forthcoming. From growth to sufficiency? A political-economic analysis of climate change responses in the UK and Canada. Ph.D. thesis, Boston College, Department of Sociology.

———. 2000. *Sharing the work, sparing the planet: Work time reduction, consumption and the environment.* London: Zed Press.

Hayden, Anders, and John M. Shandra. 2009. Hours of work and the ecological footprint of nations: An exploratory analysis. *Local Environment: The International Journal of Justice and Sustainability* 14: 575–600.

Heal, Geoffrey. 2009. Climate economics: A meta-review and some suggestions for future research. *Review of Environmental Economics and Policy* 3 (1): 4–21.

Healthcare in Malaysia. 2009. Wikipedia [database online]. Available from http://en.wikipedia.org/wiki/Healthcare_in_Malaysia (accessed August 31, 2009).

Helfand, Jessica, Akbar Sadeghi, and David Talan. 2007. Employment dynamics: Small and large firms over the business cycle. *Monthly Labor Review* (March). Available from http://www.bls.gov/opub/mlr/2007/03/art3full.pdf (accessed September 6, 2009).

Hertwich, Edgar G. 2005. Consumption and the rebound effect. *Journal of Industrial Ecology* 9 (1–2): 85–98.

Hertwich, Edgar G., and Glen P. Peters. 2009. Carbon footprint of nations: A global, trade-linked analysis. *Environmental Science & Technology* (June 15). Available from http://pubs.acs.org/doi/pdfplus/10.1021/es803496a (accessed July 21, 2009).

Hess, Charlotte, and Elinor Ostrom. 2006. *Understanding knowledge as a commons: From theory to practice.* Cambridge, Mass.: MIT Press.

Hoekstra, A. Y., and A. K. Chapagain. 2007. Water footprints of nations: Water use by people as a function of their consumption pattern. *Water Resources Management* 21: 35–48.

Holm, Stig-Olof, and Göran Englund. 2009. Increased ecoefficiency and gross rebound effect: Evidence from USA and six European countries 1960–2002. *Ecological Economics* 68 (3): 879–87.

Hunnicutt, Benjamin Kline. 1988. *Work without end: Abandoning shorter hours for the right to work.* Philadelphia: Temple University Press.

Hurlbert, Jeanne S., Valerie A. Haines, and John J. Beggs. 2000. Core networks and tie activation: What kinds of routine networks allocate resources in nonroutine situations? *American Sociological Review* 65 (4): 598–618.

HybridCars.com. 2006. Hybrid battery toxicity. Available from http://www.hybridcars .com/battery-toxicity.html (accessed June 15, 2009).

ICF International. 2009. *Climate impact of the economic stimulus package: Preliminary findings.* Available from http://www.greenpeace.org/raw/content/usa/press-center/ reports4/ghg-impact-of-the-economic-sti.pdf (accessed June 1, 2009).

Inglehart, Ronald. 1997. *Modernization and postmodernization: Cultural, economic, and political change in 43 societies.* Princeton, N.J.: Princeton University Press.

———. 1989. *Culture shift in advanced industrial society.* Princeton, N.J.: Princeton University Press.

Intergovernmental Panel on Climate Change. 2001. *Special report on emissions scenarios.* Geneva, Switzerland: IPCC Secretariat. Available from http://www.grida.no/publi cations/other/ipcc%5Fsr/?src=/climate/ipcc/emission (accessed July 4, 2009).

International Monetary Fund. 2009. Indices of primary commodity prices 1999–2009. Available from http://www.imf.org/external/np/res/commod/table1a.pdf (accessed May 25, 2009).

International Union for Conservation of Nature and Natural Resources. 2009. Wildlife in a changing world: An analysis of the 2008 IUCN red list of threatened species. Available from http://data.iucn.org/dbtw-wpd/edocs/RL-2009-001.pdf (accessed July 23, 2009).

Jackson, Jeremy B. C. 2008. Ecological extinction and evolution in the brave new ocean. *PNAS* 105 (August 12): 11458–65.

Jacobs, Jerry A., and Kathleen Gerson. 2005. *The time divide: Work, family and gender inequality.* Cambridge, Mass.: Harvard University Press.

Jakubowski, Marcin. 2009. RepRap: The end of Walmart. Open Source Ecology [database online]. Available from http://openfarmtech.org/weblog/?p=614 (accessed April 29, 2009).

———. 2008. Neocommercialization. P2P Foundation [database online]. Available from http://www.p2pfoundation.net/Neocommercialization (accessed December 30, 2008).

Jalas, Mikko. 2002. A time use perspective on the materials intensity of consumption. *Ecological Economics* 41: 109–23.

Jenkins, Henry. 1992. *Textual poachers: Television fans and participatory culture.* New York: Routledge.

Johnston, Denise, Chris Soderquist, and Donella H. Meadows. 2000. *The shrimp commodity system.* Hartland Four Corners, Vt.: Sustainability Institute.

Jones, Timothy W. 2004. Using contemporary archaeology and applied anthropology to understand food loss in the American food system. Community Composting Network [database online]. Available from http://www.communitycompost.org/info/usafood.pdf (accessed October 7, 2009).

Jowit, Juliette, and Patrick Wintour. 2008. Cost of tackling global climate change has doubled, warns Stern. *The Guardian,* June 26. Available from http://www.guardian.co.uk/environment/2008/jun/26/climatechange.scienceofclimatechange (accessed February 6, 2009).

Kahneman, Daniel, Ed Diener, and Norbert Schwarz, eds. 1999. *Well being: The foundation of hedonic psychology.* New York: Russell Sage.

Kahneman, Daniel, and Alan B. Krueger. 2006. Developments in the measurement of subjective well-being. *Journal of Economic Perspectives* 20 (1): 3–24.

Kahneman, Daniel, Alan B. Krueger, David A. Schkade, Norbert Schwarz, and Arthur A. Stone. 2006. Would you be happier if you were richer? A focusing illusion. *Science* 312 (30): 1776–80.

Kahneman, Daniel, and Amos Tversky. 2000. *Choices, values and frames.* New York: Cambridge University Press.

Kasser, Tim, and Kirk W. Brown. 2003. On time, happiness, and ecological footprints. In *Take back your time: Fighting overwork and time poverty in America,* edited by John De Graaf. San Francisco: Berrett-Koehler, 107–12.

Kasser, Tim, and Kennon M. Sheldon. 2009. Time affluence as a path towards personal happiness and ethical business practices: Empirical evidence from four studies. *Journal of Business Ethics* 84 (2): 243–55.

Keim, Brandon. 2007. Humans evolving more rapidly than ever, say scientists. *Wired Science,* December 10. Available from http://www.wired.com/wiredscience/2007/12/humans-evolving (accessed March 16, 2009).

Kellert, Stephen R. 2005. *Building for life: Designing and understanding the human-nature connection.* Washington, D.C.: Island Press.

Keynes, John Maynard. 1936. *The general theory of employment, interest, and money.* London: Macmillan.

Khazzoom, J. D. 1980. Economic implications of mandated efficiency in standards for household appliances. *Energy Journal* 1 (4): 21–40.

Kintisch, Eli. 2009. Projections of climate change go from bad to worse, scientists report. *Science* 323 (March 20): 1546–47.

Kitzes, Justin, Alessandro Galli, Marco Bagliani, John Barrett, Gorm Dige, Sharon Ede, Karlheinz Erb, et al. 2009. A research agenda for improving national ecological footprint accounts. *Ecological Economics* 68 (7) (May 15): 1991–2007.

Kleppa, Elizabeth, Bjarte Sanne, and Grethe Tell. 2008. Working overtime is associated with anxiety and depression. *Journal of Occupational and Environmental Medicine* 50 (6): 658–66.

Klinenberg, Eric. 2003. *Heat wave: A social autopsy of disaster in Chicago.* Chicago: University of Chicago.

Kolbert, Elizabeth. 2009. The sixth extinction? *The New Yorker,* May 25.

Koplow, Doug. 2007. *Subsidies in the US energy sector: Magnitude, causes and options for reform.* OECD, Subsidies and Sustainable Development: Political Economy Aspects. Available from http://www.earthtrack.net/earthtrack/library/SubsidyReform Options.pdf (accessed July 6, 2009).

Koplow, Doug, and John C. Dernbach. 2001. Federal fossil fuel subsidies and greenhouse gas emissions: A case study of increasing transparency for fiscal policy. *Annual Review of Energy and Environment* 26: 361–89.

Kremer, Michael. 1993. Population growth and technological change: One million B.C. to 1990. *The Quarterly Journal of Economics* 108 (3) (August): 681–716.

Krieger, Lisa M. 2009. Joyful, noisy Maker Faire returns for fourth boisterous year of invention. *The Oakland Tribune,* May 30. Available from http://www.insidebayarea .com/search/ci_12488182?IADID=Search-www.insidebayarea.com-www.inside bayarea.com (accessed August 12, 2009).

Kuhn, Peter, and Fernando Lozano. 2008. The expanding workweek? Understanding trends in long work hours among U.S. men, 1979–2006. *Journal of Labor Economics* 26 (2): 311–43.

Kurutz, Steven. 2008. The next little thing? *The New York Times,* September 10. Available from http://www.nytimes.com/2008/09/11/garden/11tiny.html?emc=eta1 (accessed February 2, 2009).

Lancaster, Kelvin. 1966. A new approach to consumer theory. *Journal of Political Economy* 74 (2): 132–57.

Lappé, Frances Moore, and Anna Lappé. 2002. *Hope's edge: The next diet for a small planet.* New York: Jeremy P. Tarcher/Putnam.

Lash, Scott, and John Urry. 1994. *Economies of signs and space.* London: Sage.

Lawrence, Ben. 2008. *Recycled consumerism: An exploratory study of a community of gift giving.* Unpublished, Boston University.

Layard, Richard. 2005. *Happiness: Lessons from a new science.* London: Penguin Press.

Lee, Michelle. 2003. *Fashion victim: Our love-hate relationship with dressing, shopping, and the cost of style.* New York: Broadway Books.

Leete-Guy, Laura, and Juliet B. Schor. 1992. *The great American time squeeze: Trends in work and leisure, 1969–1989.* Washington, D.C.: Economic Policy Institute.

Lemire, Beverly. 2006. *The business of everyday life: Gender, practice and social politics in England, c. 1600–1900.* Manchester, U.K.: Manchester University Press.

Lenzen, Manfred, and Shauna A. Murray. 2001. A modified footprint model and its application to Australia. *Ecological Economics* 31: 227–55.

Levine, Robert. 1997. *A geography of time: The temporal misadventures of a social psychologist, or how every culture keeps time just a little bit differently.* New York: Basic Books.

Le Quéré, Corinne, Christian Rödenbeck, Erik T. Buitenhuis, Thomas J. Conway, Ray Langenfelds, Antony Gomez, Casper Labuschagne, et al. 2007. Saturation of the southern ocean CO_2 sink due to recent climate change. *Science* 316 (June 22): 1735–38. Available from http://www.sciencemag.org/cgi/rapidpdf/316/5832/1735.pdf?ijkey=7hkt7KrW5Ov.w&keytype=ref&siteid=sci (accessed July 22, 2009).

Lippincott, Mathew. 2009. Why I'm not a true fan anymore. Open Source Ecology [database online]. Available from http://factorefarm.org/content/why-im-not-true-fan-anymore#comment-111 (accessed April 29, 2009).

Loewenstein, George, Ted O'Donoghue, and Matthew Rabin. 2003. Projection bias in predicting future utility. *The Quarterly Journal of Economics* 118 (3): 1209–48.

Loser, Claudio M. 2009. Global financial turmoil and emerging market economies: Major contagion and a shocking loss of wealth? Asian Development Bank. Available from http://www.adb.org/media/Articles/2009/12818-global-financial-crisis/Major-Contagion-and-a-shocking-loss-of-wealth.pdf (accessed May 28, 2009).

Lovelock, James. 2006. *The revenge of Gaia.* New York: Basic Books.

Lowe, Sarah Ryan, Christian Chan, and Jean Rhodes. Forthcoming. Pre-hurricane social support protects against psychological distress: A longitudinal analysis of young, low-income, predominantly African-American mothers. *Journal of Clinical and Consulting Psychology.*

Luedicke, Marius K., Craig J. Thompson, and Markus Giesler. 2010. Consumer identity work as moral protagonism: How myth and ideology animate a brand-mediated moral conflict. *Journal of Consumer Research* 36 (April).

Luo, Michael. 2009. Still working, but making do with less. *The New York Times*, May 28. Available from http://www.nytimes.com/2009/05/29/us/29paycut.html?scp=1&sq=Michael%20Luo%20may%202009&st=cse (accessed May 30, 2009).

Luttmer, Erzo F. 2005. Neighbors as negatives: Relative earnings and well-being. *Quarterly Journal of Economics* 120 (3): 963–1002.

Lydersen, Kari. 2009. Scientists: Pace of climate change exceeds estimates. *The Washington Post*, February 15. Available from http://www.washingtonpost.com/wp-dyn/content/article/2009/02/14/AR2009021401757.html (accessed June 1, 2009).

Lynas, Mark. 2008. *Six degrees: Our future on a hotter planet.* Washington, D.C.: National Geographic Books.

Macabrey, Jean-Marie. 2009. Researchers: Sea levels may rise faster than predicted. *The New York Times*, March 11, 2009. Available from http://www.nytimes.com/cwire/2009/03/11/11climatewire-researchers-warn-that-sea-levels-will-rise-m-10080.html (accessed November 24, 2009).

Macy, Joanna, and Molly Young Brown. 1998. *Coming back to life: Practices to reconnect our lives, our world.* Gabriola Island, Canada: New Society Publishers.

Maddison, Angus. 1987. Growth and slowdown in advanced capitalist economies: Techniques of quantitative assessment. *Journal of Economic Literature* 25 (2) (June): 649–98.

Maker Faire. 2009. O'Reilly Media, Inc. [database online]. Available from http://www .makerfaire.com (accessed August 12, 2009).

Makower, Joel. 2007. London goes carbon crazy. Worldchanging [database online]. Available from http://www.worldchanging.com/archives/006818.html (accessed August 3, 2009).

Maniates, Michael, and John M. Meyer, eds. Forthcoming. *The environmental politics of sacrifice.* Cambridge, Mass.: MIT Press.

Marglin, Stephen A. 2008. *The dismal science: How thinking like an economist undermines community.* Cambridge, Mass.: Harvard University Press.

Marglin, Stephen A., and Juliet B. Schor, eds. 1990. *The golden age of capitalism: Reinterpreting the postwar experience.* Oxford: Oxford University Press.

Margo, Robert. 2000. The labor force in the nineteenth century. In *The Cambridge economic history of the United States, vol. 2.,* edited by Stanley L. Engerman and Robert E. Gallman. New York: Cambridge University Press, 207–44.

McCracken, Grant. 1990. Ever dearer in our thoughts: Patina and the representation of status before and after the eighteenth century. In *Culture and consumption.* Bloomington: Indiana University Press.

McDonough, William, and Michael Braungart. 2002. *Cradle to cradle: Remaking the way we make things.* New York: North Point Press.

McKendrick, Neil, John Brewer, and J. H. Plumb. 1982. *The birth of consumer society: The commercialization of eighteenth-century England.* London: Europa.

McKibben, Bill. 2007. Reversal of fortune. *Mother Jones,* March/April. Available from http://www.motherjones.com/politics/2007/03/reversal-fortune (accessed March 1, 2007).

McKinsey & Company. 2009. *Pathways to a low-carbon economy: Version 2 of the global greenhouse gas abatement cost curve.* https://solutions.mckinsey.com/ClimateDesk/default.aspx

———. 2007. *Reducing U.S. greenhouse gas emissions: How much at what cost? U.S. greenhouse gas abatement mapping initiative, executive report.* http://www.mckinsey.com/clientservice/ccsi/greenhousegas.asp

McNeill, John R. 2000. *Something new under the sun: An environmental history of the twentieth-century world.* New York: Norton.

McPherson, Miller, Lynn Smith-Lovin, and Matthew E. Brashears. 2006. Social isolation in America: Changes in core discussion networks over two decades. *American Sociological Review* 71: 353–75.

Meadows, Dennis L. 2005. Evaluating past forecasts: Reflections on one critique of *The limits to growth.* In *Sustainability or collapse: An integrated history and future of people on earth*, edited by Robert Costanza, Lisa J. Gramlich, and Will Steffen. Cambridge, Mass.: MIT Press.

Meadows, Donella, Jorgen Randers, and Dennis Meadows. 2004. *Limits to growth: The thirty year update*. White River Junction, Vt.: Chelsea Green Publishing.

Meadows, Donella H., Dennis Meadows, and Jorgen Randers. 1992. *Beyond the limits: Confronting global collapse; envisioning a sustainable future*. White River Junction, Vt.: Chelsea Green Publishing.

Meadows, Donella H., Dennis L. Meadows, Jorgen Randers, and William W. Behrens. 1972. *The limits to growth*. New York: Universe Books.

Millennium Ecosystem Assessment. 2005. *Ecosystems and human well-being: Synthesis*. Washington, D.C.: Island Press. Available from http://www.millenniumassess ment.org/documents/document.356.aspx.pdf (accessed July 27, 2009).

Miller, Geoffrey. 2009. *Spent: Sex, evolution, and consumer behavior*. New York: Viking.

Mishel, Lawrence, Jared Bernstein, and Heidi Shierholz. 2009. *The state of working America 2008/2009*. An Economic Policy Institute book. Ithaca, N.Y.: Cornell University Press.

Mol, Arthur P. J. 1996. Ecological modernisation and institutional reflexivity: Environmental reform in the late modern age. *Environmental Politics* 5 (2): 302–23.

———. 1995. *The refinement of production: Ecological modernization theory and the chemical industry*. Utrecht, the Netherlands: Van Arkel.

Mol, Arthur P. J., and Gert Spaargaren. 2000. Ecological modernisation theory in debate: A review. *Environmental Politics* 9 (1): 17–49.

Monastersky, Richard. 2009. Climate crunch: A burden beyond bearing. *Nature* 458: 1091–94.

Mooallem, Jon. 2009. The self-storage self. *The New York Times Magazine*, September 2. Available from http://www.nytimes.com/2009/09/06/magazine/06self-storage-t .html?ref=magazine (accessed October 9, 2009).

Morin, Rich, and Paul Taylor. 2009. *Luxury or necessity? The public makes a U-turn*. Pew Research Center. Available from http://pewresearch.org/pubs/1199/more-items-seen-as-luxury-not-necessity (accessed May 11, 2009).

Moyers, Bill. 2001. Earth on edge. PBS [database online]. Available from http://www .pbs.org/earthonedge/program/index.html (accessed July 28, 2009).

Muniz, Albert M., and Thomas C. O'Guinn. Brand community. *Journal of Consumer Research* 27 (March): 412–32.

National Association of Professional Organizers. 2009. National Association of Professional Organizers. Available from http://napo.net (accessed April 7, 2009).

National Oceanic and Atmospheric Administration. 2009. Greenhouse gases continue to climb despite economic slump. *Science Daily*, April 26. Available from http:// www.sciencedaily.com/releases/2009/04/090424195920.htm (accessed April 27, 2009).

National Research Council. 2009. *Hidden costs of energy: Unpriced consequences of energy production and use*. Washington, D.C.: National Academies Press. Available from http://www.nap.edu/openbook.php?record_id=12794&page=R1 (accessed November 18, 2009).

Nelson, Michelle R., Mark A. Rademacher, and Hye-Jin Paek. 2007. Downshifting consumer= upshifting citizen? An examination of a local freecycle community. *The Annals of the American Academy of Political and Social Science* 611 (1): 141–56.

Nestle, Marion. 2002. *Food politics.* Berkeley: University of California Press.

Noble, David F. 1986. *Forces of production.* New York: Oxford University Press.

Nordhaus, William D. 2008. *A question of balance: Weighing the options on global warming policies.* New Haven, Conn.: Yale University Press.

———. 1991. To slow or not to slow: The economics of the greenhouse effect. *The Economic Journal* 101 (407) (July): 920–37.

———. 1982. How fast should we graze the global commons? *American Economic Review* 72 (2): 242–46.

———. 1973. World dynamics: Measurement without data. *The Economic Journal* 83 (332) (December): 1156–83.

Nordhaus, William D., Robert N. Stavins, and Martin L. Weitzman. 1992. Lethal model 2: The limits to growth revisited. *Brookings Papers on Economic Activity* 1992 (2): 1–59.

Norgaard, Kari Marie. 2006a. "People want to protect themselves a little bit": Emotions, denial, and social movement nonparticipation. *Sociological Inquiry* 76 (3) (August): 372–96.

———. 2006b. "We don't really want to know": Environmental justice and socially organized denial of global warming in Norway. *Organization and Environment* 19 (3) (September 2006): 347–70.

North American Bird Conservation Initiative, U.S. Committee. 2009. *The state of the birds, United States of America, 2009.* Washington, D.C.: U.S. Department of Interior. Available from http://www.stateofthebirds.org/pdf_files/State_of_the_Birds_2009 .pdf (accessed July 27, 2009).

Organization for Economic Cooperation and Development. 2008a. GDP per capita of OECD countries. Available from http://www.swivel.com/graphs/show/27734241? limit_modifier=all&graph%5Blimit%5D=41&commit=%3E.

———. 2008b. *Measuring material flows and resource productivity: Synthesis report.* Paris: OECD.

———. 2007. *Pensions at a glance: Public policies across OECD countries.* Paris: OECD.

Ostrom, Elinor. 1990. *Governing the commons: The evolution of institutions for collective action.* New York: Cambridge University Press.

Parthasarathi, Prasannan. 2002. Toward property as share: Ownership, community, and the environment. In *Sustainable planet: Solutions for the twenty-first century,* edited by Juliet B. Schor and Betsy Taylor. Boston: Beacon Press,141–54.

Pauli, Gunter. 2000. *Upsizing: The road to zero emissions, more jobs, more income and no pollution.* Sheffield, U. K.: Greenleaf Publishing.

Pearce, Fred. 2008. *Confessions of an eco-sinner: Tracking down the sources of my stuff.* Boston: Beacon Press.

Perlez, Jane, and Lowell Bergman. 2005. Tangled strands in fight over Peru gold mine. *The New York Times,* October 25. Available from http://www.nytimes.com/2005/10/25/international/americas/25GOLD.html?_r=1&scp=1&sq=perlez%20bergman%202005%20gold&st=cse (accessed August 13, 2009).

Perlez, Jane, and Kirk Johnson. 2005. Behind gold's glitter: Torn lands and pointed questions. *The New York Times,* October 24. Available from http://www.nytimes.com/2005/10/24/international/24GOLD.html.

Piore, Michael, and Charles Sabel. 1986. *The second industrial divide: Possibilities for prosperity.* New York: Basic Books.

Pollan, Michael. 2006. *The omnivore's dilemma: A natural history of four meals.* New York: Penguin Press.

Pollin, Robert, James Heintz, and Heidi Garrett-Peltier. 2009. *The economic benefits of investing in clean energy.* Political Economy Research Institute and the Center for American Progress. Available from http://www.peri.umass.edu/236/hash/cb09819d9c/publication/350 (accessed July 23, 2009).

Post carbon cities: All actions. 2009. Post Carbon Institute [database online]. Available from http://postcarboncities.net/actions/table?sort=desc&order=Population (accessed August 5, 2009).

Pouwels, Babette, Jacques Siegers, and Jan Dirk Vlasblom. 2008. Income, working hours and happiness. *Economics Letters* 99: 72–74.

Putnam, Robert D. 2000. *Bowling alone: The collapse and revival of American community.* New York: Simon and Schuster.

Putnam, Robert D., Robert Leonardi, and Raffaella Y. Nanetti. 1994. *Making democracy work: Civic traditions in modern Italy.* Princeton, N.J.: Princeton University Press.

Rampell, Catherine. 2009. Outsourced chores come back home. *The New York Times,* January 16. Available from http://www.nytimes.com/2009/01/17/business/17services.html?_r=1&emc=eta1 (accessed September 7, 2009).

Rasmussen Reports. 2009. *Just 53% say capitalism better than socialism.* Available from http://www.rasmussenreports.com/public_content/politics/general_politics/april_2009/just_53_say_capitalism_better_than_socialism (accessed September 27, 2009).

Raver, Anne. 2009. The grass *is* greener at Harvard. *The New York Times,* September 24.

Reinhardt, Uwe E. 2009. An economist's mea culpa. *The New York Times* Economix Blog, January 9. Available from http://economix.blogs.nytimes.com/2009/01/09/an-economists-mea-culpa (accessed June 9, 2009).

Repetto, Robert, and Daniel Dias. 2006. Equity analysis: The true picture? Environmental Finance (July–August): 44–45. Available from http://www.trucost.com/Trucva%20-%20Environmental%20Finance%20-%20July%2006.pdf (accessed June 11, 2009).

Repetto, Robert, William Magrath, Michael Wells, and Christine Beer. 1989. *Wasting assets: Natural resources in the national income accounts.* Washington, D.C.: World Resources Institute.

Research and Innovative Technology Administration. 2009. North American transborder freight data. Bureau of Transportation Statistics [database online]. Available from http://www.bts.gov.proxy.bc.edu/programs/international/transborder/ TBDR_QA.html. Accessed January 15, 2007.

Resources for Life. 2009. Small house society. Resources for Life [database online]. Available from http://www.resourcesforlife.com/small-house-society (accessed February 2, 2009).

Revkin, Andrew C. 2009. Among climate scientists, a dispute over "tipping points." *The New York Times*, March 29. Available from http://www.nytimes.com/2009/03/29/ weekinreview/29revkin.html?scp=1&sq=revkin%20march%2029%202009&st=cse (accessed July 23, 2009).

Richards, John F. 2003. *The unending frontier: An environmental history of the early modern world.* Berkeley: University of California Press.

Richtel, Matt. 2008. More companies are cutting labor costs without layoffs. *The New York Times*, December 22. Available from http://www.nytimes.com/2008/12/22/ business/22layoffs.html?scp=1&sq=richtel%20december%2022%202008&st=cse (accessed January 7, 2009).

Rignot, Eric, and Pannir Kanagaratnam. 2006. Changes in the velocity structure of the Greenland ice sheet. *Science* 311 (February 17): 986–90.

Ritzer, George. 2005. *Enchanting a disenchanted world.* Thousand Oaks, Calif.: Pine Forge Press.

Roche, Daniel. 1994. *The culture of clothing: Dress and fashion in the Ancien Régime.* New York: Cambridge University Press.

Rockström, Johan, Will Steffen, Kevin Noone, Åsa Persson, Chapin F. Stuart III, Eric F. Lambin, Timothy M. Lenton, et al. 2009. A safe operating space for humanity. *Nature* 461 (September 24): 472–75.

Romero-Ávila, Diego. 2008. Questioning the empirical basis of the environmental Kuznets curve for CO_2. *Ecological Economics* 64: 559–74.

Romm, Joseph. 2009. Half of world's population could face climate-driven food crisis by 2100. Climate Progress. Available at http://climateprogress.org/2009/01/11/ half-of-worlds-population-could-face-climate-driven-food-crisis-by-2100 (accessed June 30, 2009).

———. 2008. Cleaning up on carbon. *Nature Reports Climate Change* (June 19). Available at http://climateprogress.org/2008/06/19/nature-publishes-my-climate-analysis-and-solution (accessed September 12, 2009).

Røpke, Inge. 2005. Trends in the development of ecological economics from the late 1980s to the early 2000s. *Ecological Economics* 55 (2): 262–90.

———. 2004. The early history of modern ecological economics. *Ecological Economics* 50 (3–4): 293–314.

Rosen, Ellen. 2002. *Making sweatshops: The globalization of the U.S. apparel industry.* Berkeley: University of California Press.

Rosenthal, Elisabeth. 2008. No furnaces but heat aplenty in "passive houses." *The New*

York Times, December 26. Available at http://www.nytimes.com/2008/12/27/ world/europe/27house.html?emc=eta1 (accessed February 7, 2009).

Rosnick, David, and Mark Weisbrot. 2006. *Are shorter work hours good for the environment? A comparison of U.S. and European energy consumption.* Washington, D.C.: Center for Economic and Policy Research.

Ross, Andrew, ed. 1997. *No sweat: Fashion, free trade, and the rights of garment workers.* New York: Verso.

Ross, Robert J. S. 2004. *Slaves to fashion: Poverty and abuse in the new sweatshops.* Ann Arbor: University of Michigan Press.

Rubin, Jeff, and Benjamin Tal. 2007. Does energy efficiency save energy? *StrategEcon* (November 27). Available from http://research.cibcwm.com/economic_public/ download/snov07.pdf (accessed January 28, 2009).

Saad, Gad. 2007. *The evolutionary bases of consumption behavior.* Danvers, Mass.: Lawrence Erlbaum.

Sachs, Jeffrey D. 2008. *Common wealth: Economics for a crowded planet.* New York: Penguin Press.

Sachs, Wolfgang, Reinhard Loske, and Manfred Linz. 1998. *Greening the north: A post-industrial blueprint for ecology and equity.* London: Zed Books.

Saez, Emmanuel. 2008. *Striking it richer: The evolution of top incomes in the United States (update using 2006 preliminary estimates).* Available from http://elsa.berkeley .edu/~saez/saez-UStopincomes-2006prel.pdf (accessed July 6, 2009).

Sarkisian, Natalia, Mariana Gerena, and Naomi Gerstel. 2006. Extended family ties among Mexicans, Puerto Ricans, and Whites: Superintegration or disintegration? *Family Relations* 55 (3) (July): 331–44.

Sarkisian, Natalia, and Naomi Gerstel. 2004. Kin support among blacks and whites: Race and family organization. *American Sociological Review* 69 (4) (December): 812–37.

Schnaiberg, Allan. 1980. *The environment: From surplus to scarcity.* New York: Oxford University Press.

Schor, Juliet B. Forthcoming. Consumer-topia: Social transformation and the politics of the new consumer movement. In *Consumerism and its discontents.* New York: Oxford University Press.

———. 2008. *The expansion of fast-fashion: A macro-material analysis of trends in US consumption, 1998–2005.* Unpublished mimeo ed., available from author.

———. 2005. Sustainable consumption and worktime reduction. *Journal of Industrial Ecology, Special Issue on Sustainable Consumption* 9 (1): 37–50.

———. 2002. Cleaning the closet: Toward a new ethic of fashion. In *Sustainable planet: Solutions for the 21st century,* edited by Juliet B. Schor and Betsy Taylor. Boston: Beacon Press, 45–60.

———. 2000. Voluntary downshifting in the 1990s. In *Power, employment and accumulation: Social structures in economic theory and practice,* edited by James Stanford. Armonk, N.Y.: M.E. Sharpe.

————. 1998. *The overspent American: Upscaling, downshifting and the new consumer.* New York: Basic Books.

————. 1995. Can the north stop consumption growth? Escaping the cycle of work and spend. In *The north, the south and the environment,* edited by V. Bhaskar and Andrew Glyn. London: Earthscan.

————. 1992. *The overworked American: The unexpected decline of leisure.* New York: Basic Books.

————. 1991. Global inequality and environmental crisis: An argument for reducing working hours in the north. *World Development* 19 (1): 73–84.

Schor, Juliet B., and Jong-il You, eds. 1995. *Capital, the state and labour: A global perspective.* Cheltenham, U.K.: Edward Elgar.

Schuster, Ute, and Andrew J. Watson. 2007. A variable and decreasing sink for atmospheric CO_2 in the North Atlantic. *Journal of Geophysical Research* 112: C11006.

Scotchmer, Suzanne. 1991. Standing on the shoulders of giants: Cumulative research and the patent law. *Journal of Economic Perspectives* 5 (1): 29–41.

Self Storage Association. 2008. Self storage association fact sheet. Self Storage Association [database online]. Available from http://www.selfstorage.org/SSA/Home/AM/ContentManagerNet/ContentDisplay.aspx?Section=Home&ContentID=4228 (accessed July 2, 2009).

Seyfang, Gil, and David Elliott. 2009. *The new economics of sustainable consumption: Seeds of change.* New York: Palgrave Macmillan.

Shierholz, Heidi. 2009. Jobs picture for October 2, 2009. Economic Policy Institute [database online]. Available from http://www.epi.org/analysis_and_opinion/entry/jobs_picture_for_october_2_2009 (accessed October 11, 2009).

Shiller, Robert J. 2008. Challenging the crowd in whispers, not shouts. *The New York Times,* November 1. Available from http://www.nytimes.com/2008/11/02/business/02view.html?emc=eta1 (accessed March 6, 2009).

Shiva, Vandana. 1999. *Biopiracy: The plunder of nature and knowledge.* Boston: South End Press.

Shuman, Michael H. 2006. *The small-mart revolution: How local businesses are beating the global competition.* San Francisco: Berrett-Koehler.

————. N.d. Amazing shrinking machines: The movement toward diminishing economies of scale. *New Village Journal:* Issue 2—Community Scale Economics. Available from http://www.newvillage.net/Journal/Issue2/2amazing.html (accessed May 29, 2009).

Smil, Václav, and Mao Yushi. 1998. *The economic costs of China's environmental degradation.* Cambridge, Mass.: American Academy of Arts and Sciences.

Sokolov, A. P., P. H. Stone, C. E. Forest, R. Prinn, M. C. Sarofim, M. Webster, S. Paltsev, et al. 2009. Probabilistic forecast for 21st century climate based on uncertainties in emissions (without policy) and climate parameters. *Journal of Climate* 22 (19): 5175–5204.

Solar Energy Industries Association. 2009. *US solar industry 2008 year in review.* Washington,

D.C.: Solar Energy Industries Association. Available from http://seia.org/galleries/pdf/2008_Year_in_Review-small.pdf (accessed September 7, 2009).

Solnick, Sara J., and David Hemenway. 1998. Is more always better? A survey on positional concerns. *Journal of Economic Behavior and Organization* 37: 373–83.

Solomon, Susan, Gian-Kasper Plattner, Reto Knutti, and Pierre Friedlingstein. 2009. Irreversible climate change due to carbon dioxide emissions. *PNAS* 106 (6) (February 10): 1704–1709.

Sorrell, Steve. 2007. *The rebound effect: An assessment of the evidence for economy-wide energy savings from improved energy efficiency*. London: UK Energy Research Centre.

Speth, James Gustave. 2008. *The bridge at the edge of the world: Capitalism, the environment, and crossing from crisis to sustainability*. New Haven, Conn.: Yale University Press.

Stack, Carol B. 1983. *All our kin: Strategies for survival in a black community*. New York: Basic Books.

Stanton, Elizabeth A., Frank Ackerman, and Sivan Kartha. 2009. Inside the integrated assessment models: Four issues in climate economics. *Climate and Development* 8: 1–19.

Stanton, Elizabeth A., and James K. Boyce. 2005. *Environment for the people*. Amherst, Mass.: Political Economy Research Institute. Available from http://www.peri.umass.edu/fileadmin/pdf/envtforpeople-web.pdf (accessed May 5, 2009).

Steinfeld, Henning, Pierre Gerber, Tom Wassenaar, Vincent Castel, Mauricio Rosales, and Cees de Haan. 2006. *Livestock's long shadow: Environmental issues and options*. Rome: Food and Agriculture Organization of the United Nations.

Stern, Sir Nicholas. 2006. *Stern review of the economics of climate change*. HM Treasury. Available from http://www.hm-treasury.gov.uk/sternreview_index.htm (accessed March 15, 2009).

Sterner, Thomas, and U. Martin Persson. 2008. An even sterner review: Introducing relative prices into the discounting debate. *Review of Environmental Economics and Policy* 2 (1) (Winter): 61–76.

Stevenson, Betsey, and Justin Wolfers. 2008a. Economic growth and subjective well-being: Reassessing the Easterlin paradox. *Brookings Papers on Economic Activity* 1: 1–87.

———.2008b. Happiness inequality in the United States. *The Journal of Legal Studies* 37 (s2) (June): S33–S79.

Stewart, Heather. 2009. This is how we let the credit crunch happen, ma'am . . . *The Guardian*, July 26. Available from http://www.guardian.co.uk/uk/2009/jul/26/monarchy-credit-crunch (accessed July 27, 2009).

Stiglitz, Joseph E., Amartya Sen, and Jean-Paul Fitoussi. 2009. *Report by the commission on the measurement of economic performance and social progress*. Available from www.stiglitz-sen-fitoussi.fr (accessed September 28, 2009).

Stutzer, Alois. 2003. The role of income aspirations in individual happiness. *Journal of Economic Behavior and Organization* 54: 89–109.

Sukhdev, Pavan, and European Communities. 2008. *The economics of ecosystems and biodiversity: An interim report*. Cambridge, U.K.: Banson Production. Available from http://ec.europa.eu/environment/nature/biodiversity/economics/pdf/teeb_report.pdf (accessed June 10, 2009).

Suranovic, Steve. 2007. Economic costs of combating climate change. Steve Suranovic's Blog [database online]. Available from http://stevesuranovic.blogspot.com/2007/07/economic-costs-of-combating-climate.html (accessed February 5, 2009).

Sustainable Europe Research Institute. 2009a. Download global resource extraction. Sustainable Europe Research Institute [database online]. Available from http://www.materialflows.net/mfa/index2.php# (accessed July 17, 2009).

———. 2009b. *Overconsumption? Our use of the world's natural resources.* Friends of the Earth Europe, Friends of the Earth Austria, Sustainable Europe Research Institute. Available at: http://seri.at/news/2009/09/24/overconsumption (accessed November 27, 2009).

Swan, Simone. 2009. The adobe alliance. Available from http://www.adobealliance.org (accessed October 12, 2009).

Taibbi, Matt. 2009 The great American bubble machine. *Rolling Stone,* July 18–23. Available from http://www.rollingstone.com/politics/story/29127316/the_great_american_bubble_machine (accessed July 15, 2009).

Tasch, Woody. 2008. *Inquiries into the nature of slow money: Investing as if food, farms, and fertility mattered.* White River Junction, Vt.: Chelsea Green Publishing.

Thampapillai, Dodo J., Xun Wu, and Lawrence R. Sunderaj. 2007. Economic growth, the environment and employment: Challenges for sustainable development in China. *International Journal of Environment, Workplace and Employment* 3 (1): 15–27.

Tidwell, James H., and Geoff L. Allan. 2001. Fish as food: Aquaculture's contribution. *EMBO Reports* 2 (11): 958–63. Available from http://www.nature.com/embor/journal/v2/n11/full/embor285.html (accessed March 16, 2009).

Transition Network. 2009. Tackling peak oil and climate change, together. Available from http://transitiontowns.org/TransitionNetwork/TransitionNetwork (accessed August 6, 2009).

Transition United States. 2009. Available from http://transitionus.ning.com (accessed August 6, 2009).

Turner, Graham. 2008. *A comparison of the limits to growth with thirty years of reality.* Australia: Socio-Economics and the Environment in Discussion CSIRO Working Paper Series. Available from http://www.csiro.au/files/files/plje.pdf (accessed September 12, 2009).

Udell, Emily. 2008. Your flat screen has (greenhouse) gas. Alternet.org [database online]. (accessed March 17, 2009).

Union of Concerned Scientists. 2005. How to buy a hybrid car. Available from http://www.ucsusa.org/publications/greentips/505-how-to-buy-a-hybrid-car.html (accessed June 15, 2009).

———. 1992. World scientists' warning to humanity. Available from http://www.ucsusa.org/about/1992-world-scientists.html (accessed July 21, 2009).

United Nations Development Programme. 2007. *Human development report 2007/2008.*

Available from http://hdr.undp.org/en/media/HDR_20072008_EN_Complete
.pdf (accessed March 29, 2009).

United Nations Statistics Division. 2009. Millennium development goals indicators:
The official United Nations site for the MDG indicators. Available from http://
mdgs.un.org.proxy.bc.edu/unsd/mdg/Data.aspx (accessed July 4, 2009).

———. 2005. UN commodity trade statistics database (UN comtrade). Available from
unstats.un.org/unsd/comtrade (accessed June 5, 2006).

United Nations Population Division. 2009. World population to exceed 9 billion by 2050.
Press release. Available from www.un.org/esa/population/publications/wpp2008/
pressrelease.pdf (accessed November 30, 2009).

United States Bureau of Economic Analysis. 2009. U.S. international transactions accounts data. Available from http://www.bea.gov/international/bp_web/simple
.cfm?anon=71&table_id=20&area_id=1 (accessed July 27, 2009).

United States Bureau of Labor Statistics. 2009a. Bureau of Labor Statistics databases:
Consumer price index—all urban consumers. Available from http://data.bls.gov
(accessed July 8, 2009).

———. 2009b. The employment situation—August 2009. Available from http://www
.bls.gov.proxy.bc.edu/news.release/pdf/empsit.pdf (accessed September 7, 2009).

———. 2009c. International comparisons of manufacturing productivity and unit
labor costs. Available from ftp://ftp.bls.gov/pub/special.requests/ForeignLabor/
prodsuppt01.txt (accessed September 9, 2009).

———. 2008. Employment & earnings 5 (2) (February). Available from http://www.bls
.gov.proxy.bc.edu/opub/ee/empearn200802.pdf (accessed September 10, 2009).

United States Census Bureau. 2009. Selected measures of household income disper-
sion: 1967 to 2007. Available from http://www.census.gov.proxy.bc.edu/hhes/
www/income/histinc/p60no231_tablea3.pdf (accessed July 6, 2009).

———. 2007. Characteristics of new housing. Available from http://www.census.gov
.proxy.bc.edu/const/www/highanncharac2007.html (accessed April 7, 2009).

———. 2005. Current industrial reports, apparel MQ315A (1992, 1997, and missing
data made available to author). Available from http://www.census.gov.proxy.bc
.edu/cir/www/315/mq315a.html (accessed March 15, 2005).

United States Department of Agriculture. 2006. *Livestock and poultry: World markets and
trade.* Circular Series DL&P 2-06. Washington, D.C.: United States Department of
Agriculture, Foreign Agricultural Service. Available from http://www.fas
.usda.gov/dlp/circular/2006/2006%20Annual/Livestock&Poultry.pdf (accessed
April 7, 2009).

Universal health care. 2009. Wikipedia [database online]. Available from http://
en.wikipedia.org/wiki/Universal_health_care (accessed August 31, 2009).

Van den Broek, Aylsa. 2008. IKEA organizes furniture swap. Springwise [database
online]. Available from http://springwise.com/homes_housing/ikea_organizes_
furniture_swap (accessed August 13, 2009).

Van Praag, Bernard M. S., and Paul Frijters. 1999. The measurement of welfare and well-being: The Leyden approach. In *Well being: The foundation of hedonic psychology*, edited by Daniel Kahneman, Ed Diener, and Norbert Schwarz, 413–33. New York: Russell Sage.

Venetoulis, Jason, and John Talberth. 2008. Refining the ecological footprint. *Environment, Development and Sustainability* 10 (4) (August): 441–69.

Victor, Peter A. 2008. *Managing without growth: Slower by design, not disaster*. Cheltenham, U.K.: Edward Elgar.

Virtanen, M., A. Singh-Manoux, J. E. Ferrie, D. Gimeno, M. G. Marmot, M. Elovainio, M. Jokela, J. Vahtera, and M. Kivimäki. 2009. Long working hours and cognitive function: The Whitehall II study. *American Journal of Epidemiology* 169 (5): 596–605.

Wagner, Gernot. 2001. The political economy of greening the national income accounts. *Newsletter of the Association of Environmental and Resource Economists* 21 (May): 14–18. Available from http://www.gwagner.com/writing/010501AERE_essay.pdf (accessed June 10, 2009).

Weidmann, Thomas, Jan Mix, John Barrett, and Mathis Wackernagel. 2006. Allocating ecological footprints to final consumption categories with input-output analysis. *Ecological Economics* 56: 28–48.

Weiss, Ray F., Jens Mühle, Peter K. Salameh, and Christina M. Harth. 2008. Nitrogen trifluoride in the global atmosphere. *Geophysical Research Letters* 35(20): L20821.

Weitzman, Martin L. 2009. On modeling and interpreting the economics of catastrophic climate change. *The Review of Economics and Statistics* 91 (1) (February): 1–19.

Weizsäcker, Ernst Ulrich, Amory D. Lovins, and L. Hunter Lovins. 1998. *Factor four: Doubling wealth, halving resource use*. London: Earthscan Publications.

Whybrow, Peter C. 2005. *American mania: When more is not enough*. New York: W.W. Norton.

Wickens, Jim. 2008. Hell for leather. *The Ecologist* (June 1). Available from http://www.theecologist.org/investigations/health/269813/hell_for_leather.html (accessed July 27, 2009).

Widmeyer Research and Polling. 2004. *New American dream: A public opinion poll*. Washington, D.C.: Center for a New American Dream.

Williams, Raymond. 1996. *Problems in materialism and culture: Selected essays*. New York: Verso Books.

Willis, Charles G., Brad Ruhfel, Richard B. Primack, Abraham J. Miller-Rushing, and Charles C. Davis. 2008. Phylogenetic patterns of species loss in Thoreau's woods are driven by climate change. *PNAS* 105 (44) (November 4): 17029–33.

Willis, Margaret M. 2009. "Conscious consumption" and activism: An empirical reevaluation of the apolitical and distracted consumer. M.A. thesis, Boston College, Department of Sociology.

Willis, Margaret M., and Juliet B. Schor. N.d. Does changing a light bulb lead to changing the world? Civic engagement and the ecologically conscious consumer. Unpublished, available from author.

Wiseman, Richard. 2007. *Quirkology: How we discover the big truths in small things.* New York: Basic Books.

WISERTrade. 2009. US district and port exports and imports. Available from http://www.wisertrade.org.proxy.bc.edu/home/index.jsp?content=/data.jsp (accessed June 5, 2008).

Wolff, Edward N. 2009. *Poverty and income distribution,* 2nd ed. Hoboken, N.J.: Wiley-Blackwell.

Woolhandler, Steffie, Terry Campbell, and David U. Himmelstein. 2003. Costs of health care administration in the United States and Canada. *New England Journal of Medicine* 349 (8): 768–75. Available from http://content.nejm.org/cgi/content/full/349/8/768 (accessed August 31, 2009).

World Bank. 2009a. Quick reference tables. Available from http://web.worldbank.org.proxy.bc.edu/WBSITE/EXTERNAL/DATASTATISTICS/0,,contentMDK:20399244~menuPK:1504474~pagePK:64133150~piPK:64133175~theSitePK:239419,00.html#ranking (accessed September 24, 2009).

———. 2009b.Understanding poverty. Available from http://go.worldbank.org.proxy.bc.edu/K7LWQUT9L0 (accessed February 15, 2009).

World Resources Institute. 2007. Earth trends: The environmental information portal. Available from http://earthtrends.wri.org/searchable_db/index.php?step=countries&cID%5B%5D=190&theme=9&variable_ID=573&action=select_years (accessed April 7, 2009).

Worldwatch Institute. 2008. Good stuff. Available from http://www.worldwatch.org/node/1497 (accessed April 7, 2009).

World Wildlife Fund. 2008. *Living planet report 2008.* Available from http://assets.panda.org/downloads/living_planet_report_2008.pdf (accessed June 9, 2009).

Wrigley, Edward Anthony. 1990. *Continuity, chance and change: The character of the industrial revolution in England.* New York: Cambridge University Press.

York, Richard, Eugene A. Rosa, and Thomas Dietz. 2003. STIRPAT, IPAT and ImPACT: Analytic tools for unpacking the driving forces of environmental impacts. *Ecological Economics* 46: 351–65.

Index

Page numbers in *italics* refer to figures.